# If only I'd known that a year ago ...

A practical guide to the help, services and equipment available for disabled people

## 2013

11th Edition © Disability Rights Enterprises

Ian claimed compensation with Thompsons after he lost part of his right leg in an accident at work

## "I was seen by an impressive cross section of experts brought in by Thompsons - both as part of building my case and also, in some instances, as part of providing practical help." Ian

At Thompsons, we have specialist teams with a wealth of experience in handling serious injury claims, including those for brain injury, spinal and spinal cord injury, amputations and serious burns.

- We are supported by highly reputed experts who assess care needs and every financial aspect of your claim.

- We will arrange for a lawyer to visit you and assess your case under no obligation.

- You will keep 100% of the settlement.

For no obligation advice call 08000 224 224 or visit www.thompsons.law.co.uk

### THE MOST EXPERIENCED PERSONAL INJURY FIRM IN THE UK

Thompsons Solicitors is a trading name of Thompsons Solicitors LLP and is regulated by the Solicitors Regulation Authority.

# Contents

## ACKNOWLEDGEMENTS

**If only I'd known that a year ago ...**
A practical guide to the help, services and
equipment available for disabled people

ISBN 978-1-9033355-9-8
11th edition. RRP £12.99

© Disability Rights Enterprises 2012
Published by Disability Rights Enterprises
for Disability Rights UK.
Registered Charity No. 1138585

At the time if writing, the government are
replacing its' online information resource
'DirectGov' with 'Gov' (www.gov.uk). We would
therefore warn that some links in this guide may
be subject to change.

Disability Rights UK
12 City Forum, 250 City Road
London EC1V 8AF
Tel: 020 7250 3222
www.disabilityrightsuk.org

FSC
www.fsc.org
MIX
Paper from
responsible sources
FSC® C013417

**Editor:**
Sarah Cosby

**Contributors:**
Ken Butler
Angela Cosby
Marije Davidson
Helen Dolphin
Jill Grey
Agnes Fletcher
Andrea Humphrey
Lisa Jennison
Ben Kersey
Paula McDiarmid
Dr Rachel Perkins
James Pool
Liz Sayce
Mark Shrimpton
John Stanford
Rundip Thind

**Cover images:**
Shutterstock
VisitBritain Images

**Design:**
© Anderson Fraser Partnership

**Production:**
Anderson Fraser:
Deb Kamofsky,
Paul Mckenzie and
Humphrey Weightman

**Print:**
Stephens & George Print Group

# Introduction

Nearly all of us are touched by the experience of a health condition or disability at some point in our lives. One in five of us has a long-term impairment or health condition that would be considered a 'disability' under the legislation that protects disabled people from discrimination. Add to that our involvement with older relatives, other family members, friends and colleagues who experience disability and nearly all of us know something about the experience.

But for most people it is only at 'turning point' moments that we really think about the impact on our own lives, for example:

- after an accident
- when we receive a diagnosis (from multiple sclerosis to bi-polar disorder, epilepsy to dementia)
- when a child is born disabled or diagnosed with a serious health condition early in life
- when a long-standing impairment enters a new phase
- when other circumstances change – from becoming a parent to more troubling issues like redundancy or bereavement.

At these times, life can seem strange and confusing. The life we know has suddenly changed.

The good news is that many millions of people have come through this sort of experience with a satisfying and fulfilling life. Life may not be as it was before, but as you go through your own process of change you often find that you can negotiate for changes (support at home, adjustments at work) that give you choice and control – and give you back your independent life.

Deciding what will work for you depends on knowing what's possible and where to look for support and advice.

This guide is designed to help. It provides information covering your rights, services and equipment that may help you and where to go for specialist information, practical and legal advice. It cannot be completely comprehensive – some services are provided locally and change rapidly – but it is packed with information that I hope you will find helpful.

In 2012 we merged three charities – Radar, Disability Alliance and National Centre for Independent Living – into one – Disability Rights UK. We now have more information available on more issues, a stronger campaigning voice and already half a million people have visited our website. During 2013 and 2014 there will be some significant changes that we can't fully map at this point. For example, in 2013 disability living allowance will be replaced by personal independence payment; and the Access to Work scheme, which can fund support, equipment and travel to work, is going through some changes as well. Our companion guide the *Disability Rights Handbook* has very detailed benefits information; and our website has up-to-date information as well.

I hope you find this book useful. We welcome feedback on this and all our products so if you have any suggestions for change, for example, new content, please email feedback@disabilityrightsuk.org or visit our website to complete one of our surveys.

We are grateful to all who have assisted in preparing this guide, not least the advertisers, whose support has made it possible.

*Liz Sayce*

Liz Sayce OBE
Chief Executive, Disability Rights UK

IF ONLY I'D KNOWN THAT A YEAR AGO ...

# About Disability Rights UK

Disability Rights UK was formed in January 2012 through the merger of Disability Alliance, National Centre for Independent Living and Radar. This merger of three national disabled person led organisations will enable us to offer all the services and campaigns we each did before plus much more. Disability Rights UK is the leading charity of its kind in the UK. We are run by and for people with lived experience of disability or health conditions.

Our vision is a society where everyone with lived experience of disability or health conditions can participate equally as full citizens.

Our mission is to strengthen the voice of disabled people to make our rights real, as an effective national organisation led by people with a wide range of impairments or health conditions

## What we do

We provide expertise to government to inform national and local policy; produce high quality products and services for disabled people; and partner with private and public sector organisations, with the aim of improving business practices.

## Who we represent

We campaign for the rights and equality of the 11 million people in Britain with lived experience of disability or health conditions regardless of age or impairment.

We have four key audiences:

1 Disabled people – and people living with disability or long-term health conditions
2 Disabled people's organisations
3 Policy makers and their circles of influence (parliament, government, media, think tanks, trusts)
4 Partner, ally and 'client' organisations (employers, charities, colleges, corporates, funders)

## Join Disability Rights UK

By becoming a member of Disability Rights UK you will be helping realise our vision. We encourage all individuals and organisations – whether statutory, voluntary or corporate – to support our work by becoming members. We want to involve members and work together in a spirit of co-production to campaign and influence change.

To become a member of Disability Rights UK and receive regular updates, including welfare rights Updates, contact us on:

Membership, Disability Rights UK, 12 City Forum, London EC1V 8AF
📞 020 7250 3222
📧 members@disabilityrightsuk.org; or visit
🌐 www.disabilityrightsuk.org

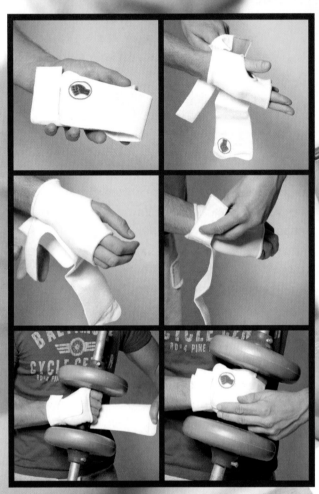

IF ONLY I'D KNOWN THAT A YEAR AGO ...

# Equipment

**This chapter provides information about finding the right equipment, clothing and footwear, technology, accessible computers and assistance dogs – to make daily life easier and provide greater control and freedom – both inside and outside the home.**

## Finding and buying equipment

Apart from standard equipment designed to make everyday tasks easier – for example, food processors or electric tin openers – other equipment is designed specifically for us as disabled people such as:

- equipment designed to overcome a particular difficulty – eg a raised toilet seat
- adapted standard equipment – eg an extended tap turner
- standard equipment with a helpful feature
- custom-made items designed for an individual's particular needs.

Equipment varies from the simple, such as a pick-up stick, grab rail, raised toilet seat, or talking kitchen scales, to the highly sophisticated, such as alarm systems and accessible computer software.

Many items of equipment can be provided by local authorities or the NHS. To find out about local authority provision of equipment, contact a social worker or occupational therapist. For NHS items, including wheelchairs, walking aids or communication aids, contact your GP.

Throughout England, Community Equipment Services bring together provision of social services and health equipment, with the exception of wheelchairs. Equipment may also be supplied that can help us in education and employment. Contact your local authority or your GP for information.

Social care departments can provide advice as part of their assessment of your needs and more generally through community occupational therapy services.

Equipment can be bought privately, which may give us a wider choice. If possible, get specialist advice and shop around, as many of the companies providing equipment add a hefty disability premium. We can get good advice from an organisation related to our specific impairment or from Disabled Living Centres (see below).

If you are paying for substantial fixed equipment, such as a stairlift, make sure it's properly installed and maintained and that you can cover the costs.

> www.livingmadeeasy.org.uk is a free and impartial website, developed by the Disabled Living Foundation. It provides valuable advice and information on daily living equipment and other aspects of independent living. It also contains a directory of suppliers of equipment around the country.

### DISABLED/INDEPENDENT LIVING CENTRES

These centres offer impartial advice on equipment for disabled people to individuals, families, carers and professionals. All centres have a range of products and information on display and many also run training days, produce leaflets and provide other services.

Some centres also operate as retail outlets, so once you've had an independent assessment from the centre, you can buy the right equipment at the same place. Information on centres throughout the UK is available from Assist UK.

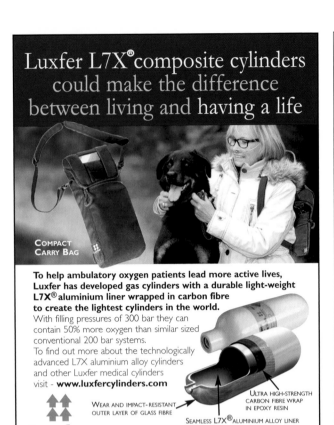

IF ONLY I'D KNOWN THAT A YEAR AGO ...

## Assist UK

Redbank House, 4 St Chad's Street, Manchester M8 8QA

☎ 0870 770 2866; textphone 0870 770 5813

✉ general.info@assist-uk.org

🌐 www.assist-uk.org

Assist UK leads a UK-wide network of Disabled Living Centres. Contact them to find the opening hours and range of services or to make an appointment at your nearest centre. Details of local centres are in the 'Useful contacts' section at the back of this book.

## British Healthcare Trades Association

New Loom House, Suite 4.06, 101 Back Church Lane, London E1 1LU

☎ 020 7702 2141

✉ bhta@bhta.net

🌐 www.bhta.net

The British Healthcare Trades Association (BHTA) represents manufacturers and suppliers of a wide range of equipment for disabled people. Members have signed up to a stringent Code of Practice, which has achieved full approval under the Office of Fair Trading (OFT) Consumer Codes Approval Scheme. An arbitration service is available in the event of any dispute and BHTA-Registered Persons are committed to a personal Code of Conduct.

> **Value added tax (VAT)**
> Some equipment is zero-rated for VAT when supplied for the personal use of a disabled person. To find out more see VAT Notice 701/7 VAT Reliefs for Disabled People from HM Revenue and Customs (http://customs.hmrc.gov.uk).

## EQUIPMENT EXHIBITIONS

A good way to find out what's available is to go to an exhibition of equipment. Some exhibitions attract visitors from across the country or even abroad, others have a more local catchment area or deal with specific types of equipment. In most cases, exhibitors include disability organisations as well as manufacturers and suppliers. News of events coming up is given in local newspapers, in the disability media and at local or regional information points. A few of the largest regular exhibitions are:

## DNEX

**Newcastle**

25-26 September 2013

🌐 www.disabilitynorth.org.uk

## NAIDEX & KIDEQUIP

**London (Excel Centre)**

October 2013

**Birmingham (National Exhibition Centre)**

30 April-2 May 2013

**SECC Glasgow**

18-19 September 2013

🌐 www.naidex.co.uk

## MOBILITY ROADSHOW

**Telford International Centre**

27-29 June 2013

🌐 www.mobilityroadshow.co.uk

---

### MANAGE AT HOME

Manage At Home is a website retailer providing an extensive range of products to aid independent daily living at home, whether that is a mobility aid to help moving around or transferring into a bath, or simply a more ergonomic utensil that is easier to use and hold than a typical design.

Our product range includes grab rails, walking aids, wheelchairs, support cushions, bath lifts, bath seats and boards, raised toilet seats, commodes, electric profiling beds, riser recliner chairs and aids for dressing and eating.

We offer free delivery on orders over £50 and are members of the BHTA.

Manage At Home Ltd is part of the Siddall and Hilton Group of companies, a family owned business that has been in existence for 110 years.

**www.manageathome.co.uk**

## WHERE CAN I FIND ...

N&C Phlexicare are leading suppliers of accessible bathrooms, kitchens, access and daily living products. Our responsibility is to supply products that allow you to live as much of a barrier free life as possible, helping you to improve quality of life for you and your loved ones. We are market leaders, continuing to introduce new innovations and products that allow greater safety, flexibility, freedom of movement and accessibility without ever compromising on design.

### One supplier that can help with all my adaptation requirements

N&C Phlexicare are unique in being the only supplier in the healthcare industry to offer the total solution for your home. We work closely with you to provide a complete adaptation solution from kitchen and bathroom adaptations to wall and flooring as well as daily living solutions and products to help you with access limitations. We are the first company to offer a complete wet room package to give you the confidence that all the components will work together perfectly. Our 'one stop shop' approach means that you benefit from operational and financial efficiencies, receiving our excellent customer service to help you along the way.

Our solutions are not just restricted to the home. As manufacturers of the RADAR locks, we have introduced a series of additional RADAR barrier free entry systems that allow access to all areas permitted allowing for an extension of the National Key Scheme (NKS). Your RADAR key now allows you greater freedom to roam in places like public footpaths, and has been adopted by The National Trust, the railways and other key organisations. Just look out for the RADAR sign.

### Designs to fit around my lifestyle

Functionality is essential, but at N&C, we believe in equality by design. Inclusive design is at the core of our very existence, as we combine the latest in innovation and the highest level of product performance testing, coupled with the latest in style to provide solutions designed around you.

As award winning suppliers, recognised for our designs, we work around your home environment and assess your living space and abilities to offer you a bespoke solution, whether a wet room, level access showering or adapted kitchen for multi-users with different levels of abilities.

### Advice and guidance

As major inventors and innovators with over 50 years of experience in the healthcare market, N&C Phlexicare have gained a great deal of pedigree in the marketplace. Offering advice with staff boasting years of expertise in the field, you gain invaluable service, something that keeps our customers loyal.

### Beautiful Showrooms for inspirational ideas

Visit the N&C Phlexicare showroom to view a wide range of accessible bathrooms and wet room displays as well the impressive, new healthcare kitchen showroom. Our kitchen team are on hand to provide help and guidance to your requirement. You also get an idea of the types of products there are available to help you around the home.

### Assistance on the level of changes I will have to make?

We have strong links with local occupational practices throughout Great Britain to help you maintain your independence at home. We offer products that allow you to manoeuvre safely and with ease whether your home is adapted – making changes to your existing room sets, or whether it is fully adapted – completely redesigned from scratch.

We are more than happy to help you with your adaptation projects. Please call 0845 605 1345 (calls charged at local rate), e-mail info@nichollsandclarke.com, visit our website.

N&C Phlexicare
www.ncdirect.co.uk

# Equipment suppliers

### Hearing and Mobility

☎ 0844 888 1338

Ⓦ www.hearingandmobility.co.uk

Hearing and Mobility (previously Keep Able) supplies a wide range of products to aid independent living through a network of over 25 retail stores around England and Wales.

### Homecraft Rolyan

Nunn Brook Road, Huthwaite, Sutton in Ashfield, Notts NG17 2HU

☎ 0844 412 4330

Ⓦ www.homecraft-rolyan.com

Homecraft Rolyan supplies a wide range of equipment for disabled people of all ages. All products are shown on the website or in a catalogue that can be ordered from the address above.

### Manage at Home Ltd

FREEPOST RSSX-TURK-KGSH

☎ 0808 231 1939

Ⓔ info@manageathome.co.uk

Ⓦ www.manageathome.co.uk

A specialist UK retailer of mobility and disability products and equipment, with an extensive range of products to aid independent daily living at home.

### Nottingham Rehab Supplies

Clinitron House, Excelsior Road, Ashby-de-la-Zouch LE65 1JG

☎ 0845 120 4522

Ⓔ customerservice@nrs-uk.co.uk

Ⓦ www.nrs-uk.co.uk

NRS stocks a range of over 3,500 products for elderly and disabled people and those in rehabilitation.

### Royal National Institute of Blind People (RNIB)

☎ 0303 123 9999

Ⓔ cservices@rnib.org.uk

Ⓦ www.rnib.org.uk

The RNIB sells thousands of products that help blind and partially sighted people – for example, talking, tactile and easy-to-see watches; telephones; kitchen equipment; and mobility aids. The RNIB has a grants programme for equipment.

### Simplyhealth

The Enterprise Centre, Duke Close, West Way, Andover SP10 5AP

☎ 0800 980 7890

Ⓦ www.simplyhealthstore.co.uk

The Simplyhealth group, which includes Totally Active, supplies independent living and mobility equipment. Orders and brochures are available on the website.

> Most of the organisations listed in this chapter sell their products online. There's no problem with this provided you know how to shop online safely. Make sure you know what the company's returns policy is. If you are unsure whether the equipment or adaptation will suit you, ask if you can borrow it or try it out first.

## HIRING EQUIPMENT

Hiring equipment on a short or medium-term basis may be a useful option in some circumstances. Your local Red Cross and some other local suppliers offer this service. Those operating on a national basis include:

### Direct Mobility Hire Ltd

Warren House, 201A Bury Street, Edmonton, London N9 9JE

☎ 0800 092 9322

Ⓔ info@directmobility.co.uk

Ⓦ www.directmobility.co.uk

Direct Mobility hires and sells a wide range of mobility, bath, toilet and bed equipment. Next-day delivery is possible in the London area.

### Theraposture Ltd

Kingdom Avenue, Northacre Industrial Park, Westbury BA13 4WE

☎ 0800 834 654

Ⓔ info@theraposture.co.uk

Ⓦ www.theraposture.co.uk

Theraposture provides a wide range of adjustable beds, chairs and other equipment. The company offers short-term rental for adjustable beds (two weeks minimum).

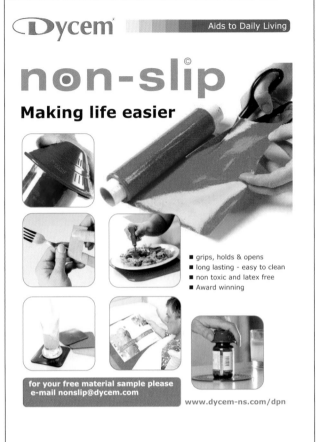

IF ONLY I'D KNOWN THAT A YEAR AGO ...

## CUSTOM-MADE EQUIPMENT

Despite the ever-expanding range and sophistication of equipment, there may not be anything that will meet your particular requirements. However, the following organisations provide bespoke equipment and may be able to help.

### Demand
### (Design & Manufacture for Disability)

The Old Chapel, Mallard Road, Abbots Langley WD5 0GQ
☎ 01923 68 1800
and
Onyx House, 303 Newmills Road, Brockholes, Holmfirth HD9 7AL
☎ 01484 66 6261
🌐 www.demand.org.uk

Demand can advise on the availability of equipment for particular needs and, if required, design and make one-off pieces of equipment.

### MERU

Unit 2 Eclipse Estate, 30 West Hill, Epsom, Surrey KT19 8JD
☎ 01372 72 5203
🌐 www.meru.org.uk

MERU is a charity that designs and makes individual pieces of equipment for disabled children and young people if there isn't a ready-made solution to meet their needs. It accepts referrals from London and southeast England.

### Remap

D9 Chaucer Business Park, Kemsing, Sevenoaks, Kent TN15 6YU
☎ 0845 130 0456
🌐 www.remap.org.uk
   www.remap-scotland.org

Remap is a nationwide network of volunteer engineers and other experts who tailor-make specific pieces of equipment that are not available commercially.

---

## BALANCE HEALTHCARE

**You don't have to tolerate seating discomfort!** Balance Healthcare is rapidly becoming very well-known across the UK for their bespoke seating and lying products.

BOSS, our orthotic support solution, uses a highly accurate digital technique to create an image of an individual's posture, and translate that into a fully upholstered soft foam mould for use as a postural management and supportive seating or lying solution.

Our digital assessment technique is quick and clean, and enables us to demonstrate to you how the finished mould will appear. It also enables us to communicate the manufacturing detail between our three factories electronically, ensuring that delivery of your perfect solution is very quick.

Our manufacturing process uses a 5 axis robotic milling machine, ensuring accuracy of the finished mould within fractions of a millimetre. Allowance can be made easily for upholstery and hoist sling thickness, clothing choice and growth factors.

Our DigitalDrapeUpholstery is also unique. Using a specially-developed CAD program, we produce contact upholstery surfaces which are tension-free, and thus highly durable and comfortable. Loose towelling covers can be provided which are also stitched to match the contours of the finished mould, providing a functional interface that maintains body temperature and can be easily laundered.

Working with virtually any chassis, Balance Healthcare can make a seating solution to fit with mobile or static lounge-type seating, hygiene or showering seating or wheelchairs and other mobility frames. We can provide a consultation appointment within two weeks, and supply your finished mould within three weeks.

To discover the difference with BOSS, call to arrange a presentation or a consultation now on 08456 588399.

**www.balancehealthcare.co.uk**

IF ONLY I'D KNOWN THAT A YEAR AGO ...

# Mobility equipment

Walking aids such as crutches, walking sticks and frames (if there is a medical need for them) can be obtained on loan from a local hospital or community equipment service.

## WHEELCHAIRS

The NHS can provide a free, long-term loan of a manual wheelchair if you have a permanent mobility need. Powered indoor/outdoor wheelchairs can be provided if you can't propel a manual one. The first step is to get a referral from your GP to the local NHS Wheelchair Service.

An occupational therapist or physiotherapist will carry out an assessment at home, in hospital or at the local NHS wheelchair service. The assessment should also consider whether you need accessories such as a cushion, armrests or trays.

In some areas, a voucher may be offered towards the cost of a privately purchased wheelchair if the assessment shows a benefit from features not available on models provided by the NHS.

Regardless of the type of wheelchair or scooter you choose, it's wise to get your equipment insured, especially against third party damage.

> *Get Mobile*, published by Disability Rights UK, is a free guide to buying a scooter or powered wheelchair, giving information on products available, assessing needs, methods of purchase, funding and operating costs.

## POWERED WHEELCHAIRS & SCOOTERS

Most powered outdoor wheelchairs and sports models have to be bought privately. As with all equipment, it is worth seeking advice from a Disabled Living Centre.

Class 3 powered wheelchairs and scooters, those capable of speeds of up to 8mph and not restricted to footpaths, must be registered for road use, be licensed in the exempt disabled taxation class and display a nil duty vehicle licence tax disc. Class 2 scooters are exempt.

Owners of mobility scooters who fail to register their vehicles face fines. In order to register and license a vehicle classified as a Class 3 'invalid carriage', you need to complete form V55/5 (for used vehicles) or V55/4 (for new vehicles) and take or send it to your nearest Driver and Vehicle Licensing Agency (DVLA) office. To get forms and local office addresses, contact the DVLA:
- ☎ 0300 790 6802
- ⓦ www.dvla.gov.uk

Some of us may find it useful to have a lightweight folding wheelchair powered with a lightweight battery. These are not widely available in this country but for information on a couple of suppliers/importers see:
- ⓦ www.steeringdevelopments.co.uk
- ⓦ www.sasaki.co.uk

## LOAN SERVICES

If you receive the higher rate mobility component of disability living allowance (or the enhanced rate of personal independence payment which the government will be introducing in 2013), you could consider using the Motability Scooter and Powered Wheelchair Scheme to lease a powered scooter or wheelchair on hire purchase over one to four years. For information, ring 0800 953 3060.

Local Red Cross branches operate a short-term medical equipment loan service for wheelchairs, other mobility aids and some other equipment. Contact details are in local phone or web directories or can be obtained from:

**British Red Cross**
44 Moorfields, London EC2Y 9AL
- ☎ 020 7138 7900
- ⓔ information@redcross.org.uk
- ⓦ www.redcross.org.uk

A similar service may be available from local disability organisations. Some equipment suppliers also offer a hire service.

## ORTHOPAEDIC FOOTWEAR

### All you need to know

If you or your child have just found out that you need to wear orthopaedic footwear, there is usually an "oh no", or gasp as perceptions of orthopaedic footwear are that they are frumpy and unfashionable. That's where Piedro® and G&M can help! Piedro® have been developing and manufacturing children's and adult's orthopaedic footwear for over 50 years and have designed an extensive range of high quality, stylish shoes, boots, sandals and trainers. Distributed by G&M, all styles are available in a wide range of colours, sizes and widths to provide a perfect fit.

Made on unique lasts that cannot be found on the high street, each pair of Piedro® footwear is handcrafted and made using only high quality materials, creating footwear that lasts, fits and provides support for feet, exactly where they need it. Every pair has removable anatomical insoles which can be taken out to provide extra depth or to accommodate custom insoles if required. Most styles can also be modified should any adaptations, such as a shoe raise, be required.

### How do I know which style to choose?

If you or your child have been advised to wear orthopaedic footwear it's for a good reason, and that's when choosing the most supportive footwear becomes essential. By this point, most people will be have seen an Orthotist or other specialist who will have advised you on appropriate footwear and measured your feet. If you are unsure about the style, size or width you need it is always best to seek expert medical advice. In many cases orthopaedic footwear can be provided by the NHS.

### What are the most important points to consider?

**Support** – Each footwear style provides different levels of support depending on where and how much is required.
**Depth** – Footwear needs to have enough depth for your feet, especially the toes. Depth is especially important if custom insoles are worn as these need to fit inside the shoes without taking away essential foot space.
**Width** – Footwear should not squash feet or be too wide that the foot moves around inside the shoes. They should be a nice, snug fit.

### Which Style should I choose?

**Rehabilitation Footwear** – These styles provide extra depth and excellent support around the heel and both sides of the foot. They feature padding around the cuff and ankles for comfort, high toe boxes and strong toe caps to provide extra protection.
**Stability Footwear** – In addition to the Rehabilitation footwear features, Stability models provide additional support using higher and longer stiffeners inside the shoes around the heel and sides of the foot to provide increased foot control and stability.
**Multi-Purpose Footwear** – Combines the features of both Rehabilitation and Stability models, they come higher up the leg and provide extra ankle support.
**AFO Footwear** – Designed for children who have to wear a splint or Ankle Foot Orthosis (AFO). They provide the required space around the heel, foot and ankle so the splint(s) fits in the footwear correctly and the feet are in the right position within the shoe with the space they need to develop properly.
**Reverse Lasted Footwear** – Our corrective footwear range, recommended as part of the treatment for children with talipes/clubfoot, can help the foot to develop normally. It can only be prescribed by a suitably qualified medical professional.

If you know the style, size and width of footwear you need, you can order additional pairs directly from G&M. For further information or a catalogue, call our Customer Services Team on 0121 475 1101 or email marketing@gilbert-mellish.co.uk
Piedro® footwear can be ordered online from:

**www.gilbert-mellish.co.uk**

# Clothing and footwear

If you have limited dexterity or restricted movement it may be difficult to put on or fasten clothing. Some disabled people have problems finding off-the-peg clothes that fit properly, or their clothes wear out very quickly. Often these problems can be overcome by selecting clothes that are easy to wear or by altering them. Sometimes you may need to get clothes specially made or buy them by mail order from specialist suppliers. Some stores offer a shopping assistance service that might be useful.

Comfortable, correctly fitting footwear is essential. If your impairment causes shoes to wear out unevenly, it is advisable to buy shoes that can easily be repaired. If you need built-up or orthopaedic shoes, a doctor or consultant can refer you to a specialist fitter. Many people, however, find they are most comfortable in sandals or trainers or shoes with easy fittings. A chiropodist or physiotherapist should be able to advise you.

### Disabled Living Foundation
380-384 Harrow Road, London W9 2HU
**T** 020 7289 6111; textphone 020 7432 8009
**E** info@dlf.org.uk
**W** www.dlf.org.uk
The DLF has many information sheets on daily living and mobility equipment, which can be obtained from the above address or downloaded from the website, including the following:
- clothing for people with continence issues;
- clothing for people with sensitive skin;
- clothing ideas for people who rip clothing;
- clothing ideas for wheelchair users;
- dressing for warmth;
- equipment to help with dressing and putting on footwear;
- finding suitable footwear;
- specialist clothing services.

## SPECIALIST PROVIDERS
### Able 2 Wear
53 Donaldson Street, Kirkintilloch, East Dunbartonshire G66 1XG
**T** 0141 775 3738
**E** info@able2wear.co.uk
**W** www.able2wear.co.uk
Able 2 Wear designs and manufactures a wide range of adaptive clothing for wheelchair-users.

### Adaptawear
14 Murray Place, Stonehaven AB39 2GG
**T** 0845 643 9492
**E** info@adaptawear.co.uk
**W** www.adaptawear.co.uk
Supplies clothes designed to be used easily by disabled and elderly people.

### Clothing Solutions for Disabled People
Unit 1 Jubilee Mills, 30 High Street, Bradford BD1 4ZW
**T** 01274 74 6739
**E** enquiries@clothingsolutions.org.uk
**W** www.clothingsolutions.org.uk
A charity that offers a clothes-making and alterations service to disabled and elderly people. Home visits are available in the Bradford area.

### Cosyfeet
The Tanyard, Leigh Road, Street, Somerset BA16 0HR
**T** 01458 44 9035
**E** comfort@cosyfeet.co.uk
**W** www.cosyfeet.com
Suppliers of extra-wide footwear for people with very wide, swollen or bandaged feet. They stock a range of other foot and leg care products including socks, hosiery, slippers and foot creams. Orders can be made through the website, catalogue or its own outlets.

### Seenin
Aydon South Farm, Aydon, Corbridge NE45 5PL
**T** 01434 63 4457
**E** info@seenin.co.uk
**W** www.seenindesign.co.uk
Suppliers of protective wear, including bibs, kerchiefs, overalls and wheelchair covers, for disabled children and adults. Seenin can also provide bespoke garments.

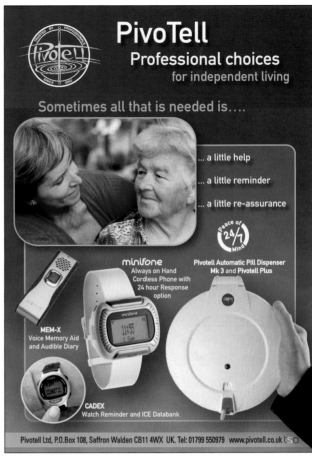

## Doing IT Differently

Information to help everyone regardless of disability, take advantage of information technology (IT) and computers. Includes advice on how to choose and use a computer, and how to adapt it to suit your needs.

Available to order from our online shop
**www.disabilityrightsuk.org**

IF ONLY I'D KNOWN THAT A YEAR AGO ...

# Monitoring and alarms

ENVIRONMENTAL CONTROL SYSTEMS

Environmental control systems can enable us to operate a wide range of equipment and appliances within our homes from a single control – for example door and window openers, electronic curtain rails and blinds, lamps, televisions and heating.

This sort of system can be provided through the NHS after an assessment by a medical consultant who acts as the environmental control assessor for the area.

An occupational therapist would be involved in the installation and the individual design and functioning of the system. The equipment is provided on loan and is maintained and serviced without charge.

TELECARE

Telecare equipment and services provide access to help when you need it. Telecare services range from pendant alarms through to more complex sensor arrangements. The system can warn you of problems by sounding an alarm, flashing lights or vibrating a box that can be kept in your pocket or under your pillow.

Most parts of the country are covered by a Telecare pendant alarm service from a local or national organisation. In recent years, local authorities, housing associations and voluntary organisations have put Telecare sensor services in place.

**How does Telecare work?**

A base unit plugs into a wall telephone socket and a nearby electrical socket. Sensors are placed around the home that will send alerts to the base unit then down the telephone line to a control centre where a response will be provided. For example, a flood detector would pick up water on the floor of a bathroom or kitchen and send a message through the base unit to the control centre.

A computer screen in the control centre gives the address and location of the detector and arrangements for calling the user or a carer, family member, response service or emergency services.

Control centre staff can generally maintain communication with the user during the emergency to provide reassurance.

Telecare services can provide information about the best sensors to use in the home to handle different situations including smoke, temperature, movement and inactivity, falls and epileptic seizures.

Telecare services are often called careline, linkline, helpline or community alarm, or they may have a local name associated with the organisation providing the service.

> *Calling for Help – a Guide to Community Alarms*, published by Ricability, contains information on various community alarm systems and points to consider when choosing one. Single copies can be obtained by sending an A4 addressed envelope with 56p in stamps to Ricability (see 'Useful contacts'.)

TELEHEALTH

A small number of local authorities and health trusts have been testing telehealth systems that can monitor respiratory and heart conditions at home. These services include regular home monitoring of blood pressure, blood sugar, weight and other vital signs. If these measurements are outside of certain levels, healthcare professionals (eg specialist nurses, community matrons) are alerted and will take appropriate follow-up action.

Schemes may be run by local authorities, voluntary organisations or commercial companies, and may be provided on a local basis or over a wider, even national, area.

## EQUIPMENT

Similarly, the level of charges and charging procedures vary. However, your social care department may be able to assist with the cost if you have been assessed as needing the service. Equipment costing under £1,000 should be provided free, but there is still likely to be a monthly connection fee.

Information on local services can be obtained from your local authority or other local information points.

**Telecare Services Association**
Suite 8 Wilmslow House, Grove Way, Wilmslow, Cheshire SK9 5AG
☎ 01625 520320
✉ admin@telecare.org.uk
🌐 www.telecare.org.uk
Represents organisations that fund, provide or operate equipment for community alarm or Telecare services. Its members conform to a code of good practice. For information about services around the country, ring the number above or visit the website.

## WEAVER VALE CARELINE

Peace of mind, independence, reassurance and safety are all words our customers have used when they have talked to us about the services we provide at Weaver Vale Careline.

Weaver Vale Careline has 25 years experience of supporting people to live both safely and independently in their own homes using personal alarm based services.

Whether this is as a preventative measure or following an event such as a fall or illness our Monitoring or Emergency Response Services are available 24 hours a day, 365 days per year.

At the touch of a button our staff can offer advice and provide a swift solution in an emergency, for example, ringing for an ambulance.

If a customer should be unable to press a button or something more is needed, a Telecare Service is available whereby discreet sensors will detect a possible problem, for example if a fall has taken place.

Although our aim is to enable people to remain independent at home, the services we offer can be used on a temporary basis such as when people are recovering from a hospital stay or family are away.

For anyone who is unsure as to what is needed, our staff will provide advice or a visit can be made to our Telecare Showflat in Cheshire, where the latest equipment can be viewed, without obligation, in a relaxed atmosphere.

We hope that people using our services rarely need to use them, but on the occasions that they do, we believe they will receive a reassuring and effective response from our trained operators at the Response Centre.

Just one of our many testimonials:
*"Being a Mum with epilepsy I was always worried about what would happen to my children if I had a fit. Being with Weaver Vale Careline now means my children and I feel safe".*

Our assistive technology enables people of all ages to enjoy life, knowing that a dedicated team is available at the touch of a button.

For more information call 01606 813448 or visit our website.

www.weavervalecareline.co.uk

# Communication and computer technology

Mainstream computers, mobile phones and TVs are increasingly being made with accessible features built in.

The terms 'assistive' or 'accessible' technology cover items of software or hardware that have been designed to facilitate the use of a computer by people with different impairments. The range of possibilities is growing all the time – from simple adaptations through to specialised computer systems, from large screens to speech recognition software. For example, if using a mouse or keyboard is difficult or not possible, you can get speech recognition software.

The best way to find out what is out there is to talk to other people – friends or organisations for people with the same impairment – and then talk to some of the experts listed at the end of this chapter.

There are a lot of options and a lot of suppliers. You don't always need to buy more expensive items. Some items may be supplied to you on loan through your health service, a Communication Aids Centre or a charity, or may be prescribed to you by your hospital consultant.

Most computers are now able to display information in a variety of sizes, talk back to the user or take commands through speech rather than the use of a mouse or pressing of buttons. To give some ideas of the options out there, here are just a few examples (there are many, many more) of access technology commonly used by people with certain disabilities or health conditions.

If you will be using IT for your work or education, explore the financial help that might be available (see the chapters on education and work). You can usually get advice on what help is available from your equipment supplier, a Citizens Advice Bureau, welfare advice agency or a voluntary organisation for people with your impairment. See the list of useful organisations at the back of this book.

## VISUAL IMPAIRMENTS

If you have problems seeing the screen or the letters on the keyboard, or have a hearing impairment, there's a wide choice of products designed to help you. Simple changes like buying large print keyboard stickers to help adapt existing keyboards and make it easier to see or buying a larger computer screen can make a real difference if you have a visual impairment. All standard computers are able to work with larger monitors.

In addition, some adaptations are free, for example, Windows has the options built in to select colour options if you can see certain colours better than others and most word-processors will allow you to increase the size of text in a document as you wish. If this standard increase in size is not enough, there is software that can increase text size further while maintaining its clarity. However, enlarging characters in this way always means that only a portion of the whole screen is visible at any time.

More expensive, stand-alone pieces of technology include closed-circuit TV systems, which enlarge pictures, print or hand-written text that is placed under it onto a screen and scanners. You can place a page from a book into the scanner and it will then convert this text onto a screen which can then be magnified or spoken back to you.

Screen readers read what is on the screen, using a synthetic voice. There is screen reading software that is compatible with most computers. Screen readers vary in their reliability and intelligence but they do make using the internet easier, providing that the websites being viewed are accessible.

Screen reading software can also produce a Braille readout of the text. What would be spoken can be displayed on a Braille strip close to your keyboard. Braille output can be used alone or combined with speech output.

## PHYSICAL DIFFICULTIES

There are a broad range of products that might be able to help by replacing a standard keyboard or even your desktop computer altogether.

Small keyboards are compatible with any computer, can be more easily positioned and are more suited to single-handed users. They can also fit between the arms of a standard wheelchair. Alternatively, ergonomic keyboards can solve problems; these are expanded keyboards that can help in situations where it is difficult for you to accurately locate the keys as the larger size gives more area to aim at.

For those of us who can't use keys or mouse buttons at all, touch pads found on most laptop computers may be easier to use. These pads are operated by sliding a finger across the surface with clicking done by lightly tapping on the surface. A more expensive option is a head controlled pointer. This is where the pointer on a screen is controlled simply by moving your head. Another alternative to the keyboard is using voice recognition software. This software enables you to talk to the computer and your words appear on the screen.

The software can even control your computer programs and compose emails by opening and closing programs as you command.

Smartphones, ipads and tablets are well worth looking at if touching the screen and pointing at what you want is easier for you than using a mouse or keyboard. These products all run apps – small computer programs – which can do all sorts of useful things. Some of the websites listed in 'Useful contacts' contain information about specialist apps of interest to disabled people.

---

If you feel you need a bit more background information before approaching the organisations listed here, or if you're not convinced that you can use a computer, read Disability Rights UK's publication *Doing IT Differently*. It's available from Disability Rights UK electronically or as a printed copy.

It answers common questions such as:
- How can I learn to use IT?
- How do I choose IT?
- What adaptations are available?
- What practical help is available?

---

## ACE CENTRE

### Communication technology
For many people effective communication is difficult because of a physical impairment, language disorder or learning disability.

We provide help and expertise in the field of communication aids. These range from simple letter boards to sophisticated computer equipment, designed to help a person to communicate more effectively. We specialise in Augmentative and Alternative Communication (AAC) and Assistive Technology (AT).

If you have communication difficulties or are a parent, carer or therapist, we can help. Our team of therapists, teachers and technicians provide a range of services including assessments, training, equipment loans, training and information, as well as project and consultancy work for statutory services.

A cost effective way of accessing a range of our services is through our Service Level Agreements, which are particularly popular with local authorities and schools.

### ACE Centres team up
We are delighted to announce that the ACE Centres based in Oldham and Oxford have now become one organisation, which will continue to operate from both areas.

**ACE Centre North** (Oldham)
Tel: 0161 358 0151
Email: enquiries@ace-north.org.uk
**ACE Centre Advisory Trust** (Oxford)
Tel: 01865 759800
Email: info@ace-centre.org.uk

www.ace-north.org.uk
www.ace-centre.org.uk

JUST REDESIGNED AND BETTER THAN EVER!

# Including You

## For those who need extra help with communications

Our Including You website is full of information for everyone. But it's especially aimed at our customers who find communications more challenging. That's why we've put our most helpful products and services all in one place.

Go to **bt.com/includingyou** for the latest on...

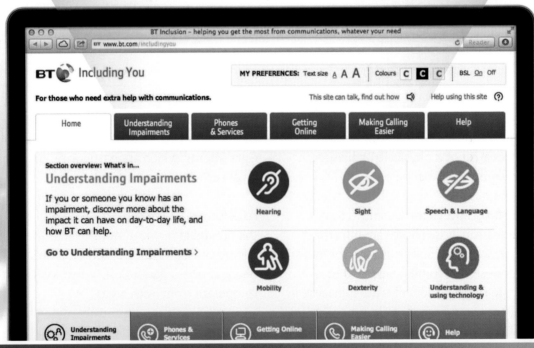

## BT.COM/INCLUDINGYOU

### A great place to start learning about communications and the internet

At BT, we think everyone should be able to get the most from the latest communications – whatever their needs. That's why we created a single website that brings together all you need to know about using our products and services.

Whether you have difficulty seeing, hearing, speaking or moving about – we have advice and products to make using your phone easier. The website contains our most helpful products and services in one place and is packed with the latest news, advice and information to make it easier for you to get more from your phone and broadband.

"The Including You website is full of useful information," explains Dave Barrett, who is responsible for accessibility and inclusion at BT. "For instance, if you have difficulty holding a phone, then there are a range of digital headsets available to overcome the problem. Or if you use hearing aids, we have lots of advice on which BT phones would be of most use to you," he said.

### Designing products and services for all

One of the phones featured on the website is the iconic 'Big Button' phone, which was redesigned and relaunched in 2012. Despite its name, the Big Button phone isn't just about 'big buttons'. The designers spoke directly to elderly people and those with mixed abilities to get direct input.

Part of the remodelling involved the designers using an impairment kit to simulate various disabilities. For instance, there are special goggles that blur vision and dexterity-limiting gloves that simulate someone who may suffer with arthritis.

"Our designers go to great lengths to ensure that the products we sell can be used by the widest audience possible," said Dave. "It's called 'inclusive design' & for us at BT, it's at the heart of everything we do."

### Designed for your needs

Indeed, this philosophy was also at the heart of creating the Including You website. We worked with technology charity AbilityNet to ensure that the new website was accessible and easy to navigate.

"It lets people find specific information about a particular disability more quickly," said Dave. "Visitors are able to alter font sizes and background colour to suit their needs. The website can also read the text out using BrowseAloud. Most information is available in BSL and you can have a conversation with BT in BSL via the site."

Whether you're in a position to help someone get online – or need help yourself – there is plenty of information about getting online and making the most of the internet plus details of how to get your hands on low cost computers.

"It's quite simple," said Dave. "The Including You website has a host of information and is the ideal place to start getting the most out of communications and the internet."

### About BT

BT is one of the world's leading providers of communications services and solutions, serving customers in more than 170 countries.

Its principal activities include the provision of networked IT services globally; local, national and international telecommunications services to its customers for use at home, at work and on the move; broadband and internet products and services and converged fixed/mobile products and services.

BT was the official communications services partner of the London 2012 Olympic and Paralympic Games.

www.btplc.com

## Assistance dogs

There is a long tradition of trained guide dogs helping blind and partially sighted people to get around. In recent years, dogs have also been trained to help a wider range of disabled people.

Assistance Dogs UK is a coalition of assistance dog organisations. It encourages the exchange of ideas and best practice, raises awareness among the general public and promotes behavioural and legislative changes to ensure the freedom, independence and rights of its clients. The following organisations are members of Assistance Dogs UK.

### Canine Partners
Mill Lane, Heyshott, Midhurst, West Sussex GU29 0ED
**T** 0845 658 0480
**E** info@caninepartners.co.uk
**W** www.caninepartners.co.uk

### Dogs for the Disabled
The Frances Hay Centre, Blacklocks Hill, Banbury Oxon OX17 2BS
**T** 01295 25 2600
**E** info@dogsforthedisabled.org
**W** www.dogsforthedisabled.org

### Guide Dogs
Burghfield Common, Reading RG7 3YG
**T** 0118 983 5555
**E** guidedogs@guidedogs.org.uk
**W** www.guidedogs.org.uk

### Hearing Dogs for Deaf People
The Grange, Wycombe Road, Saunderton, Princes Risborough HP27 9NS
**T** 01844 34 8100 (voice and textphone)
**E** info@hearingdogs.org.uk
**W** www.hearingdogs.org.uk
This UK charity selects and trains dogs, mostly from rescue centres or similar backgrounds, to alert deaf people to important sounds and danger signals. Hearing dogs provide their deaf partners with greater independence, confidence and security.

### Support Dogs
21 Jessops Riverside, Brightside Lane, Sheffield S9 2RX
**T** 0114 261 7800
**E** supportdogs@btconnect.com
**W** www.support-dogs.org.uk
In addition to training dogs to assist physically disabled people, Support Dogs trains seizure alert dogs to support people with epilepsy and some other conditions.

**Dog Assistance in Disability** provides dog training for disabled people enabling them to train their pets in general obedience and specialised tasks to help in daily life. Visit their website (www.dogaid.org.uk) or contact them at: Dog AID Office, CVS Buildings, Arthur Street, Chadsmoor, Cannock, Staffordshire WS11 5HD.

## Useful contacts

### 1 Voice – Communicating Together
PO Box 600, Chorley PR6 6JR
**T** 0845 330 7862
**E** info@1voice.info
**W** www.1voice.info
1 Voice provides a network of information and support for people who use a communication aid to act as their voice, as well as for their families and carers. It provides opportunities for personal contact in a variety of settings and also through the internet.

### Ability Magazine
**E** john.lamb@abilitymagazine.org.uk
**W** www.abilitymagazine.org.uk
Ability Magazine is a campaigning publication for people who have difficulty using IT. It has a 'useful links' page on its website.

## AbilityNet

☎ 0800 26 9545 (also textphone)
✉ enquiries@abilitynet.org.uk
ⓦ www.abilitynet.org.uk

AbilityNet, a national charity, is the UK's leading provider of advice on computing and disability. It provides a freephone advice and information line, individual assessments, a wide range of factsheets and awareness training for professionals. AbilityNet runs a number of websites including the online self-assessment site, 'My Computer My Way' (www.abilitynet.org.uk/myway) and a YouTube page that enables you to see aids and adaptations in action (www.youtube.com/abilitynet). The IT Can Help Network (www.itcanhelp.org.uk) uses skilled volunteers to assist disabled people with computer problems in their own homes, at other venues or remotely.

## Action on Hearing Loss Solutions Catalogue

Action on Hearing Loss Products Customer Services, 19-23 Featherstone Street, London EC1Y 8SL

☎ 01733 36 1199; textphone 01733 23 8020
✉ solutions@rnid.org.uk
ⓦ www.rnid.org.uk/shop

Action on Hearing Loss Solutions is a catalogue of products specifically chosen to help solve everyday problems for deaf and hard of hearing people. It contains over 200 products.

## Aidis Trust

Floor 7, 3 London Wall Buildings, London Wall, London EC2M 5PD

☎ 0808 800 0009
✉ support@aidis.org
ⓦ www.aidis.org

The Trust helps disabled people communicate more easily and effectively through the use of technology. It offers advice, assessment, installation and ongoing training and support. It runs a programme of workshops and can supply selected equipment through its website.

## Apple Vis

ⓦ www.applevis.com

A community-powered site for visually-impaired users of Apple iOS devices to share information, tips and tutorials on the accessibility of apps developed for the iPhone, iPad and iPod Touch.

## BATA (British Assistive Technology Association)

BATA Online Ltd, PO Box 52, Oldham OL3 5YY
✉ info@bataonline.org
ⓦ www.bataonline.org

BATA was established in 2009 by a group of companies and organisations to lobby for the rights and interests of those needing assistive technology, provide expert and impartial advice to government departments and to educate and inform on the benefits of assistive technology.

## British Computer Association of the Blind

c/o RNIB, 58-72 John Bright Street, Birmingham B1 1BN

☎ 0845 643 9811
✉ info@bcab.org.uk
ⓦ www.bcab.org.uk

Self-help group of visually impaired computer professionals and users.

## BT Inclusive Communications

☎ 0800 800 150
    Textphone 18001 0800 800 150
ⓦ www.btplc.com/inclusion

BT offers a number of services and products to assist people who have problems with communications. These are listed on its website and in BT's Communications Solutions Guide. This is available free by calling the above number.

## Communication Matters (ISAAC UK)

Catchpell House, Carpet Lane, Edinburgh EH6 6SP

☎ 0131 467 7487
✉ admin@communicationmatters.org.uk
ⓦ www.communicationmatters.org.uk

Communication Matters is a national charity focusing on the needs of people who have little or no clear speech and may benefit from using some form of assistive technology to help them communicate. A wide range of publications is available on its website. The Communication Matters National Symposium, regional study days and equipment road shows are organised throughout the year.

### Disabled Living Foundation (DLF)

380-384 Harrow Road, London W9 2HU

T 020 7289 6111; textphone 020 7432 8009

E info@dlf.org.uk

W www.dlf.org.uk

The DLF has many information sheets on daily living and mobility equipment, which can be obtained from the above address or downloaded from the website.

### Emptech

E info@emptech.info

W www.emptech.info

Aims to provide information resources on assistive technologies designed to help those with specific difficulties or disabilities work and study more effectively.

### Foundation for Assistive Technology

31 Scarborough Street, London E1 8DR

T 020 7264 8955

E info@fastuk.org

W www.fastuk.org

FAST promotes research and development on equipment or assistive technology for disabled people. It brings together current or prospective users of assistive technology with researchers, developers, manufacturers and other service providers to become partners in the design, development and assessment of new products.

### Karten Network

T 075 3070 2134

E ceri@karten-network.org.uk

W http://karten-network.org.uk

Operates numerous centres across the UK that provide access to adaptive computer technology.

### Learndirect

Freepost Learndirect

T 0800 101 901

W www.learndirect.co.uk

Offers computer-based courses enabling you to learn at Learndirect centres, at home or any place where you can access the internet. Some courses are also available on workbooks or CD-Rom.

### Leonard Cheshire Disability

66 South Lambeth Road, London SW8 1RL

T 020 3242 0200

E info@LCDisability.org

W www.lcdisability.org

The UK's largest voluntary sector provider of services to disabled people runs nine IT centres and an IT training and employment scheme called Workability.

### LexDis

W www.lexdis.org

Hints and tips from students at the University of Southampton but of use to anyone trying to set up their computer to suit them. Includes a strategies database.

### Mac-cessibility

W maccessibility.net

The Mac-cessibility Network brings together the best Apple resources for blind, visually impaired, and other disabled people. They list accessible apps at maccessibility.net/iphone/apps/

### Ricability

Unit G03, The Wenlock Business Centre, 50-52 Wharf Road, London N1 7EU

T 020 7427 2460; textphone 020 7427 2469

E mail@ricability.org.uk

W www.ricability.org.uk

Ricability is an independent research charity publishing practical and unbiased consumer guides for older and disabled people on a range of products and services. Reports include products for childcare, household and personal care, the use of public transport by wheelchair users, driving and car adaptations, community alarms and telecommunication equipment and services. Guides are on the Ricability website and most are available on tape and in Braille and large print. Contact them for a publications list and ordering details.

### Royal National Institute of Blind People (RNIB)

105 Judd Street, London WC1H 9NE

T 0303 123 9999

E helpline@rnib.org.uk

W www.rnib.org.uk

Leading charity offering information, support and advice to people with sight loss.

**The Sequal Trust**

3 Ploughman's Corner, Wharf Road, Ellesmere, Shropshire SW12 0EJ

☎ 01691 62 4222

✉ info@thesequaltrust.org.uk

🌐 www.thesequaltrust.org.uk

The Sequal Trust raises funds to provide communication aids and adaptations for people with speech/movement disabilities and/or learning difficulties. The aids are provided on a loan basis for as long as the need exists.

**The Speech Centre**

Speak-IT Ltd, The Computer Studio, Croft Road, Crowborough TN6 1DL

☎ 01892 66 1116

✉ speech@speechcentre.co.uk

🌐 www.speechcentre.co.uk

Provides assistive/enabling technology and computer/work-related solutions.

**TechDis**

JISC TechDis Service, The Higher Education Academy Building, Innovation Way, York Science Park, York YO10 5BR

☎ 01904 717580

✉ helpdesk@techdis.ac.uk

🌐 www.jisctechdis.ac.uk

For disabled staff and students in further, higher and specialist education.

**UCanDoIT**

1 Taylors Yard, 67 Alderbrook Road, London SW12 8AD

☎ 020 8673 3300 (also textphone)

✉ info@ucandoit.org.uk

🌐 www.ucandoit.org.uk

UCanDoIT is a charity that teaches computer and internet skills to disabled people on a one-to-one basis at home. Students are taught how to email, use the internet, and access news groups and chat rooms. The basic course consists of ten lessons lasting between one and two hours. Tutors are vetted by the police and have extensive IT backgrounds. UCanDoIT has tutors in a number of areas.

**UK online centres**

The Workstation, 15 Paternoster Row, Sheffield S1 2BX

☎ 0114 227 0010

✉ ukonlinecentres@ufi.com

🌐 www.ukonlinecentres.com

UK online centres provide access to computers and the internet as well as help and advice on how to use them. There are 3,500 centres across England, with similar provision in Wales and Scotland.

**Vodafone Disability Services**

Vodafone House, The Connection, Newbury RG14 2FN

☎ 0870 073 3222; textphone 020 8288 8038

✉ disability.access@vodafone.co.uk

🌐 www.vodafone.co.uk/Disabilityservices

Offer help and advice to make phones and services more accessible and easier to use for elderly and disabled people. Various guides and booklets describing the services are available as downloads from the website or copies can be ordered online.

IF ONLY I'D KNOWN THAT A YEAR AGO ...

# Housing

**If we begin to find it difficult to manage at home, we may be entitled to help from our local authority to adapt our home to our needs or to find a more accessible place to live. This chapter includes information about your rights to adaptations for your home, things to think about if you need to move home, when you can get help with paying your mortgage, what help is available to insulate your home (and cut energy costs) and some sheltered housing options.**

## Home adaptations

Most areas have a home improvement service to help disabled and older people with quick repairs and small adaptations like grab rails. They can also help get grants for bigger adaptations (see below). Many also offer 'handy person services' to do small jobs in the home, put in safety features and help make sure homes are suitable to return to after a spell in hospital. To find a local home improvement service contact:

### Foundations
Bleaklow House, Howard Town Mill, Glossop
SK13 8HT
- 0845 864 5210
- info@foundations.uk.com
- www.foundations.uk.com

### DISABLED FACILITIES GRANTS
For bigger adaptations such as a downstairs shower room, wider doorways or an adapted kitchen, you could apply to your local authority for a Disabled Facilities Grant.

Disabled homeowners, tenants and landlords of tenants with disabilities, can sometimes get a Disabled Facilities Grant for adaptations needed to:
- make it easier to get into and out of your home – for example, by widening doorways or installing a ramp
- improve access between your house and garden, yard or balcony
- ensure your safety and that of other people living with you – for example, by improved lighting or providing a specially adapted room where someone can be left unattended
- improve or provide a suitable heating system and adapt heating and lighting controls to make them easier for you to use
- improve access to your living room and bedroom
- make it easier for you to prepare and cook food
- provide or improve access to the kitchen, toilet, washbasin and bath or shower – for example, by installing a stairlift or downstairs bathroom
- improve access and movement around the home so you can care for another resident, such as your child or spouse.

The Disabled Facilities Grant is normally paid by your local housing authority (or your Local Housing Executive Grants Office if you are in Northern Ireland) who will give you an application form. You can apply for a grant for someone else who is disabled if you clearly state this on your application form. To approve a grant, the authority must be satisfied that the works are necessary and appropriate for your needs as well as being reasonable and practicable in relation to the property. You will usually be assessed by an occupational therapist, who will make a recommendation to the housing grants officers. Once you have filled in the formal application form you are entitled to a decision within six months. Your housing authority cannot refuse to allow you to make an application.

The maximum grant payable is £30,000 in England, £25,000 in Northern Ireland and £36,000 in Wales. A separate system operates through Housing Grants in Scotland. The amount of money you earn or the savings you have will not be taken into account if the grant is for the benefit of a disabled child. For applications from disabled adults, the amount you get from a Disabled Facilities Grant will depend on the income and savings that you and your partner have.

IF ONLY I'D KNOWN THAT A YEAR AGO ...

## HAVING BUILDING WORK DONE

- If you are applying for a Disabled Facilities Grant, do not have any work carried out until your application has been approved. If the work is urgent, contact your local council.
- Check whether you need planning permission beforehand. Many common building works and extensions will not need permission, but you must check with your local council.
- You or your builder will also need to ensure that the work complies with building regulations.
- If it's a big project, use a qualified architect or surveyor to prepare the plans and supervise the work.
- Check the reputation of builders and contractors and ensure they are members of a trade association that provides a guarantee or arbitration service, eg, the Federation of Master Builders or National Federation of Builders.
- Find out if your local authority has a list of local architects, builders, etc who have experience of carrying out adaptations.

## VAT ON BUILDING WORK

Some building work to adapt existing housing to meet the needs of a disabled occupant may be zero rated for VAT. This includes:

- building ramps or widening doorways or passages
- extending or adapting a bathroom or toilet
- installing a lift
- putting in an alarm system to call for help.

The contractor or supplier should know whether the work is zero rated. Information is available in VAT Notice 701/7, available from HM Revenue and Customs. You can get more advice from your local authority, a housing advice centre, a Home Improvement Agency or Citizens Advice Bureau or online at www.gov.uk.

## OTHER FINANCIAL ASSISTANCE

If you are awarded a Disabled Facilities Grant but the grant is not enough to cover the total cost of work you need, you may get help under other housing grant or payment schemes. Housing authorities have the power to provide discretionary assistance that might be used to top-up a Disabled Facilities Grant or help you move if that would be a better option. If you are a private householder they may provide help through low-cost loans or equity release schemes. Social care departments can sometimes provide equipment and adaptations costing up to £1,000 without charge, or loan equipment such as stairlifts.

# Energy saving

In England, the Warm Front scheme provides grants for heating and insulation improvements. Similar schemes operate in Scotland, Wales and Northern Ireland. You will be eligible if you receive certain benefits (pension credit, income support, income-related employment and support allowance or income-based jobseeker's allowance).

The scheme is designed to assist people who are most vulnerable to cold-related problems, including disabled people and people with long-term illnesses. Under the scheme, a package could include loft insulation, cavity wall insulation, draught proofing and central heating, which would help to reduce your gas or electricity bills.

Warm Front will end after March 2013 and be replaced by the Green Deal.

The Green Deal has already been launched but you cannot get help under the Scheme until January 2013. For more information visit www.gov.uk. People over 60 who aren't eligible for the full scheme can apply for a discount on the cost of installing central heating, although funds for this are limited.

To apply, or for more information, contact:
**Warm Front Scheme**
☎ 0800 316 2805
Ⓦ www.warmfront.co.uk

For free, impartial advice on energy saving in your home and cutting your fuel bills contact:
**Energy Saving Trust**
☎ 0300 123 1234 or 0800 512 012 in Scotland
Ⓦ www.energysavingtrust.org.uk

# Moving home

If your home is not suitable for adaptation or no longer suitable for your family, you might want to move.

## CAN'T AFFORD TO BUY?

If you can't afford to buy and you have a low income, contact your local authority about going on the housing register. This is a list of people who want to rent council or housing association properties. Since there are more people in need than there are homes available, councils have to prioritise. Anyone who needs to move for medical or access reasons should get priority – but check your council's policies on this.

In England, many local authorities have adopted 'choice-based lettings', which means people on the housing register are not offered a particular property but are invited to bid for any available property they think meets their needs. Properties with access features should be flagged up. Whose bid is successful depends on who has the biggest priority need.

In some areas you can get advice from a dedicated Disabled Persons Housing Service. In others, an Accessible Housing Register provides up-to-date details of accessible or adapted homes available for renting.

Local authorities have powers to pay a relocation grant to help someone move to a home that is already more accessible or could be made so more easily.

### Housing associations

Some housing associations have their own waiting lists so it's worth contacting them as well. Housing associations are non-profit organisations providing rented homes or assistance for people on low-incomes to buy a home. Some operate on a local or regional basis and others specialise in providing housing for people with particular housing needs, such as forms of supported housing.

Most vacancies in housing association properties are allocated to people nominated by the local authority for the area.

However, depending on their individual policies, associations may also accept applications from individuals or other organisations. Some associations operate partnership schemes with voluntary bodies where they provide the housing and the partner provides an agreed level of care or support for tenants.

### Shared ownership

Housing associations often run shared ownership schemes where you part buy and part rent a home. You might buy a 25%, 50% or 75% share in your home and pay a small rent on the share that you don't buy. For information go to www.shared-ownership.org.uk.

The government also has a scheme called Home Buy, which is for first-time buyers, key workers (such as teachers and nurses) and social tenants. Details are available at www.homebuy.org.uk.

## DESIGN FEATURES FOR NEW HOMES

If you're considering buying a new house, it is worth:

- checking the accessibility standards it is built to
- contacting the developer to see if they can incorporate design features that you need.

All new homes must be built to standards that enable disabled people, particularly wheelchair users and people with mobility impairments, to visit and have access to a ground floor living space and toilet. An increasing number of homes (mainly social housing) are being built to the Lifetime Homes standards (see below).

If your home needs to be wheelchair accessible – that is with the necessary circulation space and level access to provide full wheelchair use in all parts of the home – it's worth checking with local housing associations. Also try the Accessible Property Register (details in 'Useful contacts' at the end of this chapter). Disability Rights UK is pressing for more wheelchair accessible housing and for a national accessible housing register, updated by all local authorities and landlords.

**Lifetime Homes** is a design concept that aims to make new housing accessible for disabled people and easy to adapt to meet future individual requirements that may emerge. It consists of 16 design criteria that can be universally applied to new homes. Many local planning policies are already required to use the Lifetime Homes standards in new developments. In Wales and Northern Ireland, complying with the standards is a legal requirement. The scheme is administered and supported by Habinteg Housing, which encourages all social housing providers and private builders to use the standards.

The design criteria include:
- level entry to the main entrance, or a suitable alternative
- an entrance door wide enough to allow for wheelchair access
- a toilet on the entrance level that is capable of having a shower installed
- adequate circulation and door widths on the entrance floor
- switches, sockets and other controls at appropriate heights
- level or gently sloping path from a nearby parking space to the dwelling entrance
- a lift of appropriate size in blocks of flats
- walls and ceilings to which handrails and hoists can be fitted in bathrooms and adjoining bedrooms
- an area that could be used as a bedroom on the entrance floor
- staircases of a design that will facilitate the fitting of a stairlift or space for a through-floor lift.

For more information on the scheme, visit www.lifetimehomes.org.uk.

## Help with mortgage payments

If you start getting behind with your mortgage payments it's important to get advice as soon as possible. Advice is available from lenders and agencies such as Citizens Advice and Shelter. A good starting point is www.gov.uk.

Lenders are now required to consider all options before taking steps to repossess a property. These can include agreeing to reduce your mortgage payments for a set time, changing your payments to interest only, giving you a payment holiday, or letting you stay in the property while you find somewhere else to live. If you are unhappy about how your lender has been dealing with you, you can complain to the Financial Ombudsman.

**Financial Ombudsman Service**
☎ 0800 023 4567
Ⓦ www.financial-ombudsman.org.uk

**Mortgage Rescue Scheme**
In England, this scheme (and similar schemes in Wales, Scotland and Northern Ireland) may help if you are having serious difficulties making your mortgage repayments and are at risk of becoming homeless if your house were to be repossessed.

This scheme is for people with 'priority needs' – including disabled people whose household income is less than £60,000 a year. If you're eligible for the scheme, as well as financial help, you could get advice to help you stay in your home. You can be referred to the scheme by an advice agency or by contacting your local authority directly.

**Support for mortgage interest**
If you are claiming certain means-tested benefits (including pension credit, income-based jobseeker's allowance, income support and income-related employment and support allowance), you might be able to get help towards your mortgage interest payments. You can get help with a mortgage of up to £200,000 after a 13-week waiting period. If you receive pension credit, you might be able to get help immediately but only for a mortgage of up to £100,000. There is no help available for capital payments of your mortgage. If you are receiving income-based jobseeker's allowance, you can only be paid mortgage interest costs for up to 104 weeks.

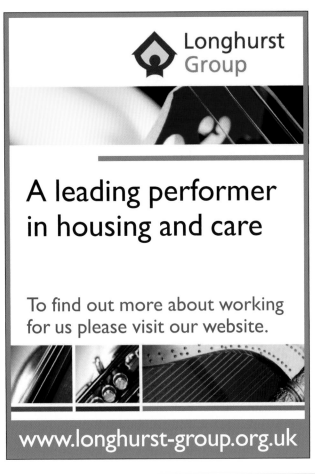

IF ONLY I'D KNOWN THAT A YEAR AGO ...

### Maximising your income

If you are ever struggling to meet your mortgage payments, it's always worth checking that you are getting all of the benefits and tax credits you are entitled to. It can make a real difference to your income and help you to meet all of your expenses. Our *Disability Rights Handbook* is a guide to benefits and services for disabled people that could help you maximise your income.

> **Housing and the Equality Act 2010**
> The Equality Act 2010 brought in legislation to ensure that disabled people are not discriminated against in relation to renting or buying property. For details, see the chapter on 'Discrimination' in this book.

## Sheltered housing

If you want housing with extra support and security but don't want to forego your independence, there are a number of options.

Sheltered housing, often but not exclusively provided for older people, comes in the form of a group of appropriately designed self-contained flats or houses with 24-hour emergency assistance plus the security of having a warden on hand. There are usually communal facilities, for example a lounge and gardens. Some schemes provide additional care services – this is often called Extra Care Housing.

Much sheltered housing is for rent and available through your local authority or housing association. Increasingly, private developers and a number of housing associations are offering a variety of purchase options to buy your own property. You can get further advice from:

**Elderly Accommodation Counsel**
3rd Floor, 89 Albert Embankment, London SE1 7TP
**T** 020 7820 1343
**E** info@firststopadvice.org.uk
**W** www.housingcare.org
Maintains a register of sheltered housing schemes, which is available on the website. They can advise older people on all matters of accommodation and related care.

**ERoSH**
PO Box 2616, Chippenham SN15 1WZ
**T** 01249 654 249
**E** info@erosh.co.uk
**W** www.erosh.co.uk
National consortium for sheltered and retirement housing. Works on behalf of older people and sheltered housing providers to improve housing and support for existing and future sheltered housing residents.

**B3LIVING**

B3Living own 4,500 homes in Broxbourne and employ 150 people. We're committed to providing better homes, better communities and running a better business. Not just better for some people but better for everyone.

We are committed to treating residents and staff fairly, responding to individual needs. To support residents with disabilities, we employ three support workers, adapt homes, provide letters in large print and our newsletter in audio and have a Disabilities Forum. We offer a community alarm and mobile warden service and some internal decorations for tenants with disabilities. We have Two Ticks Positive About Disabled People accreditation.

To find out more about what we offer residents and employees with disabilities, call us on 01992 453 700 or visit our website.

www.b3living.org.uk.

## Useful contacts

### Accessible Property Register
c/o Conrad Hodgkinson, 11 Stumperlowe Croft, Sheffield S10 3QW

T 0774 911 9385

E conradh@accessible-property.org.uk

W www.accessible-property.org.uk

The website has information on accessible and adapted housing for sale or rent, including both private and social housing. People looking for housing can place a 'Property Wanted' notice on the site.

### Community Housing Cymru
2 Ocean Way, Cardiff CF24 5TG

T 029 2067 4800

E enquiries@chcymru.org.uk

W www.chcymru.org.uk

### Counsel and Care
6 Avonmore Road, Kensington Olympia, London W14 8RL

T 0845 300 7585

E advice@counselandcare.org.uk

W www.counselandcare.org.uk

Provides information and advice for older people and their families and carers on residential and community care. Publishes guides and factsheets, downloadable from their website or available free of charge from the above address.

### Habinteg Housing Association
Holyer House, 20-21 Red Lion Court, London EC4A 3EB

T 01274 853 160 or 0845 606 2608

E info@habinteg.org.uk

W www.habinteg.org.uk

A specialist provider of accessible housing, Habinteg provides over 2,000 homes across England, of which over a quarter are designed for wheelchair users and the rest to accessibility standards. Provides advice to other housing associations on disability equality policies. Sister organisations operate in Northern Ireland, Scotland, Wales and the Irish Republic.

### Housing Ombudsman Service
81 Aldwych, London WC2B 4HN

T 0300 111 3000

E info@housing-ombudsman.org.uk

W www.housing-ombudsman.org.uk

An independent organisation that can take up complaints from residents of housing provided by social landlords, including those who have taken over properties from local authorities. You should have used your landlord's own complaints procedure before registering it with the Ombudsman. Local authority tenants should contact the Local Government Ombudsman. The Housing Ombudsman operates only in England.

### Housing Options
Stanelaw House, Sutton Lane, Sutton, Witney OX29 5RY

T 0845 456 1497

E enquiries@housingoptions.org.uk

W www.housingoptions.org.uk

An advisory service for anyone concerned with housing for people with learning disabilities, their families and carers. The website includes a wide range of information sheets, all of which can be read in Easy Read format.

### Joseph Rowntree Foundation
The Homestead, 40 Water End, York YO30 6WP

T 01904 629 241; textphone 01904 615 910

E info@jrf.org.uk

W www.jrf.org.uk

Supports a wide programme of research and development projects in housing, social care and social policy. Also carries out practical innovative projects in housing and care through the Joseph Rowntree Housing Trust, including the development of the concept of Lifetime Homes.

### Livability
50 Scrutton Street, London EC2A 4XQ

T 020 7452 2000

E info@livability.org.uk

W www.livability.org.uk

A merger of John Grooms Association and the Shaftesbury Society, includes Livability Housing. They specialise in homes designed and adapted for wheelchair users and their families.

**Mobility Friendly Homes**
99 South Street, Eastbourne BN21 4LU
**T** 0845 612 0280
**E** info@mobilityfriendlyhomes.co.uk
**W** www.mobilityfriendlyhomes.co.uk
An online estate agent for disabled people wanting to buy or rent an accessible or adapted property. It lists properties across the UK with details of access features and adaptations as well as other property details.

**National Housing Federation**
Lion Court, 25 Procter Street, London WC1V 6NY
**T** 020 7067 1010
**E** info@housing.org.uk
**W** www.housing.org.uk
Provides information on housing associations and other independent social landlords and affordable housing providers in England. It has around 1,200 members who are responsible for 2.5 million homes.

**Northern Ireland Federation of Housing Associations**
6c Citylink Business Park, Albert Street, Belfast BT12 4HB
**T** 028 9023 0446
**W** www.nifha.org

**Ownership Options in Scotland**
The Melting Pot, 5 Rose Street, Edinburgh EH2 2PR
**T** 0131 247 1400
**E** info@housingoptionsscotland.org.uk
**W** www.ownershipoptions.org.uk
A charity that provides information and advice to disabled people in Scotland to help them overcome the legal, financial and practical barriers to home ownership.

**Scottish Federation of Housing Associations**
3rd floor, Sutherland House, 149 St Vincent Street, Glasgow G2 5NW
**T** 0141 332 8113
**E** sfha@sfha.co.uk
**W** www.sfha.co.uk

**Shelter**
88 Old Street, London EC1V 9HU
**T** 0808 800 4444
**E** info@shelter.org.uk
**W** www.shelter.org.uk
The national housing and homelessness charity that campaigns for decent housing and helps people find and keep a home. It provides advice by telephone, through publications, on its website and through a network of housing advice centres around the country.

**L&Q GROUP**

L&Q Group is one of the 2,000 Housing Associations in the UK. Our main purpose is to provide high quality, affordable homes.

We manage over 66,000 homes and although most are in Greater London, we also work all over South East England.

Other things we do include:
- Building new homes and refurbishing old ones
- Creating affordable homes for sale
- Providing accommodation for key workers like nurses
- Helping people on lower incomes buy homes through shared ownership
- Helping with community projects through our Neighbourhood investment teams

All our work is about creating places where people want to live and getting the best value so that our residents get the best service possible from us.

**www.lqgroup.org.uk**

Space donated by

**A friend in Gloucester**

Space donated by

**Roger Harper Isle of Man**

Best wishes from a friend in Ladykirk

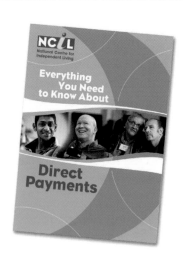

IF ONLY I'D KNOWN THAT A YEAR AGO ...

# Social care

**When we have a disability or long-term health condition, we may need practical support in order to remain living in our own home, to carry out day-to-day tasks and to do the things we want to do to lead a full life. Or we may need to move to a residential home where there might be more support. This chapter provides a brief guide to the types of practical support available, how to get the help, and what to do if we don't get the help we need. At the end of the chapter there are details of organisations that can provide further information, advice and support.**

## What is social care?

The purpose of social care is to support disabled people and to promote our independence.

Social care services may include:
- personal care at home
- care in residential or nursing homes
- domestic help
- help with shopping
- Meals on Wheels
- provision of equipment.

Local authorities are responsible for providing social care, but their resources are limited. They can charge for services or they can give a direct payment so you can buy the care you need from an independent organisation.

You have the right to be assessed for local authority care services, but whether or not you get any of these services depends on the outcome of a social care assessment and your financial situation.

### DEFINITIONS
#### Community care
The term 'community care' is simply a different term for 'social care'. There is no difference between a community care assessment and a social care assessment – they are just different terms for the same set of services.

#### Independent living
Independent living means having the practical support you need to lead a full life and having a say in how the support or care you receive is arranged and provided.

### Direct payments
Direct payments are central to the government's personalisation (self-directed support) agenda that aims to give you more choice and control over your personal care. Direct payments are not counted as income when you are claiming social security benefits or tax credits.

Direct payments are cash payments given directly to you by your local authority so you can arrange for your own care services (for example, to employ your own personal assistant or to buy your own equipment). If you receive a direct payment to pay for a particular service, the local authority social care department will not arrange or provide the service to you themselves; arranging it becomes your own responsibility.

You can spend your direct payment in any way you wish so as to meet your eligible needs. Direct payments cannot be used to pay for residential care or to buy care services directly from the local council.

By law, if the authority agrees to fund some support for you, they have to offer you a direct payment unless there are exceptional circumstances.

For more information on residential and continuing care services, please see the 'Later years' chapter in this book.

### Personal budgets

Personal budgets were introduced in England in 2008 and the government hopes that by 2013 every care service user will have one. Personal budgets are a pot of money given to you if your care assessment shows you have eligible needs. You then decide how you would like to spend your personal budget to get the help you need.

You can take your personal budget as a direct payment, leave it to social services to commission services on your behalf, or you can have a combination of the two.

Personal budgets are not counted as income when you are claiming social security benefits or tax credits.

## Who is responsible for what?

You may hear about or be referred to different people and departments when entering the social care system. The most important ones are:

### Social care department

Social care services are provided through your local authority social care department, either adult social care or children's social care.

### Care manager

Your care manager will be the person in your local authority's social care department who is responsible for supporting your support requirements.

### Direct payment support services

These services can advise and support you to manage your personal budget. They can provide many practical services such as helping you to find and employ your own personal assistant and help with drafting contracts of employment for anyone you employ to provide you a service.

### Brokerage support service

A broker provided to you through this support service is responsible for helping you identify the changes you wish to make to your life and the help you need to make those changes.

They can help you find the support you need by liaising with service providers, getting any necessary insurance in place and writing the support plan with you.

They can also help to resolve any problems you have and provide ongoing support.

> To find your local direct payment support service or brokerage support service, contact your local authority or the Disability Rights UK **Independent Living Helpline** (see 'Useful contacts' below)

## The social care assessment

The purpose of the social care assessment is to find out what difficulties you are having, so that the local authority can decide whether you need any care services and if so, which services the authority might arrange for you or which you might arrange for yourself.

You have the right to ask your council to assess your needs. If someone helps to look after you, their needs should also be taken into account.

> If you are caring for someone else, you have the right to an assessment in your own right to highlight any support you need to help with caring tasks. For more information, see the chapter on carers.

When you request an assessment, the council should arrange for a social worker to visit you at home to understand what requirements you have to enable you to live independently.

The assessment must take into account both your immediate day-to-day needs and your longer-term needs. The social worker should look at any risks there are to you which could affect your physical or mental health, either now or in the future. You can have a friend or family member with you for the assessment if you wish.

A full care assessment should look at your needs in the following areas:
- personal care
- healthcare
- transport
- employment and leisure
- help at home
- accommodation
- finance.

Make sure you explain how your disability or health condition affects your day-to-day life. Try not to underestimate the problems you have and to think of examples of when you are prevented from doing something or find it hard to manage.

For example, tell the social worker if you find it hard to prepare a cooked meal or to dress yourself, or if you would really like to go to the cinema but find it too difficult to get there or meet friends. Tell them if you have had any accidents, either at home or when you have gone out on your own.

If you are finding the assessment tiring, ask to take a break or for it to be finished on another day.

When you request an assessment for yourself or a friend or family member, ask the council how long you might have to wait for the assessment. If your request is urgent because your health or wellbeing may be at risk, tell them. The recommended maximum waiting time is four weeks from the date of request.

Your local authority should not withdraw any services from you without first reassessing your needs. You can ask for a reassessment of your needs at any time if you feel your needs have changed.

## Eligibility

Following the social care assessment, when your needs have been identified, the council will make a decision about whether you will receive any support. To make this decision they will follow government guidance called *Fair Access to Care Services.*

In *Fair Access to Care Services,* the severity of your needs and the risks to your independence are categorised into four bands: critical, substantial, moderate and low.

Each band consists of a different combination of eight risk factors, some examples of which are:
- a threat to life
- reduced choice or control over aspects of the immediate environment
- a reduced ability to carry out vital personal care or domestic routines

Some of your needs might be categorised as critical, while others may be seen as only moderate.

Any needs that you have identified in the assessment, and which meet your council's eligibility criteria, are called 'eligible needs'. If your eligible needs fall within one of the bands which the council is able to fund, then those particular needs must be met. You can ask the council for details of its eligibility criteria and the bands of need it can fund; they should publish this information. Most councils now only fund needs that are deemed critical or substantial.

Make sure you get copies of your council's information leaflets about social care assessments and eligibility criteria. The information should be available on the council's website. You can then think about how your needs fit within the eligibility criteria.

IF ONLY I'D KNOWN THAT A YEAR AGO ...

## Your care or support plan

When your assessment is complete, the social worker will put together a 'statement of needs' and an action plan to meet those needs, usually known as a 'care plan'. Alternatively, you can draw together your own statement of needs that will form a 'support plan'. When you have agreed your care or support plan you will be given a copy.

Your plan should include:
- details of your eligible needs and associated risks
- how the services provided to you will help you
- a plan to cope with emergencies
- details of the services that will be provided to you
- the date your assessment will be reviewed. This should be within three months of the date you start receiving your services and then at least once a year after that
- details of any charges you will have to pay towards services plus details of any direct payments agreed for you so you can arrange services yourself.

## Funding

### FINANCIAL ASSESSMENT

After establishing your needs and eligibility for support, the local authority will decide how much money you might need to meet your care requirements.

Even if the local authority decides that you have eligible needs it will not necessarily cover the costs of all the services required to meet those needs. Therefore, soon after your needs assessment you will be given a financial assessment to look at whether you will have to pay any charges for your services. Your financial situation should not, however, be taken into account during the care assessment.

### CHARGING CRITERIA

The way each local authority works out how much people have to pay towards their care services differs across the UK. Ask your local authority for a copy of their charging policy.

If you have savings above a certain level (currently £23,250 in England, £22,000 in Wales and £24,750 in Scotland) you may have to pay all of the costs of your support services. If you do not have savings, you may still have to contribute towards your care costs.

Local authorities decide on a case-by-case basis how much people have to contribute. Your council will look at the services you require to meet your eligible needs and the costs of these services in your area. They will then compare the costs with your available income. Some of your income will not be taken into account – for example, the mobility component of disability living allowance or earnings from work (although in Scotland your earnings will be taken into account). It is important to note that in Scotland, personal care at home is free to people over 65 and in Northern Ireland, it's free to those over 75.

You must be able to afford to pay any contribution that the local authority decides you have to pay. A contribution can be totally waived if you are unable to pay it. A service cannot be taken away from you if you cannot pay, although the local authority can take court action to recover money owed.

## How do you use your funding?

If your local authority decides it should arrange support for you and cover all or some of the costs, you will be asked to choose:

- whether you want to apply for direct payments or personal budgets, or
- whether you want to get services provided to you directly by social services, or
- whether you want a combination of both.

To get a personal budget, you will have to fill in a self-assessment questionnaire to demonstrate your needs. After you submit your questionnaire, social services will decide your Resource Allocation System. This is where an estimate of the amount of money you may need to provide the help you need is agreed and this forms your personal budget. You will then be asked to write a support plan to show how you intend to spend your personal budget. When you write this plan, think about what you find difficult in your life and how you will organise your support. A friend, family member or social worker can help you to complete the plan.

You can get support and advice on managing your personal budget and looking after your money through user-controlled trusts, a brokerage support service, your local direct payment support service or your local authority. See 'Who is responsible for what' at the beginning of this chapter for more information.

You can decide at any time to stop using personal budgets and instead get the local authority to organise your care services for you.

*Everything you need to know about direct payments*, including how to make the most of them and how to employ your own personal assistant, is a 100-page guide available from Disability Rights UK. Price: £10 including postage and packing. To order your copy, visit our online shop.

## How to complain

If you are refused a social care assessment, denied a service when you think that you meet your local authority's eligibility criteria or made to wait a long time before getting your support, you can make a complaint. The council will have its own complaints procedure and be able to tell you how to make a complaint. If you exhaust your local council's complaints procedure, you could take your issue to the relevant Ombudsman.

**Local Government Ombudsman (England)**
☎ 0300 061 0614
ⓦ www.lgo.org.uk

**Scottish Public Services Ombudsman**
☎ 0800 377 7330
ⓦ www.spso.org.uk

**Public Service Ombudsman for Wales**
☎ 0845 601 0987
ⓦ www.ombudsman-wales.org.uk

**Northern Ireland Ombudsman**
☎ 0800 34 3424
ⓦ www.ni-ombudsman.org.uk

You can get advice about your rights from a local Centre for Independent Living or from a local or national disability organisation. If you want to complain about any social care service providers, you should notify the relevant inspection agency (see 'Useful contacts' below).

# The future

In recent years, the amount of support local authorities provide has been cut back and this looks set to continue further. Remember: you cannot have your support withdrawn without first being reassessed, even if your council changes its eligibility criteria.

Being prepared for your needs assessment and understanding your council's eligibility criteria will be a huge help to you. Be prepared to persevere to get what you need.

# Useful contacts

**Communicare**
63 Headlands, Kettering, Northants NN15 9EU
📞 01536 268 807
✉ enquiries@communicare.uk.com
🌐 www.communicare.uk.com
Specialise in providing domiciliary and nursing care to clients with complex conditions including ventilator dependency, spinal cord injury, motor neurone disease, multiple sclerosis and cerebral palsy to enable them to live independently in the community. Work in partnership with the Active Assistance Group.

**Disability Rights UK – Independent Living Helpline**
📞 0845 026 4748
Provides advice on getting direct payments including information on personal budgets, funding from social services in relation to care needs and general advice on employing personal assistants.

**In Control**
Carillon House, Chapel Lane, Wythall, West Midlands B47 6JX
📞 01564 821 650
✉ admin@in-control.org.uk
🌐 www.in-control.org.uk
This is a social enterprise whose mission is to help create a new welfare system in which everyone is in control of their lives as full citizens. In Control worked with disabled people and local authorities to design the 'Self-Directed Support' scheme. It provides information on direct payments and personal budgets and on the different ways you can manage your own support services. It also runs a web-based resource called Shop4Support, where you can search for and choose a wide range of services. Visit www.shop4support.com.

**United Kingdom Home Care Association**
Group House, 2nd Floor, 52 Sutton Court Road, Sutton SM1 4SL
📞 020 8661 8188
✉ helpline@ukhca.co.uk
🌐 www.ukhca.co.uk
Represents and supports home care agencies and operates a code of practice for its members.

INSPECTION AND REGISTRATION BODIES

**Care Quality Commission**
CQC National Customer Service Centre, Citygate, Gallowgate, Newcastle upon Tyne NE1 4PA
📞 0300 061 6161
🌐 www.cqc.org.uk

**Department of Health, Social Services & Public Safety**
Castle Buildings, Stormont, Belfast BT4 3SJ
📞 028 9052 0500
✉ webmaster@dhsspsni.gov.uk
🌐 www.dhsspsni.gov.uk

**Scottish Commission for the Regulation of Care**
Compass House, 11 Riverside Drive, Dundee DD1 4NY
📞 01382 20 7100
✉ enquiries@carecommission.com
🌐 www.carecommission.com

**Care & Social Services Inspectorate Wales**
Welsh Government, Rhydycar Business Park, Merthyr Tydfil CF48 1UZ
📞 0300 062 8800
✉ cssiw@wales.gsi.gov.uk
🌐 www.cssiw.org.uk

IF ONLY I'D KNOWN THAT A YEAR AGO ...

# Carers

**Friends, parents, relatives or neighbours often provide essential care and support for disabled people. Care may be given on a regular or occasional basis. This chapter provides information about the help and support available to carers.**

## Carers and the law

There is now better recognition of the importance of the role that carers play and their need for support and assistance.

### CARERS' RIGHTS
**Carer's assessment**
Under the Carers and Disabled Children Act 2000, if you look after a disabled child or adult and your caring has a significant impact on that person's life, you can ask your social care department to carry out a carer's assessment. This can identify the effects of caring on your life and consider any support that may be available to you. For more information visit www.nhs.uk/CarersDirect.

The assessment should be provided regardless of the carer's age, so it would be available for a child caring for an adult or sibling. Carers can ask for an assessment whether or not the person they care for has had their own care needs assessed. Assessments should recognise that the carer may themselves be disabled.

The Carers (Equal Opportunities) Act 2004 places a duty on local authorities to tell carers about their rights. When carrying out an assessment, they must consider carers' wishes to work, study or carry out leisure activities. It gives authorities powers to enlist the help of health, housing and education departments to provide support for carers.

**Rights at work**
If you are caring for an adult and also work, you have the right under the Work and Families Act 2006 to request flexible working hours. If a carer is treated badly at work because of the impact of care they give to a disabled person, it may constitute discrimination. Local law centres, and the Citizens Advice Bureaux can offer advice.

> For more information see *Flexible Working and Work-Life Balance*. Ring ACAS on 0870 242 9090 or visit www.acas.org.uk.

## Carer's allowance

Carer's allowance is payable to people caring full time for a disabled child or adult who receives the middle or higher rate care component of disability living allowance or attendance allowance or either of the daily living rates of the personal independence payment. You can claim carer's allowance while a decision is being made on the payment of those three benefits. For more information see the chapter on benefits.

To be eligible for carer's allowance, you must:
- spend at least 35 hours a week caring
- be between 16 and 65 years of age at the time of claiming
- not be in full time education

- not be earning more from any employment than the current set amount after allowable expenses are deducted.

Carer's allowance is not means tested. It is taxable and can be paid at the same time as some other benefits. While it is taken into account as income for means-tested benefits, it does trigger an extra carers' premium for income support, employment and support allowance, housing benefit and council tax benefit. It also provides national insurance credits so it preserves your entitlement to retirement pension.

For further information contact Carers UK.

IF ONLY I'D KNOWN THAT A YEAR AGO ...

# Useful contacts

**Carers UK**

20 Great Dover Street, London SE1 4LX

☎ 020 7378 4999

   Advice line 0808 808 7777

✉ info@carersuk.org

🌐 www.carersuk.org

Carers UK is a national organisation that works for improved services for carers. It provides advice and information to carers and the professionals who support them through its websites, helpline, booklets and factsheets.

Around the UK you can contact:

**Carers Northern Ireland**

58 Howard Street, Belfast BT1 6PJ

☎ 028 9043 9843

✉ info@carersni.org

**Carers Scotland**

The Cottage, 21 Pearce Street, Glasgow G51 3UT

☎ 0141 445 3070

✉ info@carersscotland.org

**Carers Wales**

River House, Ynysbridge Court, Gwaelod y Garth, Cardiff CF15 9SS

☎ 029 2081 1370

✉ info@carerswales.org

**Carers Trust**

32-36 Loman Street, London SE1 0EH

☎ 0844 450 0350

✉ info@carers.org

🌐 www.carers.org

Formed in 2012 by the merger of The Princess Royal Trust for Carers and Crossroads Care, the Carers Trust works to improve support, services and recognition for anyone who is caring, unpaid, for a family member or friend who is ill, frail or disabled or who has mental health or addiction problems. With its Network Partners, it aims to ensure that information, advice and practical support are available to all carers across the UK. Visit the website to find local services – for example, a Crossroads scheme or a carers' centre.

**Carer Watch**

🌐 www.carerwatch.com

Carer Watch is a campaign group for carers across the UK run by independent, unpaid carers. They aim to provide a non-party-political campaign platform to change the way opinion-formers, politicians and journalists think about carers.

## CROSSROADS CARE

**Do you look after somebody?**

We provide support for carers and the people they care for. We work with over 43,000 individuals and their families, helping carers to make a life of their own outside caring.

**Would you like a break?**

Our staff are fully trained in all aspects of practical care and provide flexible services to people of all ages and with a range of disabilities and health conditions. Our service can be anything from providing support within the home to helping with personal care. You can choose to pay for your own Crossroads care or fund it through your personal budget/direct payment. To find out more, call us for an informal chat.

**www.gmcrossroads.co.uk**

**Working Families**

1-3 Berry Street, London EC1V 0AA

☎ 0300 012 0312 Freephone helpline for parents and carers

✉ office@workingfamilies.org.uk

🌐 www.workingfamilies.org.uk

Working Families supports and campaigns for working parents and carers. Its project *Waving not Drowning* supports parents combining paid work and caring for disabled children. A free newsletter is published for interested professionals and parents. Parents and carers can ring the helpline for advice on tax credits, flexible working and rights at work. *Make it work for you!*, a guidebook for working parents of disabled children, gives practical advice on employment rights.

IF ONLY I'D KNOWN THAT A YEAR AGO ...

# Childhood

**This chapter is about the support available to disabled children and their families and about their legal rights. It looks at the help available before your child goes to school, at short breaks and stays in hospital, and at play equipment and out-of-school activities.**

## Finding support

If your child is born with, or acquires, a disability or long-term health condition it is vitally important that you get as much information as possible about the implications. Encourage your doctor to explain any complex medical terms and help you understand the condition.

Find out as much as you can about the help and support available for you and your child.

*Children first* is a comprehensive guide to children's services. This fact-packed book is available from Disability Rights UK.

Often, the best way to learn about services and support available in your area is to talk to other parents. You can also get practical information and emotional support from a parent support group or local carer's group.

## Children's Commissioners

Disabled children have a right to the practical support they need to participate in all the things that other kids take for granted. They need to be allowed to take risks and make choices like any other child.

Every nation of the UK has its own Children's Commissioner responsible for promoting and protecting the interests and welfare of all children and young people. They scrutinise and influence policy, hold inquiries, involve children and young people in their work, and provide advice.

The Northern Ireland and Scotland Commissioners can bring, or intervene in, legal proceedings on behalf of a child. The England and Wales Commissioners cannot help with individual cases.

**Children's Commissioner for England**
33 Greycoat Street, London SW1P 2QF
☎ 020 7783 8330
✉ info.request@
    childrenscommissioner.gsi.gov.uk
🌐 www.childrenscommissioner.gov.uk

**Northern Ireland Commissioner for Children and Young People**
Millennium House, 17-25 Great Victoria Street, Belfast BT2 7BA
☎ 028 9031 1616; textphone 028 9031 6393
✉ info@niccy.org
🌐 www.niccy.org

**Scotland's Commissioner for Children and Young People**
85 Holyrood Road, Edinburgh EH8 8AU
☎ 0131 558 3733
    Young Person's Freephone 0800 019 1179
✉ inbox@sccyp.org.uk
🌐 www.sccyp.org.uk

**Children's Commissioner for Wales**
Oystermouth House, Phoenix Way, Llansamlet, Swansea SA7 9FS
☎ 01792 76 5600
☎ Young Person's Freephone 0808 801 1000
    or text 80800 (start your message with COM)
✉ post@childcomwales.org.uk
🌐 www.childcom.org.uk

# Support for parents

## FAMILY INFORMATION SERVICES

Family Information Services (FIS) provide information on services available to help you support your children up to age 20 (25 if the child is disabled). A local FIS can offer you information about appropriate play, childcare and nursery provision and links to education services, youth clubs and careers advisers. FIS can help you find details of local parent support groups and about assessments and services offered by voluntary organisations.

Your FIS will usually be located within your local council and can be contacted through them, or by visiting:

**National Association of Family Information Services (NAFIS)**
Ⓦ www.familyinformationservices.org.uk
NAFIS is a registered charity that supports, links and promotes Family Information Services. Their website gives contact details for locations throughout the UK.

> **Portage** is a home-visiting educational service for preschool children with additional support needs. It is usually provided by local authorities. Its aim is to give parents skills, confidence and practical help and ideas to encourage a child's interests. A directory of schemes can be found at www.portage.org.uk.

## SURE START

Local Sure Start schemes were established by the government to co-ordinate and develop services for children in the areas of greatest need. Although emphasis is given to young children, the remit of Sure Start extends from conception to age 14, or 16 for disabled children.

Among the services being promoted by Sure Start are children's centres, neighbourhood nurseries, extended schools and out-of-school programmes.

Unfortunately, over the past year, many Sure Start centres have been forced to close. To check if your local centre is still open, visit www.gov.uk.

There are Sure Start programmes in Northern Ireland, Scotland and Wales. In Wales, Sure Start is part of Cymorth (Children and Youth Support Fund) and administered through Children & Young People's Partnerships that have been established in each local authority.

## PARENT PARTNERSHIP SERVICES

Parent Partnership Services (PPS) are statutory services offering information, advice and support to parents and carers of children with special educational needs (SEN). PPS are also able to put parents in touch with other local and national organisations. PPS have a role in making sure that parents' views are heard and understood and that these views inform local policy and practice.

PPS are based within voluntary organisations, local authorities or Children's Trusts. They offer confidential and impartial advice on issues such as:
- how special educational needs are identified and assessed by schools
- who parents can talk to in a school or local authority about their concerns
- the SEN Code of Practice, the statutory assessment process and statements
- parents'/carers' rights and responsibilities.

## PARENT NETWORKS AND CARER SUPPORT GROUPS

Being able to share your experiences with other people in a similar situation can be a tremendous comfort for many parents. There are many support groups across the UK operating locally and nationally. Some are aimed at parents caring for children with a specific disability, while others cover a broad spectrum of impairments but in a certain area or with a focus on supporting young carers.

You should be able to get a list of local parent or carer groups from your local council. Alternatively, many specific impairment organisations (see 'Useful contacts' at the end of this book) run their own support groups for parents or carers.

# Right to short breaks for disabled children and families

From April 2011 in England and Wales, local authorities have been under an explicit duty under the Children and Young Persons Act 2008 to provide short breaks to disabled children and their families. This is intended to enable children to experience new relationships, environments and positive activities as well as to support parents. New funding has been made available to support this.

Short breaks are not just for crisis situations but enable parents and carers to maintain and improve the quality of care they give their children.

### KIDS Direct Short Breaks Service
249 Birmingham Road, Wylde Green, Sutton Coldfield B72 1EA
- 0845 453 1000
- enquiries@directshortbreaks.org.uk
- www.directshortbreaks.org.uk

KIDS Direct Short Breaks enables parents to access a short break service through a secure, easy-to-use website.

### Shared Care Network
Units 34-36 Easton Business Centre, Felix Road, Bristol BS5 0HE
- 0117 941 5361
- rob.foundtain@sharedcarenetwork.org.uk
- www.sharedcarenetwork.org.uk

This charity operates in England, Wales and Northern Ireland to promote short breaks for disabled children.

In Scotland:
### Shared Care Scotland
Unit 7, Dunfermline Business Centre, Izatt Avenue, Dunfermline KY11 3BZ
- 01383 622462
- office@sharedcarescotland.com
- www.sharedcarescotland.org.uk

**Contact a Family** provide information about short breaks for disabled children on their website. Visit www.cafamily.org.uk to find out more.

# Childcare

### FINDING SUITABLE CHILDCARE
Under the Childcare Act 2006, local authorities in England and Wales are required to ensure there is sufficient childcare available to working parents with children up to the age of 14, or 18 for disabled children.

Childcare providers – including childminders, nurseries, preschools and after-school clubs have duties not to discriminate against disabled children and to make reasonable adjustments so their services are accessible and inclusive.

It can be difficult to find accessible, affordable, suitable, high-quality childcare for your disabled child. To find out about childcare in your area, contact your Family Information Services. Talk to other parents for recommendations.

Check out online information about childcare providers near you, including Ofsted inspection reports for England, with links to the rest of the UK at:
- http://childcarefinder.direct.gov.uk
- http://schoolsfinder.direct.gov.uk

The Daycare Trust has a Family Information Directory, which enables you to search for local childcare online (www.daycaretrust.org.uk).

### Help with costs
Make sure you are getting all the financial help available. Every 3- and 4-year-old child is eligible for a free part-time nursery or childcare place at the start of the term after their third birthday. You can have up to 15 hours a week, to be taken over 38 weeks of the year.

Families with a low income may also get free places for 2-year-olds. Criteria are different in Scotland, Wales and Northern Ireland; check entitlements with your local FIS.

If you are on a low income, tax credits can help with the costs of childcare (see the benefits chapter for more information). The Daycare Trust's Paying for Childcare website (www.payingforchildcare.org.uk) includes a tax credit checker and information to help you understand what financial support you may be able to get for your childcare costs.

You can ask your employer to join the Childcare Voucher Scheme. Childcare vouchers are currently exempt from tax and national insurance, up to £243 a month for anyone who joined the scheme before 6 April 2011.

There are limitations on savings for people paying higher and additional tax rates and for people who joined the scheme on or after 6 April 2011.

You may be able to use direct payments to help pay for childcare. See the chapter on social care for more information.

> *Everything you need to know about direct payments*, published by Disability Rights UK, provides guidance on direct payments. It includes information about employing a personal assistant and includes example contracts of employment. You can order a copy for £10 including p&p, from our online shop.

## Stays in hospital

For children in hospital, visiting hours are usually unrestricted and you may be able to stay with your child overnight. Discuss your child's particular needs with one of the nurses so that everyone will look after your child in the appropriate way. Your child's social worker will help with organising your visits and dealing with your responsibilities at home while your child is in hospital. If you experience any problems with care in hospital, the hospital's Patient Advisory Liaison Service (PALS) may be able to help. There should be clear signposting in the hospital to the PALS.

The local authority is responsible for ensuring that school-aged children have appropriate opportunities to continue their education while in hospital.

A prolonged stay, or frequent stays, in hospital can affect entitlement to benefits:
- Child benefit will be affected if a child is in hospital for over 12 weeks, unless it can be shown that the benefit is used for visits, to buy clothing, magazines, etc
- Disability living allowance and carer's allowance are affected after 12 weeks for children under 16. Short stays in hospital will be linked if they are less than 28 days apart

- Carer's allowance will stop if the carer is in hospital for longer than 12 weeks.

**Action for Sick Children**
32b Buxton Road, High Lane, Stockport SK6 8BH
📞 0800 074 4519
📧 enquiries@actionforsickchildren.org
🌐 www.actionforsickchildren.org
Action for Sick Children has guidelines for the care of sick children before, during and after a stay in hospital in England. It also has information leaflets for parents.

For Scotland and Wales contact:

**Action for Sick Children Scotland**
22 Laurie Street, Edinburgh EH6 7AB
📞 0131 553 6553
🌐 www.ascscotland.org.uk

**Association for the Welfare of Children in Hospital (Wales)**
31 Penyrheol Drive, Sketty, Swansea SA2 9JT
📞 01792 20 5227
📧 awchwales.org.uk@tiscali.co.uk
🌐 www.awchwales.org.uk

### Sick Children's Trust

3rd Floor, Willow House, 17-23 Willow Place,
London SW1P 1JH

T 020 7931 8695
E info@sickchildrenstrust.org
W www.sickchildrenstrust.org

Provides accommodation for parents and other family members close to major children's hospitals. The Trust currently has seven houses offering clean, comfortable accommodation. They also work with hospitals, supporting them in their role and providing complementary support to the families.

### Together for Short Lives

4th Floor, Bridge House, 48-52 Baldwin Street,
Bristol BS1 1QB

T 0117 989 7820
E info@childhospice.org.uk
W www.togetherforshortlives.org.uk

Represents children's hospice services in Britain including those in the process of being established. It is concerned with developing best professional practice; improving the provision, regulation and funding of children's hospice services; and promoting the needs of children with life-limiting conditions and their families.

## Play and other equipment

Some toys and play equipment are useful in helping with the development of disabled children. Your local library may have a section for borrowing such toys free of charge. Toy libraries can also be another great place to meet and network with other parents. The following organisations will be able to offer advice and information on more specific disability-related equipment and resources.

### Action for Kids

Ability House, 15A Tottenham Lane, London N8 9DJ

T 020 8347 8111; textphone 020 8347 3486
E info@actionforkids.org
W www.actionforkids.org

Action for Kids runs a national mobility equipment service for disabled children and young people and a wheelchair maintenance and repair service. It also offers nationwide family support services, including a telephone helpline (0845 300 0237) and work-related learning services in parts of London and Hertfordshire.

### Fledglings

Wendens Court, Station Approach, Wendens Ambo, Saffron Walden CB11 4LB

T 0845 458 1124
E enquiries@fledglings.org.uk
W www.fledglings.org.uk

Fledglings is a not-for-profit organisation that helps parents find specialist equipment, toys and clothing to encourage their children's development. Publishes a regular newsletter.

### Go Kids Go!

206 Norwood, Beverley, East Yorkshire HU17 9JA

T 01482 887163
E roy@go-kids-go.org.uk
W www.go-kids-go.org.uk

A small national charity that aims to enable young wheelchair-users throughout the UK to become independently mobile. It provides specialist wheelchair training, assessments and advice through one, two and three-day free mobility skills training courses in all parts of the UK and Ireland.

### Letterbox Library

Unit 151 Stratford Workshops, Burford Road,
London E15 2SP

T 020 7503 4801
E info@letterboxlibrary.com
W www.letterboxlibrary.com

Letterbox Library provides children's books by mail order. Their list includes a diverse and broad collection, including books on disability issues.

### MERU

Unit 2, Eclipse Estate, 30 West Hill, Epsom, Surrey KT19 8JD

T 01372 725203
E info@meru.org.uk
W www.meru.org.uk

MERU is a charity that designs and manufactures equipment for disabled children and young people. It accepts referrals from London and southeast England.

MERU manufactures Bugzi – a powered wheelchair for the under-5s, the Moozi low-profile switch joystick, Flexzi – a system for mounting small items and equipment conveniently for the user, and Rokzi – add-on accessories that make standard school chairs safer and more comfortable for disabled children.

**Play Matters**
8 Wakley Street, London EC1V 7QE
Ⓔ admin@playmatters.co.uk
Ⓦ www.ncb.org.uk/play-matters
Play Matters supports play opportunities in communities around England and Northern Ireland through toy libraries and other initiatives. Toy libraries lend carefully selected toys, including specialist toys for disabled children. Many also run play sessions and provide a meeting place for parents and carers. There are over 1,000 toy libraries throughout the UK.

In Scotland:
**Smartplay Network**
Gilmerton Community Centre, 4 Drum Street, Edinburgh EH17 8QG
Ⓣ 0131 664 2746
Ⓦ www.smartplaynetwork.org

In Wales:
**Play Wales**
Baltic House, Mount Stuart Square, Cardiff CF10 5FH
Ⓣ 029 2048 6050; Welsh line 029 2043 6927
Ⓔ mail@playwales.org.uk
Ⓦ www.playwales.org.uk

**Whizz-Kidz**
4th floor, Portland House, Bressenden Place, London SW1E 5BH
Ⓣ 020 7233 6600
Ⓔ info@whizz-kidz.org.uk
Ⓦ www.whizz-kidz.org.uk
Whizz-Kidz provides customised mobility equipment, help and advice to children and their families, and raises awareness of mobility-related issues. It also provides a wide range of specialised mobility equipment not available through the NHS. A network of qualified mobility therapists assesses each child for their individual needs. It operates specialist mobility centres for children in Birmingham, London and Newcastle.

## Out-of-school activities

Your local Family Information Services should be able to provide information about the range of out-of-school activities available in your area. These may include programmes during holidays and information about services and special activities such as sports taster days and arts workshops.

Disabled children and young people have the right to use mainstream play and leisure facilities. Service providers are required to make reasonable adjustments to enable them to do so.

Some voluntary organisations arrange children's breaks combining activities with peer support and training.

For information on schemes in your area, contact:

**KIDS**
Ⓦ www.kids.org.uk
A national charity providing a range of services for disabled children, their families and siblings. These are organised from regional offices around England and include home learning (Portage), family support, information, training, play and leisure. KIDS National Development Department provides workforce development and support, training, publications and guidance on the inclusion of disabled children and young people in universal play, childcare, youth and leisure. The website has contact details for the different services and offices.

# Useful contacts

**Brainwave Centre**

Ⓦ www.brainwave.org.uk

This charity helps children with physical and cognitive disabilities. Therapy programmes are tailored to the needs of the individual child and parents are taught by the Brainwave therapy team how to carry out the programme in their own homes. Regional support workers are available if required. Centres in Somerset (01278 42 9089), Essex (01376 50 5290) and Warrington (01925 82 5547).

---

### THE BRAIN INJURY HUB

This new website offers information to families of children affected by acquired brain injury. Featuring a wealth of fully-referenced information about childhood acquired brain injury, the website includes practical advice and the facts about a condition that is often misunderstood.

The website draws on the expertise of the clinicians at the national charity The Children's Trust, Tadworth and includes information and classroom strategies for education professionals.

Alongside this information, an open online forum gives families the opportunity to share their experiences and offer mutual support.

The smartphone-ready site can be accessed by families at any stage of their journey, whether they need a definition for a word they've heard at hospital, or they're looking for practical tips back at home.

The site also includes accessible, 'easy read' text, and was recently awarded the Department of Health's Information Standard quality mark in recognition of its accurate and impartial information.

www.braininjuryhub.co.uk

**British Youth Council**

CAN Mezzanine, 49-51 East Road, London N1 6AH

Ⓣ 0845 458 1489

Ⓔ mail@byc.org.uk

Ⓦ www.byc.org.uk

Represents and involves young people both individually and as members of youth organisations. It aims to:

- provide a voice for young people
- promote equality for young people
- help young people to be more involved in decisions that affect their lives
- advance young people's participation in society and civic life.

**ChildLine**

Ⓣ 0800 1111

See website for text message numbers

Ⓦ www.childline.org.uk

ChildLine offers a free and confidential telephone service for children and young people to speak to a trained volunteer counsellor about any type of problem or issue.

**Contact a Family**

209-211 City Road, London EC1V 1JN

Ⓣ 0808 808 3555; textphone 0808 808 3556

Ⓔ info@cafamily.org.uk

Ⓦ www.cafamily.org.uk

Provides support, information and advice to support the families of disabled children so that they can live the lives they want and achieve their full potential – whatever their disability.

**Gingerbread**

520 Highgate Studios, 53-79 Highgate Road, London NW5 1TL

Ⓣ 020 7428 5400; helpline 0808 802 0925

Ⓦ www.gingerbread.org.uk

Gingerbread provides advice and one-to-one help and support on problems facing single parents bringing up disabled children. Runs live online advice sessions and an online forum.

In Scotland:

**One Parent Families Scotland**

13 Gayfield Square, Edinburgh EH1 3NX

📞 0131 556 3899; helpline 0808 801 0323

📧 info@opfs.org.uk

🌐 www.opfs.org.uk

**I CAN**

8 Wakely Street, London EC1V 7QE

📞 020 7843 2552

📧 info@ican.org.uk

🌐 www.ican.org.uk

I CAN supports children and parents of children with speech, language and communication difficulties.

**National Children's Bureau**

8 Wakley Street, London EC1V 7QE

📞 020 7843 6000

📧 enquiries@ncb.org.uk

🌐 www.ncb.org.uk

An umbrella body for voluntary and statutory organisations concerned with children, childcare and family policy in England. It provides information and advice to organisations and policy makers, acts as a focal point for campaigns, and produces publications. They host a number of specialist bodies including the Council for Disabled Children.

Similar bodies in other parts of the UK are:

**Children in Northern Ireland**

Unit 9, 40 Montgomery Road, Belfast BT6 9HL

📞 028 9040 1290

📧 info@ci-ni.org.uk

🌐 www.ci-ni.org.uk

**Children in Scotland**

Princes House, 5 Shandwick Place, Edinburgh EH2 4RG

📞 0131 228 8484

📧 info@childreninscotland.org.uk

🌐 www.childreninscotland.org.uk

**Children in Wales**

25 Windsor Place, Cardiff CF10 3BZ

📞 029 2034 2434

📧 info@childreninwales.org.uk

🌐 www.childreninwales.org.uk

**YoungMinds**

Suite 11, Baden Place, Crosby Row, London SE1 1YW

📞 020 7089 5050
Parents' helpline 0808 802 5544

🌐 www.youngminds.org.uk

YoungMinds is a national charity working to improve the mental health and emotional well-being of children and young people. It has a wide range of publications and information on its website aimed at children, young people, parents and professionals.

IF ONLY I'D KNOWN THAT A YEAR AGO ...

# Education and skills

**Disabled children, young people and adults have the same rights as everyone else to a high-quality education, to learn new skills, and to reach their potential. Freedom from discrimination and getting practical, tailored support are essential if disabled people are to participate in learning on an equal basis. Parents, carers and learners can sometimes struggle to secure this support. This chapter explains your rights and provides information on the support available to disabled children and adults pursuing an education or lifelong learning.**

## Your legal rights to equality

The Equality Act 2010 aims to protect disabled people and prevent disability discrimination. Under the Act, education and training providers have a duty to not discriminate against potential, current or former students. The Act covers all aspects of studying – including course admissions, the provision of education, access to any benefit, facility or service and exclusions. See the chapter on discrimination for the definition of disability and for other details of the Equality Act.

### Reasonable adjustments

Education and training providers must make 'reasonable adjustments' for disabled learners so they are not placed at a substantial disadvantage compared to non-disabled learners.

Adjustments can include:
- changes to practices or procedures
- changes to buildings to make them physically accessible
- providing equipment and human support such as readers or note-takers and specialist tuition support.

Further information is available from the Equality and Human Rights Commission, which has a range of publications covering rights and duties under the Act available on their website:
Ⓦ www.equalityhumanrights.com

### WHAT TO DO ABOUT DISCRIMINATION

If you feel you or your child has experienced discrimination, you should first raise the issue informally with a member of staff such as the teacher, personal tutor or disability adviser.

If this does not resolve the issue, then make an internal complaint. There should be an internal complaints procedure for you to follow.

If you are not satisfied with the outcome of the complaint, you can take your complaint to an external body. You should contact the Equality Advisory and Support Service or the Disability Rights UK student helpline for further advice.

**Equality Advisory and Support Service**
FREEPOST Equality Advisory Support Service FPN4431
☏ 0800 444 205 or 0800 444 206 (textphone)
Open 09:00 to 20:00 Monday to Friday and 10:00 to 14:00 Saturday
This new service replaces the helpline run by the Equality and Human Rights Commission. The Helpline is for people who think they may have experienced discrimination. The service aims to support individuals referred from local organisations, advisory groups, faith-based organisations and other groups working within the community, that support people experiencing discrimination. It provides advice and information on discrimination and human rights issues.

Disability Rights UK's booklets *Adjustments for disabled students* and *Understanding the Equality Act: Information for disabled students* are available on our website. You can also contact our student helpline to obtain a copy. Contact details are available in the 'Useful contacts' section in this chapter.

## Public Sector Equality Duty

The Public Sector Equality Duty came into force in April 2011, harmonising the three previous duties on disability, race and gender.

In carrying out their functions, the duty requires public bodies, including schools, colleges and universities, to consider how they could positively contribute to the advancement of equality.

In summary, public bodies must consider the need to:

- eliminate unlawful discrimination, harassment and victimisation
- advance equality of opportunity between different groups
- foster good relations between different groups.

Public bodies must publish, at least annually, information to demonstrate how they are complying with the equality duty and they must also publish equality objectives at least once every four years.

## Special educational needs

This section is aimed at parents and carers of disabled children.

A child with special educational needs (SEN) is one who has a learning difficulty or a disability that makes it harder for them to learn than other children of the same age. SEN includes communication, physical, sensory and emotional difficulties that require support.

### THE CODE OF PRACTICE

All publicly funded pre-schools and nurseries, state schools and local authorities must take account of the SEN Code of Practice. The Code provides practical advice for early education settings, state schools, local authorities and others involved in identifying, assessing and providing help for children with SEN to help them carry out their statutory duties under the Education Act 1996 and the Special Educational Needs and Disability Act 2001.

The SEN Code of Practice sets out five fundamental principles that support inclusive education. These are:
- children with special educational needs should have their needs met
- children's special educational needs will normally be met in mainstream schools or settings
- the views of the child should be sought and taken into account

- parents have a vital role to play in supporting their child's education and children with special educational needs should be offered full access to broad, balanced and relevant education.

All schools must have a SEN policy and a designated Special Educational Needs Co-ordinator (SENCO). This will normally be a senior member of staff who does not have other school-wide responsibilities. In small schools it may be the head or deputy head and in large ones there may be a SEN team. The SENCO's responsibilities will include: co-ordinating provision for pupils with special educational needs and overseeing record keeping; liaising with teachers, learning support assistants, parents and external organisations; and generally carrying out the school's SEN policy.

The Code describes how help for children with special educational needs should be made by a 'graduated approach', which recognises that children learn in different ways and can have different levels of special needs. The graduated approach is a model of action and intervention in schools and early education settings to help children with special educational needs.

> The *SEN Code of Practice* and the *SEN Guide for Parents and Carers* can be found at www.education.gov.uk.

Schools try to identify SEN as early as possible so that they can bring in specialist expertise to help children with special educational needs. The school must tell you when they first start giving extra or different help because your child has special educational needs. This could be using a different way of teaching certain things, using particular equipment or help from an extra adult. This is called 'School Action'.

## WHAT TO DO IF YOU ARE CONCERNED ABOUT YOUR CHILD

If you have concerns about your child's progress you can approach their teacher and talk to the SENCO.

Any extra help that your child needs will be set out in an Individual Education Plan, which should include:

- provision to be put in place
- teaching strategies to be used
- how often your child will receive help
- who is providing the help
- targets for your child to work towards
- when the plan will be reviewed.

The plan should be reviewed at least twice a year. If your child does not make enough progress, the teacher or SENCO should talk to you about bringing in specialist help from outside the school. This kind of help is called 'School Action Plus' and could involve a speech and language therapist, a specialist teacher or an educational psychologist. Again, you and your child should be involved in the discussions.

The system is similar in pre-school settings but the stages are called Early Action and Early Action Plus.

### A statutory assessment

If help provided through School Action or School Action Plus does not meet your child's needs, you or the school can formally request a statutory assessment from the local authority. After receiving a request for a statutory assessment, the authority has up to six weeks in which to consider whether or not to make a statutory assessment. This includes the 29 days you are given to submit your evidence.

If the local authority decides to make a statutory assessment, it must write to you setting out the procedures involved, time scales, and details of a local authority officer who can be contacted for more advice and provide details of the local Parent Partnership Service.

The assessment will involve outside professionals and the local authority will seek advice from educational, medical, psychological and social services and from parents. The local authority will consult your child's school for information about the support already in place, your child's progress and the school's view of your child's SEN. You can ask for the views of professionals and organisations who know your child to be taken into account. The assessment should also give due consideration to your child's views.

When the local authority has received all the advice it must decide whether to issue a Statement of SEN. It has ten weeks to make the statutory assessment and decide on whether to issue a Statement.

If the local authority decides not to issue a Statement it must notify you and the school, explaining why a Statement is not appropriate and provide information on the right to appeal.

If the local authority decides that the child's SEN can be met by the school's resources and decides not to issue a Statement, it may issue a 'Note in Lieu' Statement outlining your child's SEN and provide the school with guidance in supporting the child. All the advice received during the assessment should be attached to the Note in Lieu.

If the local authority decides that it will issue a Statement of SEN you will be sent a 'proposed statement' for further discussion and approval.

A Statement will include a description of the child's current SEN and the provision that will be made to meet those needs. You have 15 days from receiving the proposed statement to give your opinion about it to the authority and express preference for a school.

As long as the school is suitable for your child's needs (see the *SEN Guide for Parents and Carers* for further information), the local authority must support your preference. Within eight weeks of issuing the proposed statement, the authority must issue a final statement. The process can take around 26 weeks in total.

Local authorities are legally obliged to provide the educational help specified in a Statement. The Statement should be reviewed at least annually and can be amended by agreement to meet changing circumstances.

## CHALLENGING DECISIONS

At all stages in this process, you should have the opportunity to challenge decisions that you don't agree with. You may want to negotiate directly with the local authority or you can ask an advocacy organisation for help, or use a local authority conciliation or dispute settlement system. These systems are established by local authorities but contain an independent element.

### In England and Wales

If negotiation doesn't result in a satisfactory outcome, you can appeal against a local authority decision to the First-tier Tribunal (Special Educational Needs and Disability), an independent body established by the government.

The Tribunal operates a telephone helpline on SEN queries.

**Special Educational Needs and Disability Tribunal**
Mowden Hall, Staindrop Road, Darlington DL3 9BG
☎ Helpline 01325 39 2760
✉ sendistqueries@hmcts.gsi.gov.uk
🌐 www.justice.gov.uk

**SEN Tribunal for Wales**
Unit 32, Ddole Road Enterprise Park, Llandrindod Wells, Powys LD1 6DF
☎ Helpline 01597 82 9800
✉ tribunalenquiries@wales.gsi.gov.uk
🌐 www.sentw.gov.uk
The SEN Tribunal for Wales is responsible for hearing and deciding SEN appeals against local authorities in Wales.

### In Northern Ireland

Northern Ireland has equivalent legislation – see www.education-support.org.uk for details. The Education and Library Boards are responsible for meeting special educational needs.

**Special Educational Needs and Disability Tribunal Northern Ireland**
Floor 3, Bedford House, 16-22 Bedford Street, Belfast BT2 7TF
☎ 02890 728 757
✉ SENDtribunal@courtsni.gov.uk
🌐 www.courtsni.gov.uk

### In Scotland

Legislation is different in Scotland – the relevant framework is Additional Support for Learning. For further information, contact Enquire.

**Enquire, the Scottish Advice Service for Additional Support for Learning**
5 Shandwick Place, Edinburgh EH2 4RG
☎ 0845 123 2303; textphone 0131 222 2439
✉ info@enquire.org.uk
🌐 www.enquire.org.uk
Enquire is funded by the Scottish Government and managed by Children in Scotland. It provides information, advice and mediation to families with young children and young people with educational needs.

## PREPARATION FOR LEAVING SCHOOL
**Transition planning**

If your child has a Statement of SEN, from Year 9 onwards a transition plan will be prepared. This plan looks at your child's needs in preparation for leaving school and beginning adult life. The head teacher should write to you and your child inviting you to a review meeting to prepare the plan. Local services can also be invited – for example, social services, health professionals, a Connexions Adviser, a relevant teacher, and carers.

Transition plans are about your child's hopes and aspirations for the future and what support they'll need to live as independently as possible. In preparing for the meeting, your child will need to consider what subjects they want to study in the time remaining at school, what they want to do when they leave school and what support they might need to achieve their goals.

After the meeting, you and your child should get a copy of the transition plan and a copy will go to the headteacher and other relevant professionals. The local authority is responsible for ensuring that your child receives all the services identified as necessary in the transition plan. The plan should be reviewed at all subsequent annual reviews.

## INFORMATION AND ADVICE
### Parent Partnership Services
Established in each local authority area in England and Wales, Parent Partnership Services aim to give information, advice and guidance to parents and carers of children with special educational needs so that they can make informed decisions on their child's education. They provide an initial point of contact outside of school for parents who are concerned that their child has or may have special educational needs. They can provide a link to an Independent Parental Supporter and also offer information on voluntary organisations, self-help groups and other relevant organisations.

### The National Parent Partnership
The National Parent Partnership Network was established by the Council for Disabled Children with funding from the Department for Education and Skills. The Network provides a forum for local services to share learning, experience and information. Their website includes addresses for Parent Partnership Services throughout England:
Ⓦ www.parentpartnership.org.uk.

## OTHER SOURCES OF ADVICE AND SUPPORT

### The Alliance for Inclusive Education
336 Brixton Road, London SW9 7AA
Ⓣ 020 7737 6030
Ⓔ info@allfie.org.uk
Ⓦ www.allfie.org.uk
The Alliance for Inclusion Education is a network of local groups and individuals working for a fully inclusive education system. It publishes briefings and campaign materials.

### Centre for Studies on Inclusive Education (CSIE)
The Park, Daventry Road, Knowle, Bristol BS4 1DQ
Ⓣ 0117 353 3150
Ⓔ admin@csie.org.uk
Ⓦ www.csie.org.uk
CSIE gives information and advice on the special educational needs of pre-school children and school pupils up to the age of 19. Its activities include lobbying and campaigning for inclusion, producing publications and organising seminars and training on issues relating to inclusive education. CISE publishes the *Index for Inclusion* for early years and schools to help break down educational barriers.

### Contact a Family
209-211 City Road, London EC1V 1JN
Ⓣ Helpline 0808 808 3555
Ⓔ helpline@cafamily.org.uk
Ⓦ www.cafamily.org.uk
Contact a Family gives advice and information to families who have children with special educational needs. It also provides a range of factsheets and booklets.

### Independent Parental Special Education Advice (IPSEA)
Hunters Court, Debden Road, Saffron Walden CB11 4AA
Ⓣ 01799 582030
Advice line 0800 018 4016
Tribunal Helpline 0845 602 9579
Ⓦ www.ipsea.org.uk
IPSEA provides free, legally based independent advice and support in England and Wales. Its advice line offers help with issues such as problems with schools, requesting statutory assessment, proposed statements, annual reviews, possible disability discrimination and exclusion from school. It also runs a tribunal helpline and tribunal support service.

**National Association of Independent Schools and Non-Maintained Special Schools (NASS)**
PO Box 705, York YO30 6WW
T 01904 62 4446
W www.nasschools.org.uk
NASS represents the interests of voluntary and private special schools and seeks to promote high standards and appropriate practices. A list of member schools is included on its website.

**Network 81**
10 Boleyn Way, West Clacton, Essex CO15 2NJ
T Helpline 0845 077 4055
E network81@hotmail.co.uk
W www.network81.org
A national network of parents working for properly resourced inclusive education for children with special educational needs. Network 81 offers support and information through a helpline, publications, training, information days and a network of befrienders and supporters.

**Parents for Inclusion**
336 Brixton Road, London SW9 7AA
T 020 7738 3888
   Helpline 0800 652 3145
E info@parentsforinclusion.org
W www.parentsforinclusion.org
Parents for Inclusion is a network of parents of disabled children and children with special needs. It provides support for parents through a helpline, represent parents' views to government and in the media and also offers training and consultancy service on inclusive education.

**SOS!SEN**
T 020 8538 3731
   Open 09:30 to 12.30 and 2:00 to 5:00
   Monday to Friday
W www.sossen.org.uk
SOS!SEN offers advice, initially by telephone, to parents or others concerned about children with special educational needs. It can help interpret the SEN Code of Practice, check proposed and amended SEN statements, advise on preparing appeals and help with complaints to the Local Government Ombudsman. There are drop-in centres in Twickenham, Aldershot and Thornton Heath. See the website for more details.

**The Good Schools Guide**
3 Craven Mews, London SW11 5PW
T 020 3286 6824
W www.goodschoolsguide.co.uk
The Good Schools Guide collates public information on a wide range of schools with the comments submitted by parents and other independent, interested people. A number of schools catering for children with special needs are highlighted, including some mainstream schools that 'do well by' pupils with special needs. The Guide is expanding the coverage of such schools and welcomes help in identifying them.

RESOURCES
The following organisations have developed educational computer software and other resources to help pupils with special educational needs.

**Inclusive Technology Ltd**
Riverside Court, Huddersfield Road, Delph, Oldham OL3 5FZ
T 01457 81 9790
W www.inclusive.co.uk

**LDA**
Pintail Close, Victoria Business Park, Nottingham NG4 2SG
T 0845 120 4776
E enquiries@ldalearning.com
W www.ldalearning.com

**SEMERC**
Angel House, Sherston, Malmesbury SN16 0LH
T 0800 258 5991
W www.semerc.com
SEMERC offers SENCOs, teachers and parents support and specialised resources and services for learners of all ages with special educational needs. These include a comprehensive range of award-winning SEN and general curriculum software and specialist hardware and consultancy services.

# Children with medical needs

The SEN Code of Practice stresses that a disability does not necessarily imply special educational needs but accepts that some children have medical conditions that could hinder their access to education. Medical conditions cover a range of conditions like chronic fatigue syndrome (CFS), mental health conditions, asthma, epilepsy, anaphylaxis and diabetes.

Schools should have written policies on support for children with long-term medical needs, covering matters such as managing medication and supporting pupils who regularly miss school because of a long-term health condition. If your child has medical needs they may benefit from a healthcare plan that identifies the level of support that they need.

Local authorities are responsible for arranging suitable education for children with long-term health conditions who are regularly missing school or likely to be away from school for more than 15 working days. Authorities must ensure that children have access to education and receive an education of similar quality to that available in school. This may mean arranging access to home teaching, a hospital teaching service or an integrated hospital/home education service. Local authorities must ensure that children receive their minimum entitlement of five hours teaching per week if they are educated at home because of illness, as long as their health permits it.

Schools also need to provide practical help for children who aren't able to be in school. This means letting them know what's happening at school, helping them stay in touch with fellow pupils through visits or videos, providing work packs in advance if they have to be in hospital on a regular basis, and helping them settle back into the school routine when they are ready.

## FOR FURTHER INFORMATION

### England
National statutory guidelines for schools and local authorities in England. are set out in *Access to education for children and young people with medical needs*. You can get a copy by visiting:
Ⓦ www.education.gov.uk

### Northern Ireland
Although there are no published guidelines, each Education and Library Board should have a local policy on the education of sick children that should be available from the Special Education Officer of each Board.

### Scotland
Policy guidance to education authorities is set out in *Guidance on education of children absent from school through ill-health* available from:
Ⓦ http://home.scotland.gov.uk

Or ring the Scottish Executive Head of Pupil Support and Inclusion Division:
Ⓣ 0131 244 7847

Local policies should be available from the local council.

### Wales
Circular 57/94 *The Education of Sick Children* sets out recommendations for arrangements to be made by local education authorities for the provision of education for sick children:
Ⓦ www.wales.gov.uk

Or ring the National Assembly for Wales:
Ⓣ 029 2082 5111

Local policies should be available from local education authorities.

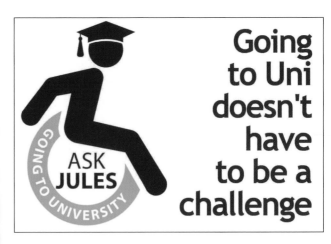

IF ONLY I'D KNOWN THAT A YEAR AGO ...

# Further education

Further education is usually for people aged 16 years or over and takes place in colleges, training centres, the workplace or a combination of these.

**The Education Funding Agency** funds people aged between 16 and 19 years old, or up to the age of 25 if they have a Section 139a Learning Difficulty and/or Disability Assessment in England.

It is important you let your education provider know as soon as possible if you need any adjustments to make the course accessible to you. The best time to do this is before you start your course. You should speak to the staff member responsible for supporting disabled students – they are often called the Additional or Extended Learning Support Adviser or the Disability Co-ordinator. Talk to them about your needs and discuss particular adjustments and how to arrange them.

Under the Equality Act, colleges are obliged to make reasonable adjustments for disabled students and receive money from their funding body to do this. The type of support a college might provide can include additional teaching for dyslexic students, an interpreter for deaf students, materials in alternative formats, and specialist computer software.

**Section 139a Learning Difficulty/
Disability Assessment (s139a LDA)**
If you have a Statement of Special Educational Needs, it will remain in force until you are 19 as long as you remain in school. The local authority has a duty to arrange an s139a LDA if you have a Statement of SEN and are leaving school to receive post-16 education or training. The s139a LDA replaces the Statement of SEN in terms of support needs.

After your s139a LDA has been done, a comprehensive report is written covering the support you'll need to ensure you are able to succeed in post-16 education. The report includes information on your disability, future plans and career aims, courses you want to attend, and areas of support needed.

This could include mobility, health, care, travel provision and adult learner support. A good s139 LDA can be used by the education provider to request funding to enable them to provide the support you need.

The Connexions Adviser is responsible for writing the s139 LDA but it is good practice for them to include contributions from you, your parents or carer, your school, social worker and other relevant professional's working with you. Evidence from your Statement of SEN is also used.

The s139a LDA should inform future education providers about the type of provision required to realistically meet your needs. It will help the college to plan for the support you need. Having an s139a LDA also means that the local authority is responsible for education, training and support needs, in some cases up to the age of 25.

The s139a LDA should always be updated if your support needs change.

**ASK JULES**

Ask Jules is an Independent Lifestyle, Recruitment and Care Management service specialising in assisting disabled university students achieve independent living and their outcomes.

We help students recruit, employ and manage their own support staff to provide not only health and social care but also student support and note taking. In short, we do everything to ensure our client gets the best services that money can buy from their Personal Budget and Disabled Students Allowance.

For further details visit our website.
Telephone: 01784 482 767
Follow us on Twitter @AskJulesCare
Like us on Facebook.com/AskJulesCare

**www.askjules.co.uk/university**

*Distinguish yourself*

# Make your mark: train to teach at King's College London

King's PGCE students train to teach in:

- Biology
- Chemistry
- Classics
- English
- Information & Communication Technology with Computing
- Mathematics
- Modern Foreign Languages (French, German, Spanish)
- Physics
- Religious Education

The PGCE programme at King's was graded 'outstanding' in the 2009-10 Ofsted inspection and offers 60 credits towards a master's degree in education once you have qualified. We're dedicated to supporting the development of our students so that they become skilled and confident teachers. Stay with us and we'll encourage you every step of the way.

We welcome applications from recent graduates, mature students from all backgrounds and those who have had other careers before teaching. For further information please contact our Admissions Team.

Contact:
Postgraduate Officer,
Centre for Arts & Sciences Admissions (CASA)

Tel: (0) 20 7848 7207
Fax: (0) 20 7848 7200
Email: pgceadmissions@kcl.ac.uk

Website: www.kcl.ac.uk/pgce

Ofsted
Outstanding
2009|2010

IF ONLY I'D KNOWN THAT A YEAR AGO ...

**Specialist colleges**

A number of colleges offer further education courses for disabled students whose needs are not met by local provision. Funding for a placement at these specialist colleges will only be considered if your s139a LDA has identified that your needs cannot be met at a local college or school. They generally operate on a residential basis and include training in life skills and other vocational and academic courses. They may liaise with mainstream colleges in the area and their courses may provide students with a stepping-stone to other training or education possibilities.

**The Association of National Specialist Colleges**
Ⓦ www.natspec.org.uk
The Association of National Specialist Colleges represents specialist further education colleges. It aims to promote opportunities for education and training, in residential or day settings, for students with disabilities and learning difficulties.

The Association's website provides help choosing and applying to specialist colleges, with a searchable directory of members.

For more specific advice, contact Disability Rights UK's **Disabled Student Helpline** which provides information, advice and guidance to disabled students and their families to support them in making decisions about post-16 opportunities including further and higher education, training and employment after leaving school.

Booklets and factsheets on applying to further education colleges and getting funding for further education are available on our website in the student publication section.

Contact details and opening times are in 'Useful contacts' at the end of this chapter.

# Higher education

Higher education is a valuable opportunity to take your education to a higher level such as a Bachelor's degree, Foundation degree or diploma. Research from the Association of Graduate Careers Advisory Services shows that disabled people have radically improved job prospects if we continue with our education. At graduate level, disabled people achieve very similar levels of job success to non-disabled people.

Every college and university has an officer or department with responsibility for advising and co-ordinating services for disabled students and prospective students. This includes making sure that any reasonable adjustments you need are in place.

Every year the number of disabled people considering higher education increases. The processes to help make sure we have a good learning experience are well understood and recognised by most institutions.

**DISABLED STUDENTS' ALLOWANCES**
Disabled students' allowances (DSAs) can help with extra study-related costs students may incur because of their impairment.

Disability Rights UK publishes *Into Higher Education*, a guide for disabled people planning to study in higher education.

It answers disabled students' common questions and provides the information you need to make the right choices including:
- choosing where to study
- disability support services
- how to apply to university
- telling people about your disability
- applying for disabled students' allowances.

The latest edition covers the new student finance system and has up-to-date information on tuition fees, repayment methods and the support that will be in place for 2013 entry. It includes a list of useful resources and inspiring profiles written by disabled people about their experiences of university.

The guide is available free from the Disability Rights UK Disabled Student Helpline (see 'Useful contacts' at the end of this chapter for details).

## KING'S COLLEGE LONDON

### Support for disabled students
The Disability and Dyslexia Service at King's College London provides applicants, students and staff with information, advice and guidance on disability support issues.

**What we provide:**

- Students with long-term medical conditions or disabilities may benefit from personal or technical support, or changes in delivery to enable access to their course.
- Staff can refer to the service to increase their awareness of inclusivity and accessibility and learn about initiatives to support disabled students and visitors.
- Managers of disabled staff can get advice on support strategies.

We also offer an MA in Inclusive Education and Technology, taught initially through face-to-face teaching then online. For details contact Chris Abbott (chris.abbott@kcl.ac.uk).

For more information about our support for disabled students, email disability@kcl.ac.uk or visit our website.

www.kcl.ac.uk/
campuslife/services/disability

*Bridging the Gap: a guide to the disabled students' allowances in higher education* can be downloaded from www.gov.uk.

Support provided depends on individual requirements and may include the cost of specialist equipment, non-medical helpers and travel. DSAs are not means tested and do not have to be repaid. They are available for full-time study on both undergraduate and postgraduate courses and to part-time students who are studying at least 25% of the full-time equivalent. Depending on where you live, you should apply to one of the following agencies:

**Student Finance England**
T 0845 300 5090; textphone 0845 604 4434
W www.gov.uk/disabled-students-allowances

**Student Finance Wales**
T 0845 602 8845; textphone 0845 603 1693
W www.studentfinancewales.co.uk

**Student Finance Northern Ireland**
T 0845 600 0662; textphone 0845 604 4434
W www.studentfinanceni.co.uk

**Student Awards Agency for Scotland**
T 0300 555 0505; textphone 0131 244 5107
W www.saas.gov.uk

For NHS-funded courses, you need to apply for an NHS Student Bursary.

**NHS BSA Student Bursaries**
Hesketh House, 200-220 Broadway, Fleetwood FY7 8SS
T 0845 358 6655
   Open 08:00 to 18:00 Monday to Friday and 09:00 to 15:00 Saturday
E nhsbsa.sbaccount@nhs.net
W www.nhsbsa.nhs.uk/students

# Adult learning

You may have been out of education for a while or missed out on qualifications when you were at school to enable you to go on to formal higher or further education. You still have the opportunity to return to education. A wide range of adult learning opportunities are open to anyone over the age of 18. If you are not sure where to begin, there are many services that offer free, impartial advice about learning, careers and courses.

**LearnDirect**
Dearing House, 1 Young Street, Sheffield S1 4UP
T 0800 101 901
W www.learndirect.co.uk
LearnDirect provides courses in computers, skills for life, management and languages. Courses are delivered online and at local learning centres throughout England and Wales.

**ContinYou**

Unit C1, Grovelands Court, Grovelands Estate, Longford Road, Exhall, Coventry CV7 9NE

📞 024 7658 8440

✉ generalenquiries@continyou.org.uk

🌐 www.continyou.org.uk

ContinYou provides a range of programmes to encourage people of all ages to take up learning opportunities. ContinYou seeks to establish links between education, health and employment – particularly for people who have gained the least from formal education and training.

**National Careers Service**

📞 0800 100 900

🌐 http://nationalcareersservice.direct.gov.uk

The National Careers Service provides information, advice and guidance to help people make decisions on learning, training and work opportunities. It can help develop CVs, search and apply for jobs, search for courses and training schemes, find funding to support any learning and explore career options. You can meet a trained adviser face-to-face, have a conversation over the phone or contact an adviser by email.

## Distance and home learning

Studying from home has advantages for some disabled people and carers. As the benefits of improved technology become more widely available, distance learning has moved on from being simply correspondence courses to much more interactive learning environments.

**National Extension College**

Michael Young Centre, Purbeck Road, Cambridge CB2 8HN

📞 0800 389 2839

✉ info@nec.ac.uk

🌐 www.nec.ac.uk

The National Extension College supports 20,000 people a year on over 100 home study courses. Programmes specifically for people who need to fit studies around caring responsibilities have been developed through their Carers into Education Project.

**Open College of the Arts**

Michael Young Arts Centre, Redbrook Business Park, Wilthorpe Road, Barnsley S75 1JN

📞 0800 731 2116

✉ enquiries@oca-uk.com

🌐 www.oca-uk.com

The Open College of the Arts is an open-access college offering home-study courses on painting, drawing, textiles, photography, music, writing and design. No formal qualifications are required and there are no age limits. The tutors are all practising artists, photographers, composers, writers or designers.

**Open & Distance Learning Quality Council**

79 Barnfield Wood Road, Beckenham, Kent BR3 6ST

✉ info@odlqc.org.uk

🌐 http://odlqc.org.uk

The Council is an independent body that registers providers of home study, distance and online learning and other open learning courses. To register, providers have to meet certain standards, which are then monitored. If anything goes wrong with a course from an accredited provider, the Council can help sort out the problem. Most accredited organisations are concerned with professional and vocational qualifications but some work with school-age learners and others provide more general or academic courses.

**The Open University (OU)**

Walton Hall, Milton Keynes MK7 6AA

📞 0845 300 6090

🌐 www.open.ac.uk

Since its foundation, the OU has welcomed disabled students and developed services for them. It now has more disabled students than the entire student numbers at some universities. A wide range of advice and guidance for OU students with a disability is available online and in the leaflet *Open to your needs*, which summarises the support services and facilities that are available to students.

## Conductive Education

Conductive Education (CE) is a teaching system designed to meet the needs of people with a range of movement disabilities. It teaches people the skills they need to control their bodies and achieve greater independence in their everyday lives. Specially trained 'conductors' work with the individual to achieve their specific goals

**Foundation for Conductive Education**
Cannon Hill House, Russell Road, Moseley, Birmingham B13 8RD
☎ 0121 442 5540
✉ ldebono@conductive-education.org.uk
🌐 www.conductive-education.org.uk
The Foundation offers workshops, courses and services for people of all ages.

Their services include:
- free parent and child service for up to 3-year-olds
- early intervention service between the ages of three and five with short-term or continuous service
- primary school group for 5 to 11-year-olds;
- sessional services for teenagers and children with dyspraxia
- sessional services for adults with Parkinson's, multiple sclerosis, strokes, head injuries and cerebral palsy and courses for the carers of people with those conditions.

Their website includes a list of other accredited Conductive Education centres.

## Useful contacts

**ACE Centre Advisory Trust**
92 Windmill Road, Headington, Oxford OX3 7DR
☎ 01865 75 9800
✉ info@ace-centre.org.uk
🌐 www.ace-centre.org.uk
The ACE Centre provides a focus on information and expertise in the use of technology as an aid to communication. ACE provides an assessment service, which sets out clear and realistic recommendations for an individual's special needs to improve their physical and communication difficulties. It offers training to teachers and teaching assistants, therapists, nursery nurses and parents to ensure that technology is used appropriately with the people they support

In Scotland contact:
**The CALL Centre (Communication Aids for Language and Learning)**
University of Edinburgh, Paterson's Land, Holyrood Road, Edinburgh EH8 8AQ
☎ 0131 651 6235
✉ info@callcentrescotland.org.uk
🌐 www.callscotland.org.uk

**Disability Rights UK**
12 City Forum, 250 City Road, London EC1V 8AF
☎ Disabled Student Helpline 0800 328 5050
  Open 11.30 to 13:30 Tuesday
  and 13:30 to 15:30 Thursday
✉ skill4disabledstudents@disabilityrightsuk.org
🌐 www.disabilityrightsuk.org
Our student helpline provides information, advice and guidance to disabled students and their families to support them in making decisions about their education, training and employment after leaving school. We also publish online information and guides.

**Linking Education and Disability (LEAD) Scotland**
Princes House, 5 Shandwick Place, Edinburgh EH2 4RG
☎ 0131 228 9441; helpline 0800 999 2568
  Open 14:00 to 16:00 Tuesdays and
  Wednesdays and 10:00 to 12:00
  Thursdays and Fridays
✉ info@lead.org.uk
🌐 www.lead.org.uk
LEAD has a range of booklets and a helpline that provides information on: applying for courses, funding and support for disabled learners, the Equality Act and discrimination. LEAD is also involved in policy and campaigning work.

## The Makaton Charity

Manor House, 46 London Road, Blackwater, Camberley, Surrey GU17 0AA

☎ 01276 60 6760

✉ info@makaton.org

🌐 www.makaton.org

The Makaton Charity aims to ensure that all people living with learning and communication disabilities have the tools and resources they need to communicate. It provides a wide range of resources (books, videos, training packs, etc) for parents, carers and professionals, provides advice and support for families and professionals, and works in partnership to influence society and employers. Makaton is a language programme of signs, symbols and speech. It has been developed for children with severe communication and learning disabilities to encourage communication, language and literacy skills. Often it serves as a voice to communicate with family members, teachers, friends and others. A network of qualified, licensed tutors provides training on a regional and local basis for people wishing to learn Makaton and how teach it to people with learning difficulties.

## Nasen

Nasen House, 4/5 Amber Business Village, Amber Close, Amington, Tamworth B77 4RP

☎ 01827 311 500

✉ welcome@nasen.org.uk

🌐 www.nasen.org.uk

Nasen, formerly the National Association for Special Educational Needs, aims to promote the education and training of all those with special educational needs and provide a forum for those involved in the field, both professionals and parents. A wide range of publications is issued and other activities include conferences, courses and exhibitions.

## OAASIS

The Croft, Vicars Hill, Boldre, Lymington SO41 5QB

☎ 0800 197 3907

✉ oaasis@cambiangroup.com

🌐 www.oaasis.co.uk

OAASIS aims to give impartial advice and information to parents and teachers of children with autism, Asperger's syndrome and other learning disabilities. It is part of Cambian Education Services, a provider of independent special schools and colleges.

**Richard Rieser** is an expert disabled international equality trainer, consultant and teacher who used to run Disability Equality in Education, a charity providing training and resources to education bodies promoting the full inclusion of disabled people in the education system. These resources and other useful information are available free from his website: www.worldofinclusion.com

## Scottish Sensory Centre

Moray House School of Education, University of Edinburgh, Holyrood Road, Edinburgh EH8 8AQ

☎ 0131 651 6501; textphone 0131 651 6067

🌐 www.ssc.education.ed.ac.uk

The SSC promotes and supports new and effective practices in the education of children and young people with sensory impairments. It organises short courses and produces a regular newsletter and other publications and videos. Bibliographies and resource documents are available online. Individual enquiries should be from Scotland on behalf of people aged up to 19.

## Social, Emotional and Behavioural Difficulties Association (SEBDA)

✉ admin@sebda.org

🌐 www.sebda.org

SEBDA provides its members with up-to-date information, support and professional development through its magazine/newsletter, research journal, networking and website. Its members are teachers and others working with children and young people who are disaffected with behavioural difficulties or who have mental health difficulties.

## Children First

A guide for everyone involved in the care and support of disabled children. It covers a wide range of topics including health, play, children's services, school and benefits.

Available to order from our online shop
**www.disabilityrightsuk.org**

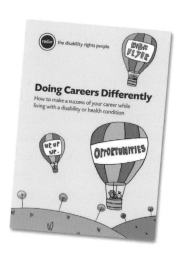

## Doing Careers Differently

Packed with useful information, this guide includes stories from disabled people who have built satisfying careers, from part-time flexible work to a first-time management role and beyond.

Available to order from our online shop
**www.disabilityrightsuk.org**

## Doing Work Differently

Explores practical solutions to real questions related to work. This guide can help you overcome barriers and shows how small adjustments can make a big difference.

Available to order from our online shop
**www.disabilityrightsuk.org**

## Doing Money Differently

Explores new ways of making, saving and looking after your money. This guide covers where your money comes from, where to keep it, where it goes and what to do if you are in debt.

Available to order from our online shop
**www.disabilityrightsuk.org**

# Relationships and life events

**This chapter provides helpful information on issues concerning sex and relationships, parenthood, and bereavement. It also provides brief details of the help available if you are unfortunate enough to experience violence or abuse.**

## Sex and relationships

### SEXUALITY

Having a disability or long-term health condition need not stop us from enjoying our sexuality. We may just have to rethink our approach to sex and make practical adjustments.

Anyone may have sexual problems from time to time, and there is a lot of practical advice and peer support available. You should be able to access mainstream services through a referral from your GP or you may want to access services provided by disability organisations. You should have the same access to sex and relationship education, contraception and sexual healthcare as anyone else, especially as a young person. You need to understand:

- how your body works and grows
- what changes to expect at puberty
- relationships and responsibility
- how society expects you to act in public
- keeping safe
- how to prevent an unwanted pregnancy
- how to prevent sexually transmitted diseases.

For general information on sex and contraception, contact one of the following mainstream organisations:

**Brook**

421 Highgate Studios, 53-79 Highgate Road, London NW5 1TL
☎ 020 7284 6040
✉ admin@brookcentres.org.uk
🌐 www.brook.org.uk
Brook Advisory Centres provide confidential advice on sex and contraception for people aged under 25. The Ask Brook confidential information and enquiry line for young people can be contacted on 0808 802 1234. The Brook website has a great deal of information on sex and disability.

**FPA**

50 Featherstone Street, London EC1Y 8QU
☎ 020 7608 5240; helpline 0845 122 8690
🌐 www.fpa.org.uk
FPA (previously the Family Planning Association), works to improve people's sexual health and reproductive rights. It has a wide range of publications available to download from its website or to buy, including titles specifically for people with disabilities. The FPA Helpline is a confidential service on all aspects of sexual and reproductive health. It is open on weekdays.

Around the UK:

**FPA Northern Ireland**

3rd Floor, 67 Ascot House, 24-31 Shaftesbury Avenue, Belfast BT2 7DB
☎ 0845 122 8687

**FPA Scotland**

Unit 10, Firhill Business Centre, 76 Firhill Road, Glasgow G20 7BA
☎ 0845 122 8676

**FPA Wales**

Suite D1, Canton House, 435-451 Cowbridge Road East, Cardiff CF5 1JH
☎ 029 2064 4034

*Learning disabilities, sex and the law*, published by the FPA, is a guide to legislation regarding sexual activity and people with learning disabilities including capacity to consent, intimate care, the use of sex workers and contraception. It's available from FPA Direct; price £14.99. Ring 0845 122 8600 or email fpadirect@fpa.org.uk.

## SPECIALIST ORGANISATIONS

There are also specialist organisations and resources for disabled people that provide information, advice and peer support on relationships and sexuality.

### In Touch

W www.lcdisability.org/?lid=11901

Project run by Leonard Cheshire Disability that aims to improve access to sexual health education and services through a multitude of online resources.

Several national disability organisations provide information and advice on sex and relationships:

*Sex Matters*, published by the Spinal Injuries Association, contains advice for anyone who is experiencing difficulties with their sex life. Ring the helpline on 0800 980 0501 for a booklet or to speak to someone directly.

A section of the Multiple Sclerosis Society website is devoted to sex, intimacy and relationships. Ring their helpline (0808 800 8000), email helpline@mssociety.org.uk, or visit www.mssociety.org.uk.

*Relationships, Intimacy and Arthritis*, published by Arthritis Care, is available to download at www.arthritiscare.org.uk.

The Stroke Association factsheet *Sex after stroke* is available from www.stroke.org.uk or the Stroke helpline (0845 3033 100).

*Relationships and Sex Matters Disability Information File*, produced by Warrington Disability Partnership, includes information on sexual health and sex aids. Visit www.disabilitypartnership.org.uk, email info@disabilitypartnership.org.uk or ring 01925 24 0064.

### Outsiders

4S Leroy House, 435 Essex Road, London N1 3QP

T 020 7354 8291

E sexdis@Outsiders.org.uk

W www.outsiders.org.uk

Social and peer support network of disabled people and the leading authority on the sexual and relationship needs of disabled people. Runs regular social events so that members can meet and gain confidence. Anyone over 16 may join. Members receive a magazine, membership list and a book giving information on the problems existing members have overcome. Individual advice is available by ringing the Sex and Disability Helpline on 0707 499 3527 or emailing (see address above).

### Regard

BM Regard, London WC1N 3XX

E secretary@regard.org.uk

W www.regard.org.uk

National organisation of disabled lesbians, gay men, bisexuals and transgendered people. It aims to raise awareness of disability issues within these communities, and of sexuality issues within the disability communities. It works to combat social isolation among its membership and campaigns on issues specifically affecting disabled lesbians, gay men, bisexuals and transgendered people.

### Relate

Premier House, Caroline Court, Lakeside, Doncaster DN4 5RA

T 0300 100 1234

E enquiries@relate.org.uk

W www.relate.org.uk

The largest organisation in the country providing advice, relationship counselling, sex therapy and other forms of support. It operates from 600 locations in England, Wales and Northern Ireland providing services face-to-face, by telephone and over the internet.

In Scotland similar services are provided by:

**Relationships Scotland**

18 York Place, Edinburgh EH1 3EP

T 0845 119 2020

W www.relationships-scotland.org.uk

## Parenting

The right to have children is a basic human right and social care and health services should support you. A social care assessment (see the chapter on 'Social care') should cover any support you need to carry out your parenting responsibilities.

If you are a parent-to-be, letting the social care team know about your situation before your baby is born can help them plan support for you.

The Equality Act protects disabled parents and prospective parents from unlawful discrimination. For example, classes for parents-to-be should make 'reasonable adjustments' to make them accessible; you should not be denied fertility treatment because of your disability; and you can't be treated unfairly by adoption and fostering services. Childcare providers and schools also have duties under the Act to make their services accessible to you.

Some of the following organisations may be able to support you or put you in touch with other disabled parents:

**Deaf Parenting UK (DPUK)**
T SMS: 077 8902 7186
E info@deafparent.org.uk
W www.deafparent.org.uk
DPUK is open to all deaf adults with responsibility for children. It works to empower and support deaf parents and improve access to information and services.

**Disability Pregnancy & Parenthood International (DPPI)**
336 Brixton Road, London SW9 7AA
T 0800 018 4730
E info@dppi.org.uk
W www.dppi.org.uk
A national information charity run by disabled parents. It promotes better awareness and support for disabled people during and after pregnancy and as parents. It has a number of publications, offers training for health and social work professionals and provides a UK information service.

**Disabled Parents Network**
Poynters House, Poynters Road, Dunstable LU5 4TP
T 0300 3300 639
W www.disabledparentsnetwork.org.uk
A membership organisation of disabled parents. It operates a peer support/contact register, issues a newsletter and runs a helpline operated by disabled parent volunteers. It campaigns for improved services for disabled parents, collaborates on research projects and provides training sessions for professionals and other interested organisations.

## Bereavement

Losing a loved one is a painful and distressing experience and dealing with the administrative procedures that need to be followed can be an additional burden. There may also be many practical issues to be dealt with. This process, combined with the emotional effects of bereavement, can be difficult to cope with. You may be able to get practical help and advice from a funeral director, GP, solicitor, religious organisation, social care department or Citizens Advice Bureau.

Refer to the chapter on 'Advocacy and decision making' for information on advance directives (living wills).

DWP leaflets *What to do after a death in England and Wales* and *What to do after a death in Scotland* provide advice and information. These can be downloaded from www.dwp.gov.uk. You may also find the BBC booklet *Planning a good death* helpful. It can be downloaded from www.bbc.co.uk/health.

Other sources of information and support are:

**Child Bereavement UK**
The Saunderton Estate, Wycombe Road,
Saunderton Buckinghamshire HP14 4BF
T 01494 56 8900
E enquiries@childbereavement.org.uk
W www.childbereavement.org.uk
Provides support, information and training to
everyone involved both when a child dies or when
they are bereaved of someone important in their
lives.

**Cruse Bereavement Care**
PO Box 800, Richmond, Surrey TW9 1RG
T 020 8939 9530; helpline 0844 477 9400
E helpline@cruse.org.uk
W www.crusebereavementcare.org.uk
W www.rd4u.org.uk (written by and for
young people)
Charity providing advice, counselling and
information on practical matters for anyone who
is bereaved. It has 134 branches and over 5,500
volunteers across the UK and offers training and
publications to those working with bereaved
people. It also aims to increase public awareness
of the needs of bereaved people through
education and information services.

Around the UK:

**Cruse Bereavement Care Northern Ireland**
10 College Green, Belfast BT7 1LN
T 028 9023 2695
E crusebelfast@btconnect.com
W www.cruse.org.uk/NorthernIreland

**Cruse Bereavement Care Scotland**
Riverview House, Friarton Road, Perth PH2 8DF
T 0845 600 2227
E info@crusescotland.org.uk
W www.crusescotland.org.uk

**Cruse Bereavement Care Cymru**
St David's Priory, Richmond Hill, Holyhead Ynys
Mon LL65 2HH
T 0844 561 7856
W www.crusenorthwalesarea.btck.co.uk

**National Council for Palliative Care**
The Fitzpatrick Building, 188-194 York Way,
London N7 9AS
T 020 7697 1520
E enquiries@ncpc.org.uk
W www.ncpc.org.uk
Works to ensure that people with life-threatening
and life-limiting conditions receive the palliative
care they need. They established the Dying
Matters Coalition following the publication by
the Department of Health of the *End of Life Care
Strategy* in 2008. For more information visit
www.dyingmatters.org.

# Violence and abuse

Sexual violence, financial abuse and other forms
of violence and abuse including neglect are all
crimes, whether they happen in your home, in the
community or in institutions.

> If violence or abuse involves an element
> of hostility to someone because of their
> disability, it can be classed as 'disability hate
> crime'. For more information see the chapter
> on 'Discrimination'.

Social and health care providers are required to
carry out criminal record checks and other checks
on staff to make sure they have not abused,
neglected or harmed the people they care for. If
you are employing your own personal assistant,
you have the right to ask for these checks. Contact
your local authority for information on how to
organise these checks.

If you or someone you know is facing violence,
abuse or neglect it's vital to tell the police and
your local council, or otherwise seek support.

Your local council and local disability organisation should be able to provide support or advice and information, as should the organisations listed below.

### Action on Elder Abuse

PO Box 60001, Streatham, London SW16 9BY

T 020 8835 9280
    UK helpline 080 8808 8141
    Ireland helpline 1800 940 010
E enquiries@elderabuse.org.uk
W www.elderabuse.org.uk

Works in the UK and Ireland to protect and prevent the abuse of vulnerable older adults.

### Victim Support

Hallam House, 56-60 Hallam Street, London W1W 6JL

T 0845 303 0900
W www.victimsupport.org.uk

An independent charity that helps people in England and Wales cope with the effects of crime. It provides free and confidential support and information through its Victim Support Line, a network of local offices, and representatives in all magistrates' and Crown Courts.

### Victim Support Northern Ireland

3rd Floor Annsgate House, 70/74 Ann Street, Belfast BT1 4EH

T 028 9024 4039
E info@victimsupportni.org.uk

### Victim Support Scotland

15/23 Hardwell Close, Edinburgh EH8 9RX

T 0131 668 4486
E info@victimsupportsco.org.uk

### Voice UK

100-106 Kelvin House, RTC Business Centre, London Road, Derby DE24 8UP

T 01332 29 2042; helpline 0808 802 8686
E voice@voiceuk.org.uk
W www.voiceuk.org.uk

A national charity supporting people with learning disabilities and other vulnerable people who have experienced crime or abuse.

### Women's Aid

PO Box 391, Bristol BS99 7WS

T 24-hour helpline 0808 200 0247
    General enquiries 0117 944 4411
E info@womensaid.org.uk
W www.womensaid.org.uk

A national charity working to end domestic violence against women and children. It supports a network of services across England.

### Women's Aid Federation of Northern Ireland

T 0800 917 1414; 24-hour helpline
E info@womensaidni.org
W www.womensaidni.org

### Scottish Women's Aid

T 0131 226 6606
    0800 027 1234 24-hour helpline
E contact@scottishwomensaid.org.uk
W www.scottishwomensaid.org.uk

### Welsh Women's Aid

T 24-hour helpline 0808 801 0800
W www.welshwomensaid.org.uk

## Staying steady
Improving your strength and balance

Improving later life

Health & wellbeing

AgeUKIG14

## Managing incontinence
Commonly experienced problems and how to deal with them

Improving later life

Health & wellbeing

AgeUKIG15

## Healthy living
Maintaining a healthy body and mind

Improving later life

Health & wellbeing

AgeUKIG24

## Caring for your eyes
Making the most of your sight

Improving later life

Health & wellbeing

AgeUKIG37

IF ONLY I'D KNOWN THAT A YEAR AGO ...

# Later years

**As we grow older, many of us are likely to develop a range of health conditions. Hearing and vision decline, we may experience reduced mobility, and mild health conditions can worsen. Some mental health conditions emerge or become more severe. It takes longer to recover from injury and we can be left with a chronic problem (mild or severe). We may start to need some help at home or, if our care needs are significant, we might choose residential care. This chapter covers the support and age-related benefits and concessions that can make life easier and help us to stay independent.**

## Health issues

### MOBILITY PROBLEMS

As we get older we may become less mobile and need to rely on mobility aids to get around. Some of us may have trouble bending, so a simple piece of equipment like a long-handled shoehorn can be a great help in maintaining dignity and independence. See the chapter on equipment for details of mobility aids that might help.

Getting out and about can become more difficult. For information on bus, train or air travel, see the chapter on public transport and if you are able to get around by car, see the chapter on motoring.

### SLIPS AND FALLS

According to Age UK, one in three over-65s and one in two over-85s will have a fall. Although most injuries are likely to be minor, the consequences for some people can be devastating. They can lead to long-term impaired mobility and loss of confidence and independence. People with osteoporosis (whose bones are more fragile) are at greater risk of breaking bones after a fall and those with osteoarthritis may experience additional pain and reduced mobility.

If you need help with walking or getting around, see the mobility topic in the chapter on equipment.

> **Age UK** runs a *Falls Awareness* campaign offering information, support and advice on how to prevent falls through exercise. Visit www.ageuk.org.uk for more information.

### EYESIGHT AND HEARING

A common problem associated with getting older is that our senses start to deteriorate. Common eye diseases like cataracts can lead to loss of vision and blindness. Deterioration in the ears through conditions such as Ménière's disease, tinnitus and vertigo can result in loss of hearing and balance.

If you are troubled by loss of hearing or vision, you can ask your GP for referral to an ophthalmologist or ear, nose and throat (ENT) specialist.

You can get advice and information from the Royal National Institute for Blind People (RNIB) or Action on Hearing Loss. Contact details are at the end of this chapter.

The chapter on health services includes sources of practical help for declining sight and hearing.

### DISEASES

The risk of being affected by certain health conditions increases with age. The probability of developing diabetes or cancer is higher if your family has a history of the disease.

Diabetes is not curable but it can be managed through diet and medicines and it is possible to lead a normal life. A person develops diabetes when the glucose level in their blood is too high and can't be regulated by the insulin hormone produced by the pancreas. This can have a negative effect on the heart, kidneys and eyesight.

Cancer occurs when cells in the body's organs and tissues don't reproduce properly and form a tumour, which may spread. There are over 200 forms of cancer and many are treatable if caught at an early stage.

Organisations such as Macmillan Cancer Support and Diabetes UK (see 'Useful contacts' at the end of this chapter) have a wealth of information on symptoms and treatments.

### HEART AND LUNGS

As we get older many of us get problems with our heart or lungs. Chronic obstructive pulmonary disease (COPD) occurs when the air sacs in the lungs get smaller, resulting in shortness of breath. Heart diseases such as angina are also more common. Maintaining a healthy lifestyle through good diet and regular exercise, stopping smoking, and reducing consumption of alcohol can help to stave off the development of these diseases – and many other health conditions.

For more information, contact the British Heart Foundation or the British Lung Foundation. Contact details are at the end of this chapter.

### DEMENTIA, PARKINSON'S DISEASE AND STROKES

As we age, our brains are not as agile as they once were. Some of us might just be a bit forgetful now and again. For others, the brain may be more vulnerable to conditions such as dementia, Parkinson's disease or stroke.

The term dementia describes a range of symptoms including memory loss, problems with reasoning and communication skills, and a reduced ability to carry out daily activities. According to the Alzheimer's Research Trust, there are about 820,000 people in the UK with dementia and some will be undiagnosed. The longer a person lives, the higher the risk of developing a type of dementia. Information and help is available from Dementia UK and the Alzheimer's Society.

Parkinson's disease affects the brain and central nervous system, having an effect on speech and mobility.

A stroke occurs when the brain is starved of blood through an arterial clot or bleed. The sooner a stroke is treated, the less brain damage there will be.

For more information on illnesses affecting the brain, contact the Alzheimer's Society, Dementia UK, the Stroke Association or Parkinson's UK. Contact details are at the end of this chapter.

### INFECTIONS AND VIRUSES

Because our immune system weakens as we get older, we are more susceptible to infections and viruses. The flu virus affects many older people and can lead to more serious illnesses such as pneumonia. If you are 65 or over, see your GP to get your flu jab every year, particularly if you have a heart or lung condition, or diabetes, or if you have had a stroke.

### INCONTINENCE

More than half of people aged 65 or over will experience some form of incontinence. Loss of bladder and bowel control can be uncomfortable as well as embarrassing. It can be caused by a number of things, including constipation, dehydration or infection. But it is possible to minimise incontinence. Pelvic floor exercises strengthen the muscles around the bladder, and keeping active and following a healthy diet will support recovery.

For more information, get in touch with the Bladder and Bowel Foundation. Contact details are at the end of this chapter.

### MENTAL HEALTH

Depression is one of the most common forms of mental illness. It can happen out of the blue or be triggered by a life event such as the loss of a loved one. As we get older we may become depressed about the state of our health or a loss of independence. We may feel low for a prolonged period and find it difficult to motivate ourselves.

For further information, see the chapter on 'Mental health and wellbeing'.

PREVENTION AND MANAGEMENT

Although there are greater health risks as you get older, illness or injury are not inevitable. It's possible to lead a full life even with a medical condition. Prevention is better than cure and a good way to guard against many diseases is to refrain from smoking, eat sensibly, attend well-man or well-woman clinics and maintain a healthy weight.

Staying active is one of the best ways to preserve physical and mental health. Incorporate activities such as dancing, swimming or walking into your daily routines. You can find some suggestions on keeping active in the chapter on 'Leisure activities'.

If you are concerned about any aspect of your health, your GP can advise you and if necessary refer you to a specialist.

## Housing and residential care

As we become older we may begin to find things more difficult around the home. It might be appropriate to consider changing our living arrangements. How much independence you may have to forgo will depend on your level of need.

Care homes are run by a range of providers and provide different types of care. Homes providing 'personal care' are run by private or voluntary organisations or private individuals.

**Personal care** is not defined, but to trigger the need for registration, it means assistance with bodily functions such as feeding, bathing and toileting.

**Nursing care** is provided in homes run by NHS bodies or independent organisations. They also provide personal care. Registration criteria require that they must have a suitably qualified registered nurse working at the home at all times.

## Age-related benefits

PENSION CREDIT

Pension credit is the commonly used name for state pension credit, a means-tested benefit for people who have reached qualifying pension age.

Pension credit has two elements:
- **Guarantee credit:** If your income is below a certain level, known as the 'appropriate minimum guarantee', the guarantee credit makes up the difference.
- **Savings credit:** This can be paid if you or your partner are aged 65 or over and have some savings. It is intended to provide extra money for people who have made modest provision for their retirement.

To claim pension credit you must have reached the qualifying age. This is being raised from 60 to 65 between 2010 and 2020, alongside the rise in women's state pension age. To check the qualifying age at the time you want to claim:
- see leaflet PC1L *Pension Credit*, available from Jobcentre Plus

- contact The Pension Service (0800 99 1234)
- use the state pension age calculator at www.gov.uk/calculate-state-pension.

OTHER BENEFITS

People with disabilities are eligible to apply for disability living allowance up until their 65th birthday. If you are 65 or older and need attention or supervision from another person at least daily or nightly you may be eligible instead for attendance allowance. You must have needed assistance for six months before the benefit can begin to be paid.

See the chapter on benefits for more information about other benefits you may be able to claim.

Disability Rights UK produces an annual user-friendly guide to benefits. The *Disability Rights Handbook* is published each spring and provides information and guidance on benefits and services for people living with disability or health conditions.

# Age-related concessions

### HEALTH

If you are aged 60 or over, you are entitled to free prescriptions and eye tests. You may also have to pay less towards dental treatment, glasses and the cost of travel for hospital treatments. For more information, refer to the chapter on health services.

### HEATING

If you were born before 6 January 1951, in winter 2012/13 you will be eligible for a winter fuel payment of £200 (£300 if you are over 80) to help towards your heating costs. You only need to claim once; after that, you should get your payment automatically every year.

To make a claim, call the Winter Fuel Payments Helpline:
☎ 0845 915 1515

If the weather is very cold, you may also receive a further cold weather payment of £25. This payment is made when the average temperature has been, or is expected to be, 0°C or below for seven days in a row. You will automatically receive a cold weather payment if you get pension credit or certain other means-tested benefits.

### TV LICENCES

For people aged 75 or over, the TV licence is free for your main home. Although it's free, you must apply for the over-75 licence. You need to provide TV Licensing with your date of birth and national insurance number. You can do this online or by phone:
☎ 0300 790 6131
Ⓦ www.tvlicensing.co.uk

There is a 50% discount on the licence fee for people who are registered as blind/severely sight impaired (not partially sighted). Anyone in the household (including children) can apply for this discount, but the licence must be transferred into that person's name.

### TRANSPORT

A senior railcard will entitle you to one-third off rail travel and discounts on hotels, restaurants and days out. You can apply for a railcard at your local station or online:
Ⓦ www.senior-railcard.co.uk

Free bus passes are available for older people in all four countries of the UK. Eligibility is related to the state pension age so you will need to check with your local council.

Residents of London who were born before 5 May 1951 are eligible for a Freedom Pass, issued by local authorities. It provides free travel on all buses, tubes and rail services in London. If you were born after that date, check your eligibility with your council.

### LEISURE

Many leisure activities offered by local councils or national organisations have a concession rate for older people. Cultural venues such as theatres, cinemas and galleries also often offer concessions.

If you receive disability living allowance or attendance allowance, or are registered blind, you will be eligible for a national Cinema Exhibitors' Association Card, which entitles you to a free cinema ticket for a person accompanying you to the cinema.
For more information visit:
Ⓦ www.ceacard.co.uk

# Useful contacts

**Action on Hearing Loss (formerly the RNID)**
19-23 Featherstone Street, London EC1Y 8SL
℡ 0808 808 0123; textphone 0808 808 9000
✉ informationline@hearingloss.org.uk
⊕ www.actiononhearingloss.org.uk

**Age UK**
Tavis House, 1-6 Tavistock Square, London WC1H 9NA
℡ 0800 169 6565
⊕ www.ageuk.org.uk

**Alzheimer's Society**
Devon House, 58 St Katherine's Way, London E1W 1LB
℡ 020 7423 3500
✉ enquiries@alzheimers.org.uk
⊕ www.alzheimers.org.uk

**Bladder and Bowel Foundation**
Rockingham Road, Kettering, Northants NN16 9JH
℡ 01536 53 3255; helpline 0845 345 0165
✉ info@bladderandbowelfoundation.org
⊕ www.bladderandbowelfoundation.org

**British Heart Foundation**
Greater London House, 180 Hampstead Road, London NW1 7AW
℡ 0300 330 3311
   Textphone 18001 020 7554 0000
⊕ www.bhf.org.uk

**British Lung Foundation**
British Lung Foundation, 73-75 Goswell Road, London EC1V 7ER
℡ 0300 003 0555
⊕ www.blf.org.uk

**Dementia UK**
6 Camden High Street, London NW1 0JH
℡ 020 7874 7200
✉ info@demetiauk.org
⊕ www.dementiauk.org

**Diabetes UK**
Macleod House, 10 Parkway, London NW1 7AA
℡ 0845 120 2960
✉ careline@diabetes.org.uk
⊕ www.diabetes.org.uk

**Macmillan Cancer Support**
89 Albert Embankment, London SE1 7UQ
℡ 0808 808 0000
⊕ www.macmillan.org.uk

**National Osteoporosis Society**
Camerton, Bath BA2 0PJ
℡ 0845 450 0230
✉ info@nos.org.uk
⊕ www.nos.org.uk

**Parkinson's UK**
215 Vauxhall Bridge Road, London SW1V 1EJ
℡ 0808 800 0303
✉ hello@parkinsons.org.uk
⊕ www.parkinsons.org.uk

**Royal National Institute for Blind People (RNIB)**
105 Judd Street, London WC1H 9NE
℡ 0303 123 9999
✉ helpline@rnib.org.uk
⊕ www.rnib.org.uk

**Stroke Association**
Stroke House, 240 City Road, London EC1V 2PR
℡ 0303 303 3100
✉ info@stroke.org.uk
⊕ www.stroke.org.uk

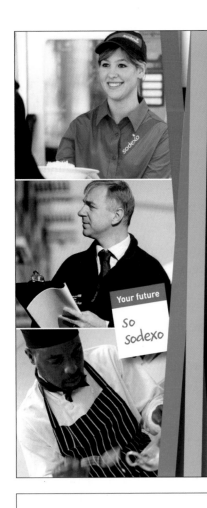

IF ONLY I'D KNOWN THAT A YEAR AGO ...

# Work

**Many disabled people want to work. It's an opportunity to earn an income, have a role and position in society, meet colleagues and develop social networks. For anyone, getting a job that suits their skills, abilities and aspirations is no easy task – and disabled people may find it even more difficult. Some of the difficulties can be due to employers' lack of disability awareness and the range of support systems available. But there is increasing government and employer support for disabled workers – and there are legal rights to protect us from discrimination when looking for work and when we are in work.**

## Your legal rights

### RIGHTS FOR DISABLED WORKERS

As well as the same general employment rights as other workers, there are particular rights for disabled workers. The Equality Act 2010 protects anyone who has a physical or mental impairment that has a substantial and long-term adverse effect on their ability to perform normal day-to-day activities. This includes people with a wide range of mental, sensory and physical impairments or health conditions (some from the point of diagnosis) including HIV, cancer, depression, dementia and learning disabilities among many others.

A wide range of work situations are also covered by the Act. It is unlawful for employers to discriminate in their application forms, interview arrangements, aptitude or proficiency tests, job offers, terms of employment including pay, promotion, transfer and training opportunities, work-related benefits such as access to recreation or refreshment facilities, dismissal or redundancy and discipline and grievances. For more information, see the 'Discrimination' chapter.

Discrimination in employment can include:
- where a disabled person is treated less favourably than a non-disabled person
- where a disabled person is treated worse because of something connected with their disability (indirect discrimination)
- where a person is discriminated against because they are associated with a disabled person or are wrongly thought to be disabled
- where a person is harassed because of their disability
- where someone complains about disability discrimination and is victimised because of it
- where reasonable adjustments are not made (see below).

### Reasonable adjustments

In order to avoid discrimination against disabled people, an employer is expected to make 'reasonable adjustments': that is, changes to their standard procedures and practices so that a disabled person will not be disadvantaged. This does not mean they are expected to do everything demanded – it must be 'reasonable'. If an adjustment is too expensive, for example, a court may not consider it 'reasonable'. Decisions need to be 'fair and balanced'.

Reasonable adjustments can apply to any aspect of your work including where, how and when it is carried out. These may include for example:
- more flexible working hours (for example, to avoid rush-hours or enable medication to be taken at the right times)
- more breaks
- using new, different or adapted equipment (a different sort of desk, telephone or computer, for example)
- time-off (for appointments, dialysis, counselling)
- additional training
- changes or adaptations to your workplace (anything from ramps or colour-schemes to the speed of automated processes)
- providing assistance (including, for example, a reader or interpreter)
- providing alternative duties or tasks.

IF ONLY I'D KNOWN THAT A YEAR AGO ...

You may want to find out what adjustments others have found useful – talk to your disabled staff network if there is one, your trade union, a local disability organisation or an organisation of people with a similar injury, illness, impairment or disability. It's much easier for your line manager if you present a solution rather than just a problem.

### What to do about discrimination

As a first step, it may help to have an informal discussion with your employer about your needs and why you feel you are experiencing discrimination. If your line manager is part of the problem, talk to the human resources department or your manager's line manager. You may wish to take a friend, advocate, assistant or someone from your trade union to the meeting. The problem may simply be that your employer is unaware of your rights and their responsibilities under the Equality Act 2010.

If this does not resolve the situation, you could make a complaint about your treatment through your employer's internal grievance procedure.

If you are still not satisfied, you might want to contact ACAS (Advisory, Arbitration and Conciliation Service) or take your complaint to an employment tribunal. It is best to raise a formal grievance before making a complaint to an employment tribunal, otherwise the tribunal may reduce the compensation they award.

There is a process under the Equality Act 2010 to obtain information before taking a possible discrimination claim against an employer. The process uses 'discrimination and other prohibited conduct' forms – one form is for your questions and another is for your employer's answers.

An employment tribunal can make a judgment on your discrimination claim, make recommendations to your employer and/ or award you with compensation for past or future loss of earnings and/or hurt feelings. It is important to adhere to employment tribunal deadlines. You must make your complaint within three months of the alleged discrimination. At the time of writing, there is no charge to take a claim to an employment tribunal, but fees will be introduced from summer 2013.

Before raising a complaint about discrimination it's important to seek advice from your trade union or local welfare advice or disability organisation.

### FURTHER INFORMATION

#### ACAS (Advisory, Arbitration and Conciliation Service)
☏ 0845 747 4747
   Textphone 18001 0845 747 4747
Ⓦ www.acas.org.uk

#### Citizens Advice Bureaux
You can get details of a local Citizens Advice Bureau from their website:
Ⓦ www.citizensadvice.org.uk

#### Community Legal Advice
☏ 0845 345 4345
Ⓦ http://legaladviserfinder.justice.gov.uk
Community Legal Advice provide details of legal advisers and legal aid eligibility

#### Disability Champions @ Work
Ⓦ www.disabilitychampions.com
Disability Champions is a project set up by Amicus and TUC Education to recruit and train union members to help disabled people negotiate with employers to meet their needs and generally raise awareness of disability issues at work. There are over 1,200 disability champions around the country.

#### Employment Tribunal Service
☏ 0845 795 9775; textphone 0845 757 3722
Ⓦ www.justice.gov.uk/contacts/hmcts/
   tribunals/employment

#### Equality and Human Rights Commission
The Equality and Human Rights Commission website has useful information about bringing a discrimination case.
Ⓦ www.equalityhumanrights.com

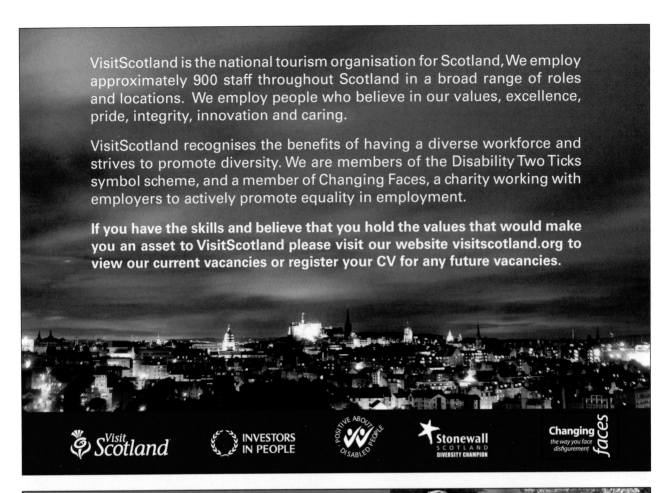

VisitScotland is the national tourism organisation for Scotland, We employ approximately 900 staff throughout Scotland in a broad range of roles and locations. We employ people who believe in our values, excellence, pride, integrity, innovation and caring.

VisitScotland recognises the benefits of having a diverse workforce and strives to promote diversity. We are members of the Disability Two Ticks symbol scheme, and a member of Changing Faces, a charity working with employers to actively promote equality in employment.

**If you have the skills and believe that you hold the values that would make you an asset to VisitScotland please visit our website visitscotland.org to view our current vacancies or register your CV for any future vacancies.**

# The biggest challenges
# The best opportunities
# The only place to apply

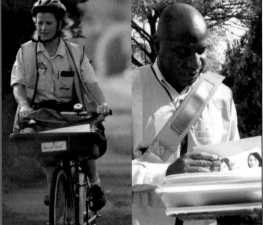

Did you know that the Royal Mail Group is the only business that reaches 99% of UK addresses every day? This means that we deliver more than 80 million items to 28 million addresses – a network of real people reaching all our customers every single day.

More than 140,000 people work across the wider Royal Mail Group (Post Office™, Royal Mail and Parcelforce Worldwide) and, along with our global distribution mail and logistical partnerships, collect, process and deliver the mail every day. We have vacancies across the business in delivery, collections and mail centres. Our mission is to make sure we continue to further improve on our successes, which is why we're going through a programme of modernisation and transformation across our operations business.

And that's why we need people like you in our business; ambitious people who can bring fresh thinking and new energy to the Royal Mail business, and perhaps even become our leaders of the future. With your help, our business will take on this new shape – and start setting the standards that others aim for in this competitive marketplace.

To find out more about us, the opportunities available and to apply, please visit: **www.royalmail.com/jobs**

At Royal Mail we take equality and inclusion seriously and are proud to employ a diverse mix of people. This is why we encourage and welcome applications from all parts of the community, particularly women who are currently under-represented. We are positive about Disability. Royal Mail, the cruciform and the colour red are registered trademarks of the Royal Mail Group Ltd. © Royal Mail Group 2010. All rights reserved.

**Equality Advisory and Support Service**

FREEPOST Equality Advisory Support Service FPN4431

☎ 0800 444 205; textphone 0800 444 206
09:00 to 20:00 Monday to Friday
10:00 to 14:00 Saturday

This new service replaces the helpline run by the Equality and Human Rights Commission. The Helpline is for individuals who think they may have experienced discrimination. The service aims to support individuals referred from local organisations, advisory groups, faith based organisations and other groups working within the community that support people experiencing discrimination and provides advice and information on discrimination and human rights issues.

**TUC**

Congress House, Great Russell Street, London WC1B 3LS

☎ 020 7636 4030

🌐 www.tuc.org.uk

The TUC can help you find a union relevant to your work.

**FACING DISCRIMINATION AT WORK?**

Trade Unions can help you if you are being discriminated against or having work place problems. Trade Unions offer a range of support for members including protection and representation at work, advice on workplace rights, help with pay and terms and conditions, health and safety information and support and legal and welfare services.

If you think that you are facing discrimination in the workplace or are having workplace problems the first step should be to speak to your workplace Union Representative to discuss your options. They can give you advice, support and represent you if necessary.

If you are not already a member of a union then the TUC can help you find a union relevant to your work.

www.tuc.org.uk

**TUC**

## Finding and keeping work

### CAREERS ADVICE

Local authorities in England should provide careers advice up until the age of 25 if you have a Section 139A Learning Difficulty Assessment.

Alternatively, you can use the new National Careers Service. If you're aged 13 to 19 you can ring for advice or email questions through their website. Adults aged 20 and over can also get face-to-face guidance – call to make an appointment with an adviser at your nearest National Careers Service Centre. If you have a disability, learning difficulty or health condition, you should be able to get at least three sessions of face-to-face advice.

☎ 0800 100 900 (Appointments)

🌐 https://nationalcareersservice.direct.gov.uk

Careers advice is also available from Skills Development Scotland and Careers Wales.

### DISABILITY-FRIENDLY EMPLOYERS

There are many disability-friendly employers. They may demonstrate they are positive about employing disabled people by placing the Jobcentre Plus 'two ticks' symbol on job adverts and application forms. Many employers have proactive equal opportunities policies – for example, job adverts might positively encourage disabled people to apply and application forms may be available in different formats.

**Business Disability Forum**

Nutmeg House, 60 Gainsford Street, London SE1 2NY

☎ 020 7403 3020; textphone 020 7403 0040

🌐 www.efd.org.uk

The forum promotes and develops good practice among employers in the employment of disabled people and service to disabled customers. It provides advice and information to a large number of member companies.

IF ONLY I'D KNOWN THAT A YEAR AGO ...

**Telling prospective employers about your disability**

When applying for a job, you might be unsure whether you should disclose information about your disability or whether a prospective employer can ask about your health or disability. You might be concerned about discrimination or lack of confidentiality.

Under the Equality Act, it is against the law for an employer to ask questions about your health or disability before a job offer is made.

The only kind of questions allowed are questions about whether you need a reasonable adjustment for an interview, questions asked for anonymous monitoring purposes, questions asked because of a function that is absolutely necessary for the job, or questions about whether you have a particular disability if the employer wants to recruit a person with a (specific) disability.

If you believe a question asked is not allowed or if you think you may have been discriminated against in any other way, see above under 'What to do about discrimination', and take advice.

> Under health and safety rules, you are obliged to tell your employer about any health condition that might cause an accident or other health and safety problem in the workplace.

In some cases it may be in your interests to disclose details of your disability. Several possible reasons may be:

- you may have more protection under the Equality Act if you later face discrimination if you can show you disclosed your disability
- some employers are keen to employ disabled people
- adjustments can be put in place earlier
- it is an opportunity to describe your disability positively.

## LIFE SUPPORT

While a raft of legislation now exists to protect the rights of those with a disability within the workplace, it is still a rare organisation that truly embraces the concept of inclusivity within its workforce.

"At Ernst & Young it was so much more effortless", Heather tells us. She joined Ernst & Young four years ago, having previously struggled to gain the support her physical disability and dyslexia entitles her to. "Everything that I've needed has been provided without question."

This goes beyond applying the letter of the law and looks instead at providing the tools to help ensure success at work. "I've got a lightweight laptop and I work from home one day per week. It's lovely to get that flexibility which I don't think all employers will give." Heather continues, "I'm part of the disability working group whose main focus is on education – to help people be more aware of their colleagues and to know what support is available as well."

Barry's story is a similar one. In 2004 Barry had an operation to replace a faulty heart valve. "The way the partners gathered around, and the ways colleagues on teams worked around me, that was a real affirming experience," he tells us. "We all worked around the obstacles. The technology, being Skyped up and online from home, it all worked a treat."

Ernst & Young understands that every individual has equally individual requirements and that an organisation will only tap into their very best performance, if they embrace and enable these differences. Internal networks are one of the key ways Ernst & Young remain attuned to the needs of their people.

This desire to add value to everyone's career was recently reflected in Ernst & Young winning Business Disability Forum's Best Talent award. A reflection of success, it's also an incentive to continue to do more.

www.ey.com

**EY ERNST & YOUNG**
*Quality In Everything We Do*

IF ONLY I'D KNOWN THAT A YEAR AGO ...

## SERVICES AND PROGRAMMES

There are some services and programmes designed to help us get and remain in work. Some schemes pay allowances or provide services to make finding work easier, others seek to compel you to find work by cutting or removing your benefit if you do not take certain actions recommended by your personal adviser.

### Jobcentre Plus

Jobcentre Plus is the government agency that provides employment services and employment-related benefits for people of working age. Jobcentre Plus offices offer a range of services to disabled people who are having problems finding or keeping a job. You can also ask them which benefits or allowances to claim. Your Jobcentre can also give you information about the many employment support services in your area that may be provided by private or voluntary sector organisations.

### Disability employment advisers

Disability employment advisers can be contacted through your local Jobcentre Plus office and may act as a gateway to many of the services and schemes listed below. They can provide employment assessment, job-seeking advice and referral to training courses, as well as specialist advice and information on Jobcentre Plus programmes for disabled people.

If you ask to be referred to a disability employment adviser, your request should not be refused.

If you are concerned about losing your job for a reason relating to your disability or health condition, a disability employment adviser can give you and your employer advice and explore practical ways to help you keep your job.

Advice and support from a disability employment adviser is not dependent on receipt of benefits, working with the adviser will not affect your benefits, and you may be able to claim travel expenses.

## ORWELL HOUSING ASSOCIATION

Orwell Housing Association is one of Suffolk's largest employers and actively seeks applications from people with a disability. The Association holds the 'Positive About Disabled People' Two Ticks Symbol in recognition of our commitment to employing, supporting and training those with a disability and to ensure that everybody is treated fairly as individuals.

The Association provides affordable housing for those unable to meet the expense of buying or renting privately, alongside a variety of support and care services. We respect and value equality, diversity and inclusion in all that we do and this has been recognised in our being awarded the Investors in Diversity stage 1 accreditation, the first Housing Association in the East of England to do so.

Orwell Housing Association wants to achieve greater balance across the organisation by employing more disabled people. We believe that workers with a disability are as capable, independent & productive as any other employees.

We offer a range of employment opportunities including property maintenance and development, finance, HR, administration, care and support. When recruiting we also recognise those looking to carry on working, start work or get back into work, with support from specialist rehabilitation and disability services.

We interview all applicants with a disability who meet the criteria for a job vacancy and consider all applicants on their abilities. Once employed, we regularly discuss ways in which we can help staff to develop and use their abilities and to feel part of a successful, vibrant and growing business.

For further information contact Diane Stirton, HR Manager.

www.orwell-housing.co.uk

We own 4,500 homes in Broxbourne and employ 150 people. We're committed to providing better homes, better communities and running a better business - not just better for some people, but better for everyone.

To find out what we offer residents and employees with disabilties:
call us on **01992 453 700**
visit us at **www.b3living.org.uk**

## Doing Work Differently

Explores practical solutions to real questions related to work. This guide can help you overcome barriers and shows how small adjustments can make a big difference.

Available to order from our online shop
**www.disabilityrightsuk.org**

Admiral wish
Disability Rights UK
a successful year.

www.admiral.com

Best wishes to Disability Rights UK
**From Quest Analysis**

DIVERSITY MATTERS IN NORTH DORSET

North Dorset District Council is committed to promoting Equality, challenging discrimination and encouraging social inclusion.

We welcome applications from all sections of the community, operate a guaranteed interview scheme for disabled persons who meet the person specification criteria, and promote flexible working arrangements.

For more information on current vacancies please visit www.dorsetforyou.com or for details on the services we provide to our diverse community please visit www.north-dorset.gov.uk

IF ONLY I'D KNOWN THAT A YEAR AGO ...

### Work Choice

Work Choice is aimed at people who are experiencing complex barriers to work due to disability or who are in work but risk losing their job because of disability.

Participation in Work Choice is voluntary. You will only be accepted if you cannot be helped through other Jobcentre Plus programmes, and you must expect to be able to work at least 16 hours a week in the long-term. Referral is through a disability employment adviser or, in some cases, other specified organisations.

There are three modules to Work Choice: Work Entry Support, In-work Support and Longer-term In-Work Support. The module that's right for you will depend on how long you've been in work and what your needs are. Your disability employment adviser can tell you more.

### Access to Work

Access to Work gives advice and support to people with a disability or health condition as defined in the Equality Act, but also to people whose impairment or health condition is only apparent in the workplace. The service is available if you are in a job, about to start a job or work trial, or self-employed.

An Access to Work grant can cover communication support at an interview (this is also available to unemployed people who need the service) or, once you're in a job, a support worker, special aids and equipment, adaptations to premises or to existing equipment, and help with additional costs of travel to work. Apprentices can apply to Access to Work to pay for work-related costs in a similar way to other employees.

Access to Work can pay up to 100% of the approved costs if you are unemployed and starting a new job, if you are self-employed or if you have been working for an employer for less than six weeks. However, it only pays a proportion of the costs of support if you have been working for your employer for six weeks or more and you need help towards equipment. The precise level of cost-sharing is described in our factsheet *Access to Work*, which can be downloaded from our website (www.disabilityrightsuk.org).

Access to Work advisers are based across England, Scotland and Wales. Contact details can be obtained from www.gov.uk.

Remploy (see 'Useful contacts' below) provides a wide range of mental health support services for Access to Work, including:

- work-focused mental health support for six months
- assessment of an individual's needs to identify coping strategies
- personalised support plans, detailing the steps needed to remain in or return to work
- advice and guidance to enable employers to fully understand mental health and how they can support employees who have a mental health condition
- identifying reasonable adjustments that can be made in the workplace.

### The Work Programme

This is the main welfare-to-work programme. Referral is normally through Jobcentre Plus, and the programme is delivered by organisations called 'providers'. The providers aim to help people find, prepare and stay in work through activities such as work experience, work trials, voluntary work and training.

For those capable of some kind of work, and in receipt of certain benefits, non-participation may result in either a suspension or reduction of benefit depending on your situation. For example, if you get jobseeker's allowance or employment and support allowance and you are in the work-related activity group, you may be required to take part. This, however, will depend on things like how long you have claimed your benefit, when you are expected to be fit for work or whether you are in certain specified groups.

> See our *Disability Rights Handbook* for more information, available from our online shop.

### TRAINING

There are many government training programmes and new initiatives are often launched. Various types of help, such as aids, equipment and adaptations, are available to enable disabled people to take part in government training programmes.

IF ONLY I'D KNOWN THAT A YEAR AGO ...

A disability employment adviser at your local Jobcentre Plus or the Careers Service may be able to tell you about what help is available. Trainees aged 18 or over who receive a wage from their employer must be paid at least the national minimum wage, which can vary for apprentices.

Three of the training programmes are:

### Work-based learning
Work-based learning covers a number of courses and programmes such as apprenticeships or combining a job with study towards a vocational qualification. If you're not employed while training, find out if a training allowance is available. If you are employed, you'll receive wages and will have more legal rights than an unemployed trainee.

### Apprenticeships
Under an apprenticeship scheme, you may be able to achieve a recognised vocational qualification at the same time as gaining relevant, practical experience in work situations. You must be paid at least the national minimum wage for apprentices. If you are aged 19 or over and have completed the first year of an apprenticeship, the full national minimum wage must be paid.

Details of the apprenticeship national minimum wage and the full national minimum wage can be found at www.gov.uk. See above for information on Access to Work for apprentices and the Remploy mental health project.

For information, including vacancy and registration details, go to:
- www.apprenticeships.org.uk
- www.skillsdevelopmentscotland.co.uk

### Work-related residential training
Residential training is available to help long-term unemployed disabled people find or retain jobs or self-employment. You must be disabled, over 18, resident in the UK and unable to find any local training. Trainees receive an allowance with residential costs. Applications are made through a disability employment adviser. For more information, including a list of colleges offering residential training, speak to a disability employment adviser.

## NEW CHARTER HOUSING TRUST GROUP

Formed in 2000 as the new landlord to own and manage homes transferred from Tameside council in Greater Manchester, the Group has a turnover of £90 million a year and a workforce of 800. We own around 18,600 homes and are one of the region's largest registered providers of social housing. We came 7th in the 2012 Sunday Times '100 Best Not-For-Profit Companies To Work For' survey.

The New Charter Group was the first organisation to support and take part in the Chartered Institute of Housing Positive Action for Disability Programme. We wanted to affirm our commitment to support and further the careers of people with a disability.

In 2009, Debbie Smith was employed on the scheme as a Trainee Debt Advisor. She had survived a life-threatening illness in 2003 and was determined to get back to work. Her drive to succeed, combined with support, training and work experience at New Charter resulted in her promotion to Debt Advice Manager, responsible for a team of Debt Advisors. Debbie was awarded the Chartered Institute of Housing/Habinteg Nicky Chapman Award for the best trainee in 2011. The judges said she was an inspiration to her colleagues and a positive role model for disabled people. Debbie has also won a 2012 Housing Heroes Award. Outside work Debbie is studying for a housing degree, plans to do a post-graduate degree in housing and has also completed an Institute of Leadership and Management certificate in team leading.

Our vision for 'Great Homes, Great Neighbourhoods and Great People' needs individuals with the right blend of skills and attitude to make a difference for our customers. New Charter is an organisation that truly values the benefits of a diverse workforce and will wherever possible give full support to our employees.

www.newcharter.co.uk

## Northern Pinetree Trust

**Specialist Micro Enterprise Support for people with disabilities**

- ▲ Enterprise awareness
- ▲ Ideas Generation
- ▲ Ideas Evaluation
- ▲ Enterprise Coaching
- ▲ One to one support
- ▲ Outreach provision
- ▲ Business Planning
- ▲ Business Start-up support
- ▲ Access to Finance (Loans and Grants)

For information:
Telephone: 0191 492 8215
Email: admin@pinetree-centre.co.uk

**www.northernpinetreetrust.co.uk**

Northern
Pinetree
Trust

Pinetree Centre, Durham Road, Birtley, County Durham, DH3 2TD

Is pleased to support
Disability Rights UK

**FOR HIS SAKE**

**DO YOUR BIT**
to support heroes
like Peter. Serving
on the front line
in Afghanistan,
Peter lost both his
legs in an explosion.

All we ask from you is to give
a couple of hours of your time.
Please help your local Poppy
Appeal this year to raise funds
for Service people like Peter
who desperately need our help.

Just choose a time and location
to suit you and you'll be making a
difference to the lives of so many
veterans, young and old.

Please call **0800 085 5924**
or visit **www.poppy.org.uk**

THE ROYAL BRITISH
LEGION

**For our
Armed Forces,
past and
present.**

Registered Charity No. 219279

IF ONLY I'D KNOWN THAT A YEAR AGO ...

# Alternative ways of working

### PART-TIME AND FLEXIBLE WORKING

You may find that a full-time job with fixed, regular hours does not meet your needs.

Part-time work may be another option. Job sharing is also becoming more popular and some organisations maintain a list of people who are willing to become job-sharers. There are also ever-increasing opportunities to work from home, using new technology.

The following organisation may be able to advise on flexible working if you are a parent or a carer:

**Working Families**
1-3 Berry Street, London EC1V 0AA
📞 0300 012 0312
📧 office@workingfamilies.org.uk
🌐 www.workingfamilies.org.uk

### SELF-EMPLOYMENT

Working for yourself can often be a good alternative to paid employment. Although it may seem daunting, self-employment can offer a degree of flexibility and personal control that suits some disabled people.

You may be able to get help under the new enterprise allowance scheme to start your own business – if you claim jobseeker's allowance, if you are regarded as having a viable business idea and if you are not on the Work Programme. The scheme includes advice from volunteer business mentors to help you develop a business plan. You may be able to get a loan of up to £1,000 to help with start-up costs and a weekly allowance for up to 26 weeks. You should speak to your Jobcentre Plus adviser about this.

General help and advice on setting up a business and overcoming or avoiding problems can be obtained from the following government-sponsored networks, which provide services online and through local operators.

**Business Link (England)**
📞 0845 600 9006; textphone 0845 606 2666
🌐 www.businesslink.gov.uk

**Invest Northern Ireland**
📞 0800 181 4422
🌐 www.investni.com

**Business Gateway (Scotland)**
📞 0845 609 6611
🌐 www.business.scotland.gov.uk

**Business Wales**
📞 0300 060 3000
🌐 business.wales.gov.uk

---

### NORTHERN PINETREE TRUST

**Social enterprise as a pathway to work**
The Northern Pinetree trust promotes enterprise for people with a disability and people from disadvantaged communities.

We work with a wide range of adults and younger people who benefit from 1:1 and additional support.

Based near Gateshead, County Durham, we provide support on an outreach service at locations across County Durham, Gateshead, Tyne & Wear, Tees Valley and Northumberland.

We offer self-employment counselling and guidance to ensure you make an informed choice about whether working for yourself or creating a social enterprise is for you.

Our services include a full programme of business and enterprise support for people with disabilities; including one-to-one support, workshops, business coaching and planning alongside confidence and personal development sessions. We can also help you access business grants or loans.

**www.northernpinetreetrust.co.uk**

**WEa**
Learning*for*Life

## Our vision

'A better world – equal, democratic and just; through adult education the WEA challenges and inspires individuals, communities and society'.

More than 70,000 learners go on WEA courses across England and Scotland each year. That's a huge number of diverse individuals, and that's why we're working to ensure that the same can be said of our teachers and staff. Work with us. Join us.

Look out for adverts in local and national press. Call 020 7426 3450 or visit www.wea.org.uk

# Royal Brompton and Harefield
## NHS Foundation Trust

Is pleased to support Disability Rights UK

Derwentside Homes

# Valuing our staff

Derwentside Homes is a not for profit housing association, registered with the Tenant Services Authority and the Charity Commission.

The diversity of our workforce and their varied backgrounds, skills and experiences help us to deliver an efficient and effective service to our tenants.

We value our employees and ensure they can work in an environment where they are supported and treated with respect and dignity.

We also encourage job applicants from all areas of society and select, develop and retain staff on merit, ensuring all our employment practices and processes are free from discrimination.

To find out more, please visit our website at www.derwentsidehomes.co.uk

TOP 100 APPRENTICE EMPLOYER 2011

business for neighbourhoods

**EXCELLENT HOMES • QUALITY SERVICE • PROUD COMMUNITIES**

Hastoe is the leading rural affordable housing specialist in England and we are passionate about developing sustainable rural homes and communities.

Achieving that aim relies on the dedication of our diverse staff team who meet the varied needs of our residents by delivering high quality services that are equally accessible to all.

We have a strong focus on ability and in order to maintain our growth, we are keen to continue to attract the best people and to help them reach their potential. We are 'Positive about Disabled People', and make every effort to to ensure that our disabled staff are supported long-term, in their working environment. We are Investor in People Bronze accredited and committed to disability awareness.

If you would be interested in joining our team in the East, South or West, please visit our website at www.hastoe.com for current vacancies.

SHIFT. SILVER

# Hastoe
Group

business for neighbourhoods   Stonewall DIVERSITY CHAMPION   INVESTORS IN PEOPLE | Bronze

Hastoe Group is an equal opportunities employer and applications from all sectors of the community are welcome.

IF ONLY I'D KNOWN THAT A YEAR AGO ...

**The Prince's Trust**

📞 0800 84 2842; textphone 020 7543 1374

📧 webinfops@princes-trust.org.uk

🌐 www.princes-trust.org.uk

The Prince's Trust assists unemployed or underemployed young people set up in business with financial help and ongoing business advice. There are 12 national and regional offices – contact details are on the website. The four national contact details are as follows:

**Northern Ireland:**

📞 028 9074 5454

📧 webinfoni@princes-trust.org.uk

**Scotland:**

📞 0141 204 4409

📧 webinfosc@princes-trust.org.uk

**Wales:**

📞 029 2043 7000

📧 webinfowa@princes-trust.org.uk

## VOLUNTEERING

Doing voluntary work is an opportunity to learn new skills, build confidence and meet people. Many areas have some sort of volunteer bureau with information about local opportunities. You can also find information on www.gov.uk and the national volunteering database www.do-it.org.uk.

If you're getting benefits and want to volunteer, ask at your Jobcentre Plus about a scheme called Work Together. Voluntary work may not affect your benefits but it is important that you check with the benefits offices before making a commitment.

Further information on volunteering is available from:

**Community Service Volunteers (CSV)**

237 Pentonville Road, London N1 9NJ

📞 020 7278 6601

📧 information@csv.org.uk

🌐 www.csv.org.uk

CSV is Britain's largest volunteer organisation and provides opportunities for people with disabilities and learning difficulties to take part in a number of its projects.

**Volunteering England**

Regents Wharf, 8 All Saints Street, London N1 9RL

📞 020 7520 8900

🌐 www.volunteering.org.uk

**Volunteer Now (Northern Ireland)**

📞 028 9023 2020

📧 info@volunteernow.org.uk

🌐 www.volunteering-ni.org

**Volunteer Development Scotland**

Jubilee House, Forthside Way, Stirling FK8 1QZ

📞 01786 47 9593

📧 vds@vds.org.uk

🌐 www.vds.org.uk

**Wales Council for Voluntary Action**

📞 0800 288 8329; textphone: 029 2043 1702

📧 help@ wcva.org.uk

🌐 www.wcva.org.uk

## Useful contacts

Many local and national organisations, including some of the disability-specific organisations listed elsewhere in the book, provide employment-related services.

In some cases, they can put you in touch with other disabled people who work or want to work.

**Association of Disabled Professionals**

BCM ADP, London WC1N 3XX

📞 01204 43 1638 (answerphone only)

📧 info@adp.org.uk

🌐 www.adp.org.uk

ADP members are disabled people who work, or have worked, in professional or managerial roles. It provides advice on employment and self-employment.

IF ONLY I'D KNOWN THAT A YEAR AGO ...

The Association for Disabled Professionals established the Disabled Entrepreneurs' Network for self-employed disabled people and those setting up and running their own businesses.
Ⓦ www.disabled-entrepreneurs.net.

**British Association for Supported Employment (BASE)**
Unit 4, 200 Bury Road, Tottington, Lancs BL8 3DX
Ⓣ 01204 88 0733
Ⓔ admin@ base-uk.org
Ⓦ www.base-uk.org
BASE supports agencies and staff providing supported employment. It represents around 200 organisations providing information, training and encouragement for the development of new services.

**Disabled Workers Co-operative**
Ⓦ www.disabledworkers.org.uk
The Disabled Workers Co-operative has a database of skills and services offered by disabled workers. Any disabled individual, sheltered workshop or organisation employing a significant number of disabled people can register free on the database, which is also free to use by visiting the website. The website also has an e-jobs portal where disabled people looking for employment can browse for jobs and employers can post their vacancies.

**Enham**
Enham Place, Enham Alamein, Andover SP11 6JS
Ⓣ 01264 34 5800
Ⓦ www.enham.org.uk
Enham provides a wide range of employment and training services for disabled people.

**Kate Nash Associates**
Ⓣ 079 0401 8939
Ⓔ info@katenashassociates.com
Ⓦ www.katenashassociates.com
The website contains advice on how to set up disabled employee networks. It includes a downloadable toolkit, *Disabled Employee Networks – a practical guide,* about how to set up or refresh a network or disability interest group.

**Remploy**
Ⓣ 0845 155 2700; textphone 0845 155 0532
Ⓔ employmentservices.osc@remploy.co.uk
Ⓦ www.remploy.co.uk
Remploy Employment Services is one of the UK's leading providers of specialist employment support for disabled and disadvantaged people.

**Shaw Trust**
Ⓦ www.shaw-trust.org.uk
The Shaw Trust supports disabled people to prepare for work, find jobs and live more independently. It is one of the government's lead partners in the delivery of employment programmes for disabled people. Visit the website to contact them.

IF ONLY I'D KNOWN THAT A YEAR AGO ...

# Careers

**This chapter introduces some of the issues we may face when trying to get into work or trying to get ahead in our job or career. It provides some tips on choosing a career and why work is so important.**

## Why careers count

A lot of our sense of ourselves, who we are and our role in society is related to the job we do. If we spend a lot of our time working, it makes sense to take it seriously, try to enjoy it and get as much out of it as we can.

It's understandable that as disabled people, especially if newly disabled, we may think it difficult enough to get a job, let alone develop it into a career. But this need not be the case.

Evidence has shown that disabled people stay in jobs longer. In part, this may be because disabled workers believe it's more difficult to change jobs. It can be, but it's far from impossible.

*Doing Careers Differently* is part of our Doing Life Differently series. It looks at career development and how to make a success of your career.

It includes stories from disabled people who have built satisfying careers – anything from part-time flexible work or self-employment to a first management job and beyond. The book is packed with useful information and visions of the possible to spark your imagination. You can buy a copy or download it from the Disability Rights UK website.

## Making a career decision

Careers today are not linear journeys up a promotion ladder. Many people have CVs showing a number of jobs with many employers, perhaps in quite different fields, or for various clients. Many are freelancers working for themselves.

Thanks to modern technology and the changing nature of the jobs we're doing, it's less and less necessary to work in a conventional setting like an office or factory. Home working is increasingly practical. Changing direction or adding a new string to your bow is also becoming more common and, as a result, easier.

When making a decision about your career –whether it's your first job, whether you're planning to return to work after a period of absence, or whether you simply fancy a change, there are four main areas to consider.

QUESTIONS TO ASK YOURSELF
**1: What do you want to do?**
What are you really interested in? What are your skills and, especially, which ones do you most enjoy using? What are the influences on your career ideas, including any experiences or messages in relation to disability that might be holding you back? Some people feel they have a vocation in life. Maybe there is something you have always wanted to do but somehow stopped yourself from trying.

You're going to spend a lot of time working so do what you want to do – not what others want you to do or think you're suitable for. Some jobs might be more difficult because of your disability but there will be others that would suit you very well and many for which it makes no difference at all.

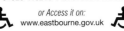
IF ONLY I'D KNOWN THAT A YEAR AGO ...

## 2: What do you need to help you do it?

You may need to find out more about the available opportunities. This might be information on different types of jobs, the work, pay and prospects as well as the skills needed and any education and training requirements. Some useful careers resources are listed at the end of this chapter. If you have access to the internet you can find information on most occupations and look up the appropriate professional body.

## 3: Is what you want to do suitable for you?

You might need some feedback about the suitability of your career ideas. There may be obstacles in your way that need addressing. Psychometric tests and computer guidance programmes can be a useful source of additional data. Adult Directions is available in most careers offices and the Prospects Planner can be accessed online by graduates (see 'Useful contacts' at the end of this chapter). A careers adviser can help you sound out your ideas and suggest alternative occupations based on what you have discovered so far.

## 4: How do you make it happen?

It's important to be open to the influences around you, taking on board any useful feedback and adapting to new situations.

- Networking is an undervalued skill, useful not just for people who want to set up their own business. Research shows that 80% of job vacancies are not advertised.
- You might need a period of study or training to acquire relevant qualifications.
- You may need to gain confidence or experience elsewhere, perhaps as a volunteer. Meeting other disabled workers and personal development may help you gain the confidence to believe you can have a career. Contact other disabled people through national and local disabled people's organisations.

There's more on training in the 'Education and skills' chapter, including details of the National Extension College, the Open and Distance Learning Quality Council, the Open College of the Arts and the Open University. You can search for volunteering opportunities through the government website www.gov.uk.

Careers advisers can assist with your job search strategy – showing you how to access vacancies, create a CV, fill out an application form or perform at an interview. They should also be able to help with disability-related questions such as discussing your impairment with an employer and how to apply for Access to Work.

## Disability means business

### BENEFITS FOR BUSINESS

The law protects our rights, but many organisations now see the business case for going beyond their legal obligations in relation to employing disabled people. An organisation that performs well for disabled people performs exceptionally for everybody and companies are learning the benefits of an inclusive and diverse workplace.

Diversity helps encourage innovation and many disabled people already have the adaptability, multi-tasking and complex problem-solving skills that jobs often require.

Customers expect diversity. Companies that appear to discriminate may lose custom and those with a diverse workforce are better placed to understand the needs of their customers.

Businesses want to differentiate themselves as an employer of choice to ensure they attract the best talent. The benefits of employing disabled people are proven: from improved image and reputation to increased employee productivity.

### YOUR RIGHTS AND RESPONSIBILITIES

You need to know your rights – these are outlined in the chapters on 'Work' and 'Discrimination'.

But in many cases, the most appropriate and constructive response is not a legal one. Discrimination often arises from ignorance or fear, so being clear about yourself, your disability and what you expect, will help your boss and your colleagues understand and work with you to build a positive working environment.

IF ONLY I'D KNOWN THAT A YEAR AGO ...

# Discussing your disability

Your employer can't make 'reasonable adjustments' if he or she doesn't know about your disability. The legal aspects of this are discussed in the chapters 'Work' and 'Discrimination', but it's also a question of how you want to present yourself in the workplace.

This may seem like something that only concerns people with invisible impairments but even those with obvious physical impairments need to think about how and when they might talk about them. This is important in the context of going to interviews or for promotion but is also relevant to your everyday working life.

What language do you want used? By discussing your impairment you can help give colleagues a vocabulary they might not otherwise have.

Regrettably, society understands some impairments even less well than others – mental health problems, for example. While being open and honest is the ideal, it would be simply untrue to suggest it is always the best policy. Of course, you're unlikely to have a long, successful career in an environment where you don't feel able to be honest about who you are, but at the same time telling all on day one may not be the best strategy either.

Building trust takes time. You need to make your own decisions based on your relationships at work and your career plans.

> Help your employer to be disability friendly. If they'd like to be but don't know how to be, suggest they talk to us at Disability Rights UK. Email sarah.cosby@disabilityrightsuk.org.

You may also want to find out about disabled employee networks. If your employer has one, join it. If not, you could help to set one up.

## Improving performance by promoting diversity and inclusion

Getting it right for your disabled customers and employing and retaining disabled staff can be key to business success.

Disability Rights UK can help you fine tune your business and add value, ensuring your products, services, recruitment and employment activities reach and support disabled people.

Our experts, some of whom have been active in the disability field for over 25 years can work with you at the highest level to deliver real business solutions for your company.

We can:
* Empower your employees to perform at their best
* Give you disability confidence to employ and manage disabled staff
* Develop and motivate your workforce through inclusive recruitment and development programmes
* Promote wellbeing in your workplace boosting productivity
* Understand what equality law means for your business and how you can benefit.

### Our credentials

We are the UK's leading disability network run by and for disabled people. We have a unique perspective on the employment aspirations and needs of disabled people.

We have worked closely with some of the UK's leading employers such as Lloyds Banking Group, VISA Europe and Royal Mail.

Email enquiries@disabilityrightsuk.org to talk about how we can help you.

## Changing jobs

One of the deterrents to changing jobs is concern about jumping through all the hoops again – what reasonable adjustments you need, how to discuss your disability with colleagues, and so on.

The practical side – a ramp or a different computer, for example – is sometimes easier to handle than the intangible benefits that come from working with people who understand your needs and your particular working arrangements.

The Employers' Forum on Disability suggests using a 'tailored adjustment agreement'.

This is a record of reasonable adjustments agreed between a disabled employee and their line manager.

By identifying the impact your disability has on your work, this agreement can help avoid re-negotiating every time you change jobs, what good days and bad days are like for you, and what you need in terms of leave, etc.

You can take the agreement with you. If you go to a new workplace, it will be a good starting point and provide evidence of what works – and this should reassure a new employer.

## Work-life balance

Don't forget that you need to be well to do a good job and enjoy a good career. If you're living with a disability or long-term health condition then you have even more reason to look after yourself.

Managing your disability means exactly that – it doesn't mean pretending it doesn't exist. Don't put so much of yourself into your work that there's nothing left of you to enjoy the rewards.

## Mentoring

A mentor is a trusted friend who can help you get where you want to go. Not so much through their contacts – although these might help – but because they've travelled a similar road themselves.

**Disability Rights UK** supports *Radiate,* a network of high-flying professionals with lived experience of disability or health conditions. Research has shown that disabled people are three times less likely to be board-level directors and out of this research, the Radiate Network was born. The network runs events where well-known disabled people talk about their experiences and experts share their knowledge. Visit the *Radiate* website (www.disabilityrightsuk.org/radiate.htm) for more information.

Research and feedback from people who have been through leadership development programmes shows that for 75% mentoring had been a useful career development tool.

Mentoring can open doors, give you insights that you may not otherwise have access to, develop transferable skills and build confidence. But it shouldn't be entered into lightly.

Find out more about how it can work and think carefully about what you want before asking someone. Look out for potential mentors through your networks at work and through disabled people's organisations.

# Useful contacts

## Adult Directions

Ⓦ www.cascaid.co.uk/adultdirections

Offers adults of all ages online career and skills matching that can support your career and employment decisions. You will need a password from a careers adviser to access this online system. To find your local careers office, contact the National Careers Service (see below).

## Association of Disabled Professionals

BCM ADP, London WC1N 3XX

Ⓣ 01204 431 638 (answerphone only)

Ⓦ www.adp.org

Registered charity drawing on the expertise of disabled professionals to improve the educational and employment opportunities of disabled people.

## CRAC: The Career Development Organisation

Ⓦ www.crac.org.uk

A not-for-profit careers resource that aims to help you make the most of your potential and talent by showing how others have used theirs.

## Disabled Workers Co-operative

130 Wells Road, Glastonbury, Somerset BA6 9AQ

Ⓦ www.disabledworkers.org.uk

Registered charity that helps disabled people become independent and achieve a greater sense of self-worth through playing an active role in the economy.

## Employers' Forum on Disability

Nutmeg House, 60 Gainsford Street, London SE1 2NY

Ⓣ 020 7403 3020

Ⓦ www.efd.org.uk

The world's leading employers' organisation focused on disability and how it affects business.

## icould

Ⓦ www.icould.com

A resource that helps you make the most of your potential and talent by showing how others have used theirs. The site offers the opportunity to search by employment sector or life theme and has career videos and written articles.

## National Careers Service

Ⓣ 0800 100 900

Ⓦ https://nationalcareersservice.direct.gov.uk

Provides information, advice and guidance to help you make decisions on learning, training and work opportunities. The service is free to everyone living in the UK. However, to arrange a face-to-face careers meeting you must be over 19.

## Prospects

Booth Street East, Manchester M13 9EP

Ⓦ www.prospects.ac.uk

Ⓣ 0161 277 5200

The official graduate careers website. The 'Prospects Planner' can help you to identify what jobs suit you based on your skills, motivations and desires and lets you access latest vacancies (www.prospects.ac.uk/myprospects_planner).

## TUC

Congress House, Great Russell Street, London WC1B 3LS

Ⓣ 020 7636 4030

Ⓦ www.tuc.org.uk

The TUC can help you find a union relevant to your work. The TUC guide *Disability and work: a trade union guide to the law and good practice* can help negotiate good policy and practice.

> **Disability Rights UK** has a range of resources that may help with your career development, including publications that are free to download. Visit the publications pages on our website (www.disabilityrightsuk.org).

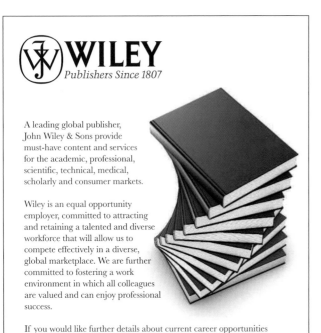
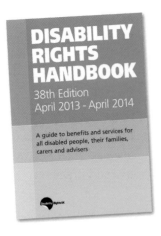

IF ONLY I'D KNOWN THAT A YEAR AGO ...

# Benefits

**As disabled people we are often forced to incur extra costs. For example, there may be extra heating costs arising from lack of mobility, you may need to buy equipment, more expensive food to meet dietary needs or use taxis rather than public transport or a private car. We may have extra costs associated with staying in work or finding work. This chapter outlines the benefits that can help with the extra costs of disability, details of how to make a claim and where to get information and advice. While benefits may not meet all your extra costs, you have a legal right to them if you meet the entitlement criteria.**

## Overview

Benefits can be divided into three broad categories:

- those provided to meet extra living costs (eg disability living allowance)
- those specifically for people whose ability to work is limited due to illness or disability (eg employment and support allowance)
- those which are are means tested and designed to top up your income (eg pension credit).

Some benefits act as a passport to others, eg receipt of income-related employment and support allowance leads to help with NHS charges (such as prescriptions) and hospital travel fares.

Some benefits overlap: that is, if you get one, you can't get another.

There are benefits for people over pension age and for people whose disability resulted from industrial injuries or service in the armed forces.

> Factsheets on all the benefits mentioned in this chapter are available to download from our website. More detailed information is available in our *Disability Rights Handbook*, a comprehensive guide to benefits and services for disabled people, which is available to order from our online shop.

## Extra costs benefits

### DISABILITY LIVING ALLOWANCE

Disability living allowance (DLA) is not means tested or taxable and can be paid in full on top of other benefits. DLA has a mobility component and a care component; these can be paid separately or together.

#### DLA mobility component

People can apply for the mobility component between the ages of 5 (or 3 for the higher rate) and 65. The upper cut-off age is important, as no alternative exists for people applying after their 65th birthday. You must have been eligible for the component for three months before your claim and likely to remain eligible for at least six months afterwards.

The mobility component is paid at two levels.

**The lower rate** is for people who are able to walk but cannot do so outdoors without guidance or supervision, a test based on ability to cope with unfamiliar routes. It is payable to people whose mobility difficulties are caused by mental health or learning difficulties as well as physical disability. For example, conditions such as panic attacks or anxiety may make you eligible for the lower rate mobility component.

Eligibility for children under 16 depends on showing that the child needs substantially more guidance or supervision than a child in normal physical and mental health would require.

The **higher rate** is for people:
- who cannot walk or are virtually unable to walk
- who are both deaf and blind
- who have been certified as severely sight impaired or blind by a consultant ophthalmologist
- who have no legs or feet
- for whom walking would lead to a serious deterioration in health or a risk to their life
- who have a severe mental impairment and receive the highest rate of the DLA care component.

When assessing 'virtual inability to walk' it is the distance, speed and manner of walking out of doors without severe discomfort that is taken into account.

### DLA care component

People are eligible to apply for the care component up until the day before their 65th birthday. There is no lower age limit for this component. Claimants must have needed help for at least three months before claiming and be likely to need it for at least a further six months.

The care component is paid at three levels:

The **lowest rate** is payable to people who require assistance with their bodily functions from another person for a significant part of the day or who cannot prepare a cooked main meal for themselves. 'Bodily functions' are actions such as hearing, seeing, eating, dressing, bathing, going to the toilet, communicating your needs, etc. The cooking test does not apply to children.

The **middle rate** is payable to people who need:
- frequent attention throughout the day in connection with their bodily functions; or
- continual supervision throughout the day to avoid substantial danger to themselves or others; or
- prolonged or repeated attention at night in connection with their bodily functions; or
- another person to be awake at night for a prolonged period or at frequent intervals to watch over them to avoid substantial danger to themselves or others.

The **highest rate** is for people who have one of the daytime needs and one of the night-time needs described above, or who are terminally ill. Children under 16 must also need substantially more care or supervision than would be needed for other children of a similar age, in order to qualify.

When assessing charges for services, social care departments can take the DLA care component, but not the mobility component, into account.

The DLA care component can be paid to people who have moved from the UK to another country in the European Economic Area.

It will not be possible to make a new claim for DLA from June 2013. This is because it will be replaced by a new benefit called the personal independence payment (PIP) that has stricter eligibility conditions. The Department for Work and Pensions estimates that around 500,000 fewer disabled people will qualify for PIP than for DLA.

Existing DLA claimants aged between 16 and 64 will be moved on to PIP from April 2013 to 2016 if they satisfy the rules for the new benefit.

### ATTENDANCE ALLOWANCE

Attendance allowance (AA) is a benefit similar to the care component of DLA, for people aged over 65. It is payable at two rates depending on whether the attention or supervision is required in the daytime or at night-time, or both daytime and night-time.

The assistance must have been needed for six months before the benefit can begin to be paid.

AA is not taxed or means tested, can be paid in addition to other benefits and does not affect eligibility for other means-tested benefits.

### PERSONAL INDEPENDENCE PAYMENT

Personal independence payment (PIP) is a new benefit to replace DLA for people aged 16 to 64. From June 2013 all new DLA claims will be for PIP.

To get the personal independence payment you must:

- be aged 16 to 64
- satisfy the daily living and/or mobility activities test for three months prior to claiming and be likely to continue to satisfy this test for at least nine months after claiming (this 9-month period is called the prospective test)
- pass a residence and presence test and a habitual residence test.

You can receive PIP whether you are in or out of work. You will not be able to claim PIP once you are 65 years old but you can stay on PIP if you received it before you reached 65.

PIP will have two components:

- a daily living component
- a mobility component.

Each component will have two rates:

- **a standard rate** – if your ability to carry out daily living activities or mobility activities is limited by your physical or mental condition
- **an enhanced rate** – if your ability to carry out daily living activities or mobility activities is severely limited by your physical or mental condition.

You may be able to get one of the two rates of the daily living component and one of the two rates of the mobility component.

If you are in a care home, you will be entitled to the mobility component so long as you satisfy the qualifying conditions.

In order to qualify for PIP, you will have to score a certain number of points in relation to nine daily living and two mobility activities.

Each activity has a set of descriptors. Points are awarded on the basis of your limitations with respect to each activity. If you can show that a descriptor applies to you for six months within a 12-month period, you will be awarded the appropriate points. If you have a fluctuating condition, the most appropriate descriptor will be the one that is likely to apply for the greatest proportion of that time.

Most people claiming PIP will be asked to attend a medical examination carried out by a healthcare professional working on behalf of the DWP. Based on this, and on any medical evidence you submit, a DWP decision maker will determine your entitlement to PIP.

## Work-related benefits

### EMPLOYMENT AND SUPPORT ALLOWANCE

Employment and support allowance (ESA) is a benefit for people who are unable to work or whose ability to work is limited by ill-health or disability. It replaced incapacity benefit and income support paid as a result of such incapacity from October 2008. Over the next few years people still receiving those benefits will be moved onto ESA.

There are two types of ESA:

- **contributory ESA** for those with sufficient national insurance contributions in certain tax years
- **income-related ESA**, which is means tested. Income-related ESA can help with mortgage interest payments (see the chapter on housing).

During the first 13 weeks of a new ESA claim (the 'assessment phase'), you will be paid at a lower rate, unless you are terminally ill.

During the assessment phase, you will go through a work capability assessment. This involves a medical examination carried out by a healthcare professional working on behalf of the DWP.

Based on the work capability assessment, and any medical evidence you submit, a DWP decision maker determines:

- whether you have a 'limited capability for work' and can stay on ESA; and
- whether you also have a 'limited capability for work-related activity'.

The 'limited capability for work-related activity' test is used to decide whether you are placed in the support group of claimants or in the work-related activity group.

Those in the work-related activity group are obliged to attend work-focused interviews with a personal adviser to discuss work prospects and draw up an action plan of activities to help you move closer to or into work. Failure to comply can result in cuts to your benefit unless you can show 'good cause' for your failure to attend or participate within a set timeframe.

If you are in the support group, you are not subject to these requirements but can see a personal adviser if you wish.

Contributory-based ESA is payable to those placed in the work-related activity group for only one year. However, it is paid indefinitely to those in the support group.

Certain levels of permitted work are allowed without affecting ESA:

- permitted work lower limit, where you can earn up to £20 a week for an unlimited period
- permitted work higher limit, where you can work for a 52-week period (or indefinitely if you are in the support group) if the work is for less than 16 hours a week and your earnings do not exceed £99.50 a week after deductions
- supported permitted work, where you must be supervised by someone employed by a public or local authority, a community interest organisation or voluntary organisation that provides or finds work for people with disabilities. You cannot earn more than £99.50 a week
- work that is part of a treatment programme done under medical supervision while you are an inpatient or regularly attending as an outpatient of a hospital or similar institution. The earnings limit is £99.50 a week.

All ESA claimants can access a work programme. These are intended to give people a tailored package of employment, training and rehabilitation.

## TAX CREDITS

**Working tax credit** is intended to help people who are in low paid work. You can get working tax credit if you are at least 16 years old and either you or your partner are working for 16 or more hours a week, provided that you also meet at least one of the following conditions:

- you are responsible for a child or young person and you are a single parent
- you are a couple, one or both of you are responsible for a child or young person, one of you works at least 16 hours a week and you work at least 24 hours a week between you
- you are a couple, one or both of you are responsible for a child or young person and one of you works at least 16 hours a week where the other partner is:
  in hospital; or
  in prison; or
  entitled to carer's allowance; or
  getting certain benefits due to sickness or disability, for example ESA or DLA
- you or your partner qualify for the disability element (see below)
- you are aged 60 or over.

To qualify for the disability element, you have to meet all of the following conditions:

- you must be working for 16 hours or more a week
- you must have a disability that makes it difficult for you to get a job
- you must be receiving, or have recently received, a qualifying sickness or disability-related benefit – or, in certain circumstances, national insurance credits.

If you do not fit into any of the above categories you may still be eligible for working tax credit if you or your partner are aged 25 or over and work at least 30 hours a week.

The amount of working tax credit paid depends on a means test and is affected by income and income from savings. You may receive an extra payment as a contribution to certain paid childcare.

**Child tax credit** is a means-tested payment for people, whether working or not, who are responsible for children or young people who are still in full-time education. You may be paid extra if you have a disabled child.

Working tax credit and child tax credit are administered by Her Majesty's Revenue and Customs (HMRC). People receiving tax credits should notify HMRC of changes in their circumstances to ensure they are getting all that they are entitled to, and to avoid overpayments that will have to be repaid in the future.

### Tax credits helpline
A helpline for enquiries and for making tax credit claims is available seven days a week. Information is also available online.
☎ 0845 300 3900; textphone 0845 300 3909
🌐 www.hmrc.gov.uk/taxcredits

## JOBSEEKER'S ALLOWANCE
Jobseeker's allowance is for people who are unemployed or working less than 16 hours a week and who are available for and actively seeking work. People who are unable to work or who have a limited capability for work due to illness or disability should claim employment and support allowance instead. People who do not have to look for work (eg carers or lone parents with responsibility for young children) may be able to claim income support.

**Contribution-based jobseeker's allowance** is a flat-rate taxable payment for people with a sufficient national insurance contribution record in certain tax years. It is payable for up to six months.

**Income-based jobseeker's allowance** can be paid to people with no or low income and no more than £16,000 in savings. It is means tested and taxable and can top up contribution-based jobseeker's allowance. It can also help with mortgage interest payments (see the chapter on housing). You cannot get jobseeker's allowance if your partner works 24 hours or more a week.

You will be required to sign a jobseeker's agreement. This will cover a description of the type of work you're looking for, the hours you are available and the action you're expected to take to look for work and improve your job prospects, plus details of any restrictions on your availability for work.

If you are providing care, you can restrict the hours you are available for work. If you have a disability you can restrict your availability on matters such as pay, hours, travel time and type of work, provided the restrictions are reasonable given your physical or mental condition. If you are a lone parent and your youngest child is under 13 you can restrict your availability for work to the child's normal school hours.

## BETTER OFF WORKING
People often think they may be worse off if they get a job and come off benefits, but often this isn't the case.

There are a number of benefits that can be paid to people in employment. These include:
- working tax credit (which can also be paid with child tax credit)
- housing benefit and council tax benefit.

In addition, depending on how long you have been unemployed and what benefits you received, you may be eligible for the following:
- return to work credit (£40 a week for 52 weeks)
- in-work credit (£40 a week – or £60 in London – for 52 weeks)
- new enterprise allowance (for those starting self-employment).

Other help includes:
- job grant, a one-off payment of £100 – or £250 if you have children – to help you bridge the gap between coming off benefits and starting work
- extended payments of housing benefit and council tax benefit for four weeks
- access to work, which can provide disabled people with grants towards extra employment costs including equipment and help with travel.

# General benefits

### INCOME SUPPORT

Income support is paid to certain people who are not expected to look for work, for example carers and certain lone parents with young children. Income support is intended to provide for basic living expenses and can be paid on top of other benefits such as carer's allowance. It can also help with mortgage payments.

The amount paid depends on your income, savings and family composition. There are supplements to the basic allowance, known as premiums, payable in respect of disability, age and caring responsibilities.

If you are already receiving income support due to incapacity for work you are likely to be moved onto ESA. For new claimants, ESA has replaced payment of income support on grounds of incapacity.

### PENSION CREDIT

Pension credit is a means-tested benefit for people on low incomes who are aged 60 or over.

There are two types of pension credit:

- **guarantee credit** – tops up your weekly income to a minimum guaranteed level. You may get more money if you or your partner have caring responsibilities or are severely disabled. It can also help with mortgage interest payments (see the chapter on housing). Between April 2010 and April 2020 the age from which you can get pension credit will gradually rise in line with the rise in the state pension age for women from 60 to 65
- **savings credit** – you may be entitled to this if you are over 65 and have made some provisions for retirement such as savings or a second pension.

### HOUSING BENEFIT & COUNCIL TAX BENEFIT

You can get housing benefit and/or council tax benefit if you:

- are liable to pay rent and/or liable to pay council tax
- are on a low income
- do not have savings above £16,000.

If you claim employment and support allowance, jobseeker's allowance, income support or pension credit, you should automatically be sent a form for housing benefit and council tax benefit. If you're not claiming these benefits, you can make a claim for housing benefit and council tax benefit direct from your local authority.

If you pay rent to a private landlord the type of housing benefit you receive is called local housing allowance and is paid straight to you, not the landlord.

### SOCIAL FUND

The social fund is administered by Jobcentre Plus.

- **The regulated social fund** makes the following non-discretionary payments: Sure Start maternity grants, funeral expenses payments, cold weather payments and winter fuel payments.
- **The discretionary social fund** provides community care grants, budgeting loans and crisis loans for urgently needed items, certain necessary journeys and emergencies. For example, payments can be made for items to help prevent someone entering residential care, to help someone returning home following such care or to ease exceptional pressure on families.

You need to receive a 'qualifying benefit' to be eligible to claim most of these regulated and discretionary social fund payments. These can include child tax credit (depending on the level of award), housing benefit, council tax benefit, income-related ESA, income-based JSA, income support, pension credit or working tax credit (if this includes an extra element for being a disabled worker or severely disabled).

From April 2013, community care grants and crisis loans will cease, apart from any loan you get pending payment of benefit (these are known as alignment loans). Instead, in England, new locally administered assistance will be provided by local authorities. In Scotland and Wales, the devolved administrations will decide the most appropriate arrangements for assistance. Budgeting loans and alignment loans will be replaced by payments on account.

## Disability arising from employment or service in the armed forces

INDUSTRIAL INJURIES DISABLEMENT BENEFIT

This is paid to people who have become disabled as a result of an accident at work or an illness or loss of hearing caused by employment. The amount depends on the nature of the disability, the extent to which care is needed and several other factors.

For information and to find out how to claim:
- Ⓦ www.gov.uk/industrial-injuries-disablement-benefit

WAR DISABLEMENT PENSION

This is payable to people who have become disabled as a result of service in the armed forces.

The amount depends on the extent of the disability and the total paid is made up of various elements. Payments are handled by the Veterans Agency, which includes the War Pensioners' Welfare Service.

For information and a claim form contact:

**Veterans UK**
Norcross, Thornton Cleveleys, Lancashire FY5 3WP
- Ⓣ 0800 169 2277; textphone 0800 169 3458
- Ⓔ veterans.help@spva.gsi.gov.uk
- Ⓦ www.veterans-uk.info

## Health costs

Most NHS treatment is free but there are some charges. You may be able to get help with NHS health costs like prescriptions, dental treatment, sight tests, glasses or contact lenses, travel costs to and from hospital, wigs, and fabric supports.

You qualify to receive the above free if you are included in an award of:
- income support
- income-based jobseeker's allowance
- income-related employment and support allowance
- pension credit guarantee credit
- working tax credit and/or child tax credit and you qualify to be issued with an NHS tax credit exemption certificate.

You may also get help with the cost of certain NHS charges if, for example, you are under 19 and still in full-time education, have a listed medical condition, have a maternity exemption certificate, get a war or service disablement pension or need prescriptions or NHS treatment for your accepted disability.

If none of the above applies and you are on a low income you may be able to get help with costs through the NHS Low Income Scheme. The amount of help you get will depend on the amount of your income and savings. You'll need to complete form HC1, which you can get from a Jobcentre Plus office, from an NHS hospital, doctor, dentist or optician, or from the Health Cost advice line (0845 850 1166).

## Benefits cap

From April 2013 there will be a limit on the total amount of benefits most people aged 16 to 64 can receive.

This benefits cap has been set at:
- £500 a week for couples
- £500 a week for lone parents whose children live with them
- £350 a week for single adults.

The cap will apply to combined income from the following benefits: bereavement allowance; carer's allowance; child benefit; child tax credits, employment and support allowance (except where the support component has been awarded); guardian's allowance; housing benefit; incapacity benefit; income support; jobseeker's allowance; maternity allowance; severe disablement allowance; widowed parent's allowance; and widow's benefit.

There will be a period of 39 weeks when you will not be capped if you (or your partner) have been doing paid work for a period of 50 weeks out of 52 weeks before claiming the above benefits and you were working at least 16 hours in your last week of work.

You will be exempt from the cap if anyone in your household is claiming:
- attendance allowance
- disability living allowance

- employment and support allowance support component
- industrial injuries benefits
- personal independence payment
- war disablement pension/armed forces compensation scheme payments (that are equivalent to industrial injuries benefits)
- war widow's or war widower's pension
- working tax credit even if you have been awarded a 'nil entitlement' (you must be working the relevant number of hours).

## Useful contacts

### WHERE TO GET HELP OR INFORMATION
You can get help from your local advice centre, such as a Citizens Advice Bureau.

For information about where to get personal advice, see our factsheet *Getting advice*, available at www.disabilityrightsuk.org.

### CONTACTING THE DWP
**For information and to make a claim**
Details of local Jobcentre Plus offices are at:
- http://los.direct.gov.uk/

Claims for benefits administered by Jobcentre Plus can be made by contacting their claim-line:
- 0800 055 6688; textphone 0800 023 4888

For details of pension centres, contact The Pension Service:
- 0845 606 0265; textphone 0845 606 0285
- http://pensions-service.direct.gov.uk/ en/find-pension-centre/home.asp

**Northern Ireland** – to find your local social security office, look in the phone book under 'Social Security' or on the website:
- www.dsdni.gov.uk

### Benefit Enquiry Line (BEL)
- 0800 882 200; textphone 0800 243 355 08:30-18.30 Monday to Friday. Calls from landlines are free.

This is a confidential telephone advice and information line for people with disabilities, carers and representatives. It covers England, Scotland and Wales. BEL can provide general benefits advice and information, but staff do not have access to any claimant records and are therefore unable to give information on the progress of a claim or benefits you are already receiving. It is a confidential service and nothing you ask or say will go on your file. For certain disability-related benefit claims, staff can fill in your claim-form over the phone and post it to you to check and sign. The form can be in Braille or large print. The service covers carer's allowance, disability living allowance and attendance allowance.

### Northern Ireland Benefit Enquiry Line (BEL)
- 0800 220 674; textphone 0800 243 787 09:00-17:00 Monday to Friday.

Staff can provide general advice on benefits for disabled people and offer a forms-completion service.

# Discrimination

**The Equality Act 2010 prohibits discrimination against disabled people and gives us the right to fair treatment in all spheres of life. This means that we should not be treated in an unfair or discriminatory manner, or face barriers to accessing education, jobs, services, housing or transport because of our disability. This chapter outlines the law around disability and the rights of disabled people. It also includes information about what to do if you are the victim of or witness to a hate crime.**

## Disability discrimination law

### CURRENT LEGISLATION

We fought hard to get disability discrimination law passed in Parliament. The Disability Discrimination Act 1995 has now been replaced by the Equality Act 2010. This Act has brought together different equalities legislation, covering: age; disability; gender reassignment; marriage and civil partnership; pregnancy and maternity; race; religion and belief; sex; and sexual orientation. These are called 'protected characteristics'.

The Equality Act relates to Great Britain. In Northern Ireland, the Disability Discrimination Act still applies.

**The Equality Act 2010 gives us:**
- the right not to be discriminated against in education – from nursery education right through to school, college, university and adult learning courses
- the right to fair treatment in recruitment and employment, including a duty on employers to make 'reasonable adjustments' to working conditions or the working environment to overcome barriers you face
- the right of access to goods, services and facilities, including the removal of physical barriers, changes to policies and extra help, where reasonable
- a right of redress against discrimination in the sale and letting of property
- the right of access to public transport – buses, trains, stations and airports (there are also rules about accessibility on new buses and trains).

The Act sets out five forms of discrimination:
- direct discrimination
- indirect discrimination
- discrimination arising from disability
- failure of reasonable adjustment duty
- harassment.

The Act states that direct discrimination, harassment and failure of reasonable adjustment duty are always unlawful. In some circumstances, indirect discrimination and discrimination arising from disability can be 'justified' – but only if the treatment is 'a proportionate means of achieving a legitimate aim'. It should be quite hard to justify discriminatory treatment. The costs of making reasonable adjustments cannot be passed on to the disabled person.

Public sector bodies – like NHS trusts, schools, local authorities and government departments – also have a duty to promote equality for disabled people, eliminate discrimination and harassment, and foster good relations, including tackling prejudice and promoting understanding.

> The Government Equalities Office has published information about the Equality Act on its website (www.equalities.gov.uk).
>
> The Equality and Diversity Forum provides information for the voluntary sector on its website (www.edf.org.uk).

### WHO IS PROTECTED AGAINST DISABILITY DISCRIMINATION?

Equality legislation protects:

- people who have, or have had, a disability that makes it substantially difficult for them to carry out normal day-to-day activities. The disability can be physical or sensory, a learning disability, a mental health condition or a long-term health problem like diabetes or sickle cell anaemia. The disability must be long term (that is, have lasted or be expected to last at least one year) or likely to recur
- people with a history of disability – for example, people who have recovered from a mental illness (that lasted more than one year) but continue to experience prejudice
- people with a severe disfigurement
- people who are registered/certified blind or partially sighted
- people with progressive conditions such as cancer, HIV infection or multiple sclerosis (MS). You are covered by the Act as soon as you are diagnosed with MS, cancer or HIV or AIDS; for other progressive conditions you are covered once your condition begins to have some effect on you.

The Equality Act also protects anyone who is victimised because they help a disabled person bring a legal case or challenge discrimination of another person under the Act.

People are also protected against direct discrimination and harassment because they are thought to be a disabled person or because of an association with a disabled person – for example, if you are a carer and get treated badly because you have time off to support a disabled child or relative.

Equality legislation is based on the idea that simply treating disabled people the same as everyone else will not necessarily lead to real equality. Often disabled people need different or better treatment in order to get the same chances and opportunities as everyone else. So the law focuses on positive action to remove barriers, change the way things are done and provide extra support that people might need ('reasonable adjustments').

It also allows disabled people to be treated more favourably than non-disabled people – for example, if two people are equally well qualified for a job an employer can decide to employ the disabled candidate.

### PUBLIC SECTOR EQUALITY DUTY

The government has acknowledged it is not fair to expect us to have to challenge discrimination after the event and that public bodies should be doing more to root out discriminatory policies and practices. Therefore, in 2006 it introduced the Disability Equality Duty, which was replaced from 6 April 2011 by the Public Sector Equality Duty, which covers all protected characteristics (except marriage and civil partnership).

It means that public authorities (that is, local authorities, NHS bodies, government departments, the police, schools and colleges) must promote equality for disabled people in everything they do.

When they are carrying out their functions (including when they are contracting out services), public sector bodies must have 'due regard' to the need to: eliminate discrimination, victimisation and harassment; advance equality of opportunities; and foster good relations between disabled and non-disabled people (including tackling prejudice and promoting understanding).

Promoting equality of opportunities can also mean taking steps to meet disabled people's needs, even if that involves more favourable treatment.

The Public Sector Equality Duty also involves looking at the impact of policies on disability equality and taking positive action. This is called the 'general duty'.

> *Lights, Camera, Action* provides guidance for public bodies on fulfilling their duty and includes information for disabled people about working with public bodies. The guide can be downloaded for free from our website (www.disabilityrightsuk.org).

Certain public bodies have further, specific duties to set equality objectives and to publish information about what they have done to meet those objectives. This information helps people to hold public bodies to account.

The general duty does not give us extra individual rights. However, if you think a public body is in breach of the general duty you could bring a claim for judicial review of a public authority's action (or inaction) or bring it to the attention of the Equality and Human Rights Commission, which has statutory powers to enforce the duty. The Commission also has powers to ensure that public bodies implement their specific duties properly.

Disabled people are using the general duty to challenge various types of unequal treatment. For example, disabled people in Harrow used it to stop the local authority restricting social care support.

### EQUALITY AND HUMAN RIGHTS COMMISSION (EHRC)

The EHRC is responsible for promoting equality for disabled people and enforcing the Equality Act, alongside promoting equality for many other groups.

The role of the EHRC is to:
- help us secure our rights and eliminate discrimination through information, advice and, sometimes, support with legal cases

- promote opportunities for us that are equal to those of non-disabled people
- promote good practice – working effectively with business and the public and voluntary sectors
- write codes of practice and guidance which explain the law in detail
- undertake enquiries and investigations
- advise government about how the legislation is working.

The EHRC can take enforcement action against organisations that persistently discriminate and is charged with monitoring and enforcing the Public Sector Equality Duty.

> The role of the EHRC has recently been restricted and all initial enquiries from individuals who feel they have experienced discrimination should now be directed to the Equality Advisory Support Service, who will refer relevant cases to the EHRC.

**Equality Advisory and Support Service**
FREEPOST Equality Advisory Support Service
FPN4431
📞 0800 444 205; textphone 0800 444 206
   09:00 to 20:00 Monday to Friday
   10:00 to 14:00 Saturday

Other organisations that might be able to help include the Disability Law Service and Law Centres Federation (see the 'Legal and consumer services' chapter for contact details).

## Education

Disabled people are protected against discrimination in all forms of education and related activities such as meals services, educational trips and student accommodation.

It is unlawful for general qualification bodies that award qualifications like GCSEs, A and AS levels, and other non-vocational exams (including Scottish and Welsh equivalents) to discriminate against us.

Candidates can expect these bodies to make reasonable adjustments, such as allowing extra time or providing exam materials in alternative formats.

For further information, see the chapter 'Education and skills'.

# Employment

It is unlawful to discriminate against us in employment. Employers cannot treat disabled people less favourably than non-disabled people when they are recruiting or in their working conditions. They have a duty to make reasonable adjustments for disabled people so we are not significantly disadvantaged in comparison to non-disabled people. It does not matter how long you've worked for an employer. For more information, see the chapter 'Work'.

It is against the law to ask questions about our health or disability before a job offer is made. There are some exceptions: the only kind of questions that will be allowed are questions about whether you need a reasonable adjustment for an interview, questions asked for anonymous monitoring purposes, questions asked because of a function that is absolutely and unarguably necessary for the job, and questions about whether you have a particular disability if the employer wants to recruit a person with a (specific) disability.

There are also specific provisions against discrimination in relation to:
- occupational pension schemes and insurance obtained through employers (for example, health insurance)
- occupations such as police officers, barristers, partnerships and office holders (such as judges and members of non-departmental public bodies)
- membership of trade organisations (for example, trade unions)
- employment services – such as employment agencies and career guidance services
- qualifying bodies that make rules about entry into a profession (for example, the Nursing and Midwifery Council).

Local councillors are also covered by the Equality Act when they are carrying out their official business. However, the Act does not apply to political appointments, local authority cabinet posts or committees.

# Goods and services

Under the Equality Act 2010, it is unlawful for the providers of goods, services and facilities to discriminate against us. All goods and services provided to the general public are covered, regardless of whether we pay for them or who provides them. This includes health, insurance and legal services, and retail, sport and leisure facilities.

This means:
- It is against the law to refuse to serve disabled customers, to give us an inferior service, or to treat us worse than other customers.
- Policies, practices and procedures must be changed (where reasonable) if they have the effect of discriminating against us (for example, restaurants may no longer refuse to admit a person with a guide dog because of a general policy not to admit animals).
- Auxiliary aids and services must be provided where this is reasonable given the size, resources and nature of the business (this means things like providing information in different formats, giving us extra help).

- If a physical barrier makes it impossible or unreasonably difficult to access a service, the service provider has a legal obligation to remove/change it, find a way of avoiding it or provide the service by reasonable alternative means (for example, by arranging a meeting at a customer's home rather than in an upstairs office).

Special rules apply to insurers. They can charge higher premiums or refuse cover only if actuarial or statistical data indicate that the disabled person presents a higher risk.

There is also special provision in the Act for guarantees and warranties given by retailers. These usually state that the goods will be replaced if they wear out within a certain period of time and have only been subject to ordinary wear and tear. A retailer may be able to justify not replacing goods on the basis that the wear and tear was greater than ordinary as a result of the purchaser's disability.

Private clubs with 25 or more members (including political parties) are not allowed to discriminate against disabled members, prospective members or guests, and must make reasonable adjustments.

Fair treatment for us in areas like policing and crime prevention, planning and public appointments (these are called 'public functions' in the legislation) are also covered by special provisions.

## Renting property

People who let property must ensure they do not discriminate against us. This covers land and business property as well as residential property. Landlords who let no more than six rooms in their own homes are not affected and nor are those who let their properties privately without advertising.

Landlords cannot refuse to let a flat to us, evict or harass us, offer us a lease on worse terms or stop us using facilities that everyone else has access to for a reason relating to our disability. Landlords must also make reasonable adjustments such as providing tenancy agreements in an accessible format, providing a portable ramp so a wheelchair user can get over a step into their home or waiving a no-animals term in a lease so that we can keep an assistance dog.

Although landlords are not required to change physical features, they do need to consider changing things like signs, doorbells and taps so they are easier to use. If we want to make adaptations to our home, landlords cannot refuse permission unreasonably.

The Equality Act also states that landlords will not be able to refuse permission to make alterations to common parts of residential premises (hallways, stairs, etc). However, at the time of writing this had not been implemented.

You can find out more by visiting:
- www.adviceguide.org.uk
- http://discrimination-disability.co.uk

## Transport

Access to stations, airports, ticketing services, etc is covered by anti-discrimination legislation and so is the use and provision of transport vehicles and services such as buses, taxis and minicabs, trains, trams, car hire and breakdown services. Essentially, transport providers cannot refuse us entry to a bus or train and must take reasonable steps to make their services accessible to us.

Ships and aircraft remain exempt from UK anti-discrimination law – although a European law on air transport gives disabled people and people with mobility problems the right not to be refused carriage and the right to certain forms of assistance.

Transport providers do not have a legal duty to overcome physical barriers to vehicles to make them accessible for individual disabled people.

There are exceptions, however. Providers of rental vehicles must consider removing the feature, altering it, providing a way of avoiding it or finding a different way of making the service available. Providers of recovery vehicles must offer an alternative method of making their service available.

Part 12 of the Equality Act gives the government power to make accessibility regulations for public service vehicles and rail vehicles. Regulations have been made requiring new buses, coaches and trains to comply with certain specified accessibility standards such as width of doors, colour contrasts, etc. All buses and coaches must comply with the regulations by 2017 and 2020 respectively. All trains must comply by 2020 at the latest. At the time of writing, the government had yet to issue taxi accessibility regulations.

There are specific provisions in the Equality Act preventing licensed taxis and minicabs from refusing to carry, or charging more for, a disabled person accompanied by a guide dog or other assistance dog.

Drivers can ask to be exempt from this duty only on medical grounds.

For more information, see the chapter on public transport and travel.

## Challenging discrimination

### EMPLOYMENT

If you are discriminated against by an employer, you can approach the conciliation service ACAS (or its Northern Ireland equivalent) to see if you can resolve the problem without having to go to court. This service is free.

### ACAS

Brandon House, 180 Borough High Street, London SE1 1LW

☎ 0845 747 4747
   Textphone 18001 0845 747 4747

🌐 www.acas.org.uk

### SERVICE PROVIDERS

For claims related to service provision, you may get free mediation. However, mediation is only possible if the service provider agrees to it. You can use free mediation services either from the courts, for money claims up to £5,000, or from LawWorks.

### LawWorks

National Pro Bono Centre, 48 Chancery Lane, London WC2A 1JF

☎ 020 7092 3940

🌐 www.lawworks.org.uk

There are professional mediation services, although they are likely to charge for their service. For a list of professional mediation services, visit:
🌐 www.civilmediation.justice.gov.uk

For further information, go to:
🌐 www.gov.uk/make-court-claim-for-money/overview

### THE PROCESS

There are time limits for bringing a legal case under the Equality Act. For employment cases, you need to apply to the Employment Tribunal within three months of the discrimination taking place and you must have tried to access your employer's grievance procedure first. For goods and services cases, you need to start a court case within six months.

There is a 'questions procedure', which is useful for getting the information you need for your case from employers or service providers.

Equality Act cases concerning schools must be brought within six months. They are heard in the First-tier Tribunal (Special Educational Needs and Disability), the Special Educational Needs Tribunal in Wales, and in similar tribunals in Northern Ireland. Discrimination cases concerning admission to maintained schools or permanent exclusions are heard by the relevant appeal panels. Scottish schools cases are heard by Additional Support Needs Tribunals. In schools cases, unlike other Equality Act cases, you cannot get compensation for injury to feelings or financial loss, although schools can be told to give an apology and put things right for you in other ways.

### GETTING REDRESS

If an employer is found guilty of discrimination, the Employment Tribunal will recommend that they take steps to stop discrimination happening in the future (for example, by training staff).

Legal action can be expensive – and there's no legal aid for employment cases. You could try to get assistance from your trade union, the Equality and Human Rights Commission (it only takes a few cases each year and will have specific criteria), a law centre, the Disability Law Service, or a Citizens Advice Bureau.

# Disability hate crime

A crime is an act that breaks the law. If someone commits a crime that is motivated by hostility or prejudice because the victim is a disabled person or is perceived as a disabled person then the crime is a disability hate crime.

## Reporting a crime

If the victim believes the crime was motivated by prejudice, it should be reported as a disability hate crime. By reporting it, you can protect yourself and help the local police tackle hate crime more effectively.

It can be reported by the victim or a witness. If you don't feel confident talking to the police on your own, take someone with you.

If you or someone else is in immediate danger, or a serious crime is taking place, ring the police using the emergency number (999). In other cases, ring the non-emergency number (101), which is available across England and Wales.

You may also be able to make a report on your local police force website. For details visit:
Ⓦ www.police.uk

You can make a report online via the True Vision website, which provides information about hate crime incidents and how to report them.
Ⓦ www.report-it.org.uk

## Getting support

A victim or a witness may be able to get help from a local disabled person's organisation, a disability hate crime third party reporting site, a local Citizens Advice Bureau, voluntary service, or Victim Support.

## Reporting someone you know

If the person who committed the crime is a friend, relative, someone you trust or someone who works with or for you, you may be worried about reprisals. It is wise to make sure you don't leave a trail that can be found by the person you are reporting.

If you report a disability hate crime online you can cover your tracks by deleting your browser history and deleting any emails relating to your report.

Three *Let's stop disability hate crime* guides have been published by Disability Rights UK in association with the Office for Disability Issues:

### A guide for disabled people

This explains what makes a crime a disability hate crime, how to avoid being a victim, what to do if you are a target, how to report it and provide evidence, and what happens if the offender is prosecuted. Also available in Easy Read.

### A guide for setting up third party reporting sites

By providing an alternative point of contact, these sites can improve the flow of intelligence from the community. This guide provides an overview of the law to assist disabled people's organisations set up these sites. Also available in Easy Read.

### A guide for non-disabled people

It is important that friends, families and people who work with and for disabled people are aware of the key issues. This guide focuses on the Police and Crown Prosecution Services definition of hate crime, to provide an understanding of how the law works.

Disability hate crime has a profound effect on disabled people's lives. Until the majority are reported there will never be a true picture of its prevalence and nothing will change.

Download our *Let's stop disability hate crime* guides at www.disabilityrightsuk.org.

# Legal and consumer services

This chapter provides information on where we can get legal advice or help – whether for personal, family or property matters or to follow up a matter of law in relation to disability discrimination, claims for benefits or compensation for wrong-doing. There are also details of organisations that can help with complaints about the quality of goods or services – including utility companies, banks, government or legal services – or the way they've been provided, or not provided.

## General legal advice

You might be put off seeking legal advice because of real or perceived problems of cost. But although it has become more difficult to get legal aid, some legal services still might not charge a fee – law centres, for example.

Agencies such as Citizens Advice Bureaux and other charities and disability organisations can offer advice, so they are a good place to start and may be able to offer or refer you to free legal services. They can also advise you if you need to seek compensation for injury or disability arising from an accident, illness, your employment or a crime committed against you.

### Citizens Advice Bureaux (CAB)

There are CABs in most towns and cities. They provide free information and advice on legal, money and other matters from over 3,200 locations across the UK. Adviceguide is their online public, self-help information service. It includes legal and consumer issues, see:
Ⓦ www.adviceguide.org.uk

To find your nearest CAB visit:
For England and Wales
Ⓦ www.citizensadvice.org.uk

For Northern Ireland
Ⓦ www.citizensadvice.co.uk

For Scotland
Ⓣ 0808 800 9060
Ⓦ www.cas.org.uk for Scotland

### Community Legal Advice
Ⓣ 0845 345 4345; textphone 0845 609 6677
Ⓦ www.legalservices.gov.uk

Community Legal Advice is a government agency that provides free, independent and confidential telephone advice in England and Wales. If you are living on a low income or benefits, you may be eligible for free specialist advice from legal advisers on issues including: benefits and tax credits; debt; education; housing; employment; and family problems. The service is available in 170 languages.

### Coram Children's Legal Centre (CCLC)
University of Essex, Wivenhoe Park, Colchester CO4 3SQ
Ⓣ 0808 802 0008
08:00 to 20:00 Monday to Friday
Ⓔ clc@essex.ac.uk
Ⓦ www.childrenslegalcentre.com
CCLC is a national charity concerned with law and policy affecting children and young people. It offers a free, confidential service – from phone advice to full legal representation. The website contains user-friendly information on many aspects of the law for young people, parents and carers.

### Disability Law Service (DLS)
39-45 Cavell Street, London E1 2BP
Ⓣ 020 7791 9800; textphone 020 7791 9801
10:00 to 17:00 Monday to Friday
Ⓦ www.dls.org.uk
The DLS is a charity providing free, confidential legal advice, information and casework services to disabled people, their families, carers and advocates. It provides specialist advice on consumer matters, community care, disability discrimination, employment, further and higher education and welfare benefits (Greater London area). It provides access to qualified legal advisers and a range of factsheets. It can refer you to other sources of help if they cannot take on your case themselves.

## WITHY KING SOLICITORS

### Helping you to get the most out of life

Our team of legal experts has a proven track record in helping people injured through no fault of their own to access justice. We work empathetically with injured people and their families to navigate the legal quagmire and secure the compensation needed to pay for their care and lifestyle needs, now and in the future.

Our specialist solicitors work with disability organisations, charities, individuals and families from all over the UK on complex Personal Injury and Clinical Negligence claims – and afterwards, providing expert advice on safeguarding and managing compensation awards.

### Personal injury

Sadly accidents occur all too often – on the road, at work, during leisure pursuits or while on holiday. We forge close working relationships with people with all manner of injuries and claims and have a national reputation for our expertise in handling brain, head and spinal injury cases.

The effects of brain and head injuries are wide ranging and can be temporary or permanent. These types of compensation claims are highly complex, requiring high-level expertise and compassion from the solicitors involved. We also have an in-depth understanding of the unseen health and mental issues. What we see on the surface often masks a range of day-to-day challenges and we take the time to ensure issues relating to work, family relationships and access to benefits, for example, are recognised and taken into account.

We offer no win-no fee agreements and are often able to secure interim payments to support clients during the legal process. We are members of the UK Acquired Brain Injury Forum (UKABIF), Brain Injury Social Work Group (BISWG), Child Brain Injury Trust as well as members of the Headway and Law Society Personal Injury panels.

### Clinical Negligence

Over the decades, we have formed long-standing relationships with people who have been injured as a result of medical negligence and their families. One of our areas of expertise relates to Cerebral Palsy – cases involving babies, children and adults whose body movements and muscle co-ordination has been affected through injury or mistreatment, often before they were born or during their birth. We know the impact that disability can have and we are skilled at securing the best possible financial outcome.

We are passionate about achieving justice for our clients and channel a lot of personal effort into raising funds for Cerebral Palsy and Erb's Palsy charities. We recently sponsored Paralympian athlete Katrina Hart whose team achieved bronze in the 4x100m relay (T37 Class). We have also lobbied hard against Government proposals to scrap Legal Aid funding for all clinical negligence cases.

### Managing your financial settlement

Working out how to make the most of your financial settlement is daunting. We have dedicated experts to help make sense of the options and come up with an arrangement which will enhance quality of life and provide for future needs. Through our Withy King Trust Corporation we can act as a professional trustee or deputy to help manage your compensation or provide support and assistance to family or friends who take on this role, providing clients with a seamless service which lasts long after compensation has been awarded.

Every person's story is different. The impact your injury has on you and your family is as individual as you are. Whatever your circumstances, we will do our utmost to try and help. For an informal, free and confidential discussion please telephone 0800 923 2073.

www.withyking.co.uk

IF ONLY I'D KNOWN THAT A YEAR AGO …

**The Independent Panel for Special Education Advice**
Hunters Court, Debden Road, Saffron Walden CB11 4AA
T 0800 018 4016
W www.ipsea.org.uk
IPSEA gives free and independent education-related legal advice and support in England and Wales through helplines, information on the website and in print, support and representation (when needed) in appeals to the Special Educational Needs and Disability Tribunal. Individual advice can be provided only by phone.

**Scottish Legal Aid Board**
T 0845 122 8686
W www.slab.org.uk

**Law Centres Federation**
PO Box 65836, London EC4P 4FX
T 020 7842 0720
W www.lawcentres.org.uk
Law centres are not-for-profit legal practices providing free legal advice and representation to disadvantaged people. There are 55 law centres in England, Wales and Northern Ireland staffed by barristers and solicitors who specialise in areas of civil law including discrimination, employment, housing, benefits, education and immigration. To find a law centre in your area, visit the website.

> Our *Disability Rights Handbook* includes information about compensation schemes, claims and compensation recovery. To order your copy, visit our online shop.

## Consumer matters

Disabled people have the right not to be discriminated against in the provision of goods or services (see 'Discrimination'). We can also call on the wider protection of consumer rights legislation.

Shops, service providers and legal professionals are providing a service and must therefore comply with the Equality Act - whether their service is free or not. You should expect an accessible service and can demand reasonable adjustments if they are not already in place.

Buying products from home, by mail order, on the internet or at the door can change the relationship between buyer and seller so there are a number of safeguards, such as cooling-off periods.

Local authority trading standards officers can take action against dishonest traders in the area. Advice and information to consumers is available from a number of sources.

**Age UK**
W www.ageuk.org.uk
Can give consumer and legal advice and provide factsheets.

**Citizens Advice consumer service**
T 0845 404 0506
   Dial 18001 for textphone options
   0845 404 0505 (Welsh language line)
W www.adviceguide.org.uk
Provides free, confidential and impartial advice on consumer issues.

In Northern Ireland a similar helpline is available:
**Consumerline**
T 0300 123 6262
W www.consumerline.org

**Financial Ombudsman Service**
South Quay Plaza, 183 Marsh Wall, London E14 9SR
T 0300 123 9123 or 0800 023 4567
E complaint.info@financial-ombudsman.org.uk
W www.financial-ombudsman.org.uk
The Financial Ombudsman Service is a free service set up by law with the power to resolve problems between consumers and financial businesses including banks, building societies, insurers or financial advisers. The Ombudsman will look at both sides of the problem and make an independent decision. If they feel that the business has acted correctly, they will explain why. If it feels that the business has done something wrong, it has the power to put it right.

## Disability Rights Handbook

Comprehensive information and guidance on benefits and services for all disabled people, their families, carers and advisers.

Available to order from our online shop
**www.disabilityrightsuk.org**

# D & HB Associates Ltd

Are pleased to support
Disability Rights UK

Supported by
Arjo Wiggins
Fine Papers
Limited

**Wishing Disability Rights UK every success**

Flixborough Industrial Estate
Scunthorpe, North Lincs
DN15 8SJ

Tel: 01724 850224
Fax: 01724 289317

**www.plantcraft.co.uk**

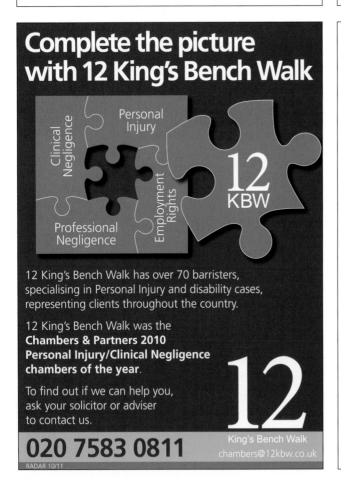

## Complete the picture with 12 King's Bench Walk

Personal Injury
Clinical Negligence
Employment Rights
Professional Negligence

12 KBW

12 King's Bench Walk has over 70 barristers, specialising in Personal Injury and disability cases, representing clients throughout the country.

12 King's Bench Walk was the
**Chambers & Partners 2010
Personal Injury/Clinical Negligence chambers of the year**.

To find out if we can help you, ask your solicitor or adviser to contact us.

**020 7583 0811**

12 King's Bench Walk
chambers@12kbw.co.uk

RADAR 10/11

## Doing Money Differently

Explores new ways of making, saving and looking after your money. This guide covers where your money comes from, where to keep it, where it goes and what to do if you are in debt.

Available to order from our online shop
**www.disabilityrightsuk.org**

## THOMPSONS SOLICITORS

*James Davies of Thompsons Solicitors looks at the funding options available to anyone wanting to pursue a civil legal claim on behalf of themselves or their child.*

With so many law firms claiming to specialise in serious injury compensation it can be difficult to know where to turn or whether you can afford to claim at all.

Serious injury claims for adults and children can be complex but cost should not be seen as a major obstacle as most good solicitors offer a free initial interview on a 'no obligation' basis and will discuss all the various funding options available.

However, from April 2013 the system will change. The government has forced through reforms of the way in which personal injury claims are funded, which will make it more difficult to find a lawyer prepared to take any case that isn't straight forward.

Up to April 2013, injured people have (rightly) been entitled to get 100% of their compensation. The government are going to make injured people start paying some of the costs of the claim themselves – denying them full compensation and boosting the profits of the insurance industry. The funding options available are:

### Legal Aid

Legal Aid is government funding intended to help people who cannot afford to pay solicitors' legal fees.

Now: available in limited circumstances and serious cases. Eligibility depends on your financial circumstances. If the case is won then usually all of the legal fees are paid by whoever pays the compensation. If the case has to be stopped or is lost, then the LSC pay the solicitor's fees.

From April 2013 it will be removed for all personal injury cases except for a very small number of claims for babies with severe disabilities as a result of clinical negligence while the baby was still in the womb, or during or after birth. To arrange Legal Aid, a solicitor must have a contract with the Legal Services Commission (LSC) so it is important to check this.

### 'No Win No Fee'

Now: 'No Win No Fee' agreements enable injured people and parents of injured children to bring a claim easily. Usually at no cost to them, whether their claim is successful or not, because the opponent's pay if you win and the opponent's legal costs are covered by insurance if you lose.

From April 2013, it will no longer be possible to get insurance to cover the costs of the other side or of outlays such as for medical experts if you lose, so you may have to pay some costs upfront. The opponent won't have to pay your solicitors bills so anything they can't get from the opponents may become your liability and the injured person will instead have to pay from their compensation.

### Other Ways of Paying Legal Fees

Motor and household insurance policies often offer additional legal expenses insurance. However, such policies will usually require that you use the insurance company's preferred firm of solicitors who may not be the most experienced or close to where you live.

### Trade Unions

Trade union members can take advantage of their union's legal services, which cover legal advice for injuries sustained at or away from work. Unions have arrangements with specialist solicitors and members will rarely suffer deductions from their damages under the trade union's funding scheme.

www.thompsons.law.co.uk

**BUSH & COMPANY**
REHABILITATION

## LEADERS IN EXPERT WITNESS, CASE MANAGEMENT & REHABILITATION SERVICES

**What We Offer**
Bush & Company are experts in the assessment, case management and rehabilitation of adults and children who have complex or severe types of injury, that require specialist knowledge and expertise.

**Our Team**
Our team, of over 100 professionals, includes nurses, occupational therapists, physiotherapists, speech and language therapists, social workers, specialist architects and assistive technology experts.

**Our Services**
- Expert Witness Quantum Reports
- Immediate Needs Assessments
- Case Management
- Vocational Rehabilitation Services
- Specialist Architect & Assistive Technology Services
- Nursing Liability Reports
- Behaviour assessment & intervention services

**To find out more, please contact:**
Rachel Bush, Director: rbush@bushco.co.uk
Karen Burgin, Director: kburgin@bushco.co.uk

**phone:** 01327 876210 **www.bushco.co.uk**

---

# LeVeNeS SOLICITORS — EDUCATION AND DISABILITY LAW

Our nationally renowned specialist team advises and represents children, students, disabled people and families on all types of problems concerning:

- **Education Law**
- **Special Education Needs Law** including disputes over placements and appropriate provisions for disabled children
- **Disability Discrimination Law**
- **Human Rights Law**

We also offer a consultancy service and training to public and private organisations and individuals

**For further information please call FREE on**

# 0800 11 88 99

Ashley House, 235-239 High Road,
Wood Green, N22 8HF
Email: education@levenes.co.uk
Website: www.levenes.co.uk

---

IF ONLY I'D KNOWN THAT A YEAR AGO ...

## UTILITIES

Utility companies are required to provide services to meet the specific needs of disabled customers. This may include special arrangements for meter reading, providing bills and other material in alternative formats and giving priority and support if there is a supply stoppage or breakdown.

If you feel you may need help, contact the company involved and ask to be placed on their priority list. This can mean faster reconnection in a power-cut or help collecting water if you get cut off. Alternatively, you could go to a CAB.

> Many utility companies can make grants to people struggling with utility and household debts. Terms vary: some are for customers only while others are for anyone living in the company's area. Applications may need to be supported by a social worker or advice worker www.charisgrants.com.

### Consumer Council for Water (CC Water)
Victoria Square House, Victoria Square, Birmingham B2 4AJ
T 0121 345 1000; textphone 0121 345 1044
W www.ccwater.org.uk
CC Water represents the interests of consumers of water and sewerage services in England and Wales. It can take up unresolved complaints that consumers have with their supply companies.

### Energy Ombudsman
PO Box 966, Warrington WA4 9DF
T 0330 440 1624; textphone 0330 440 1600
W www.energy-ombudsman.org.uk
Decides what action should be taken when a customer and energy supplier cannot reach an agreement about a complaint.

### Northern Ireland Authority for Utility Regulation
Queens House, 14 Queen Street, Belfast BT1 6ED
T 028 9031 1575
W www.niaur.gov.uk
Ensures effective regulation of electricity, gas, water and sewerage.

### Ofwat
City Centre Tower, 7 Hill Street, Birmingham B5 4UA
T 0121 644 7500
W www.ofwat.gov.uk
Ofwat is the regulator of companies providing water and sewerage services in England and Wales. It establishes minimum standards for the companies involved and monitors their performance.

### Water Industry Commission for Scotland
Ochil House, Springkerse Business Park, Stirling FK7 7XE
T 01786 43 0200
E customer.concerns@scottishwater.co.uk
W www.watercommission.co.uk

### Waterwatch Scotland
Forrester Lodge, Inglewood, Alloa FK10 2HU
E info@waterwatchscotland.org
W www.waterwatchscotland.org
Offers a similar service to CC Water.

> **The WaterSure Scheme** allows some customers to have their water bill capped at the amount of the average household. It is intended to help customers who pay for their water charges via a water meter, who experience difficulties as a result of high water usage or low income. To be eligible, customers must be on income-related benefits and have at least three children at home or a medical condition requiring extra water. Information is available from CC Water.

## TELECOMMUNICATIONS
### Ofcom
Riverside House, 2A Southwark Bridge Road, London SE1 9HA
T 0300 123 3000 or 020 7981 3000; textphone 020 7981 3043
W www.ofcom.org.uk
Ofcom is the regulatory body covering TV, radio, phone and postal services and also acts as the consumer body for most of the industry.

## Doing Careers Differently

Packed with useful information, this guide includes stories from disabled people who have built satisfying careers, from part-time flexible work to a first-time management role and beyond.

Available to order from our online shop
**www.disabilityrightsuk.org**

## Get Mobile

A guide to buying a mobility scooter or powered wheelchair. New 2012 edition.

Available to order from our online shop
**www.disabilityrightsuk.org**

## Doing IT Differently

Information to help everyone regardless of disability, take advantage of information technology (IT) and computers. Includes advice on how to choose and use a computer, and how to adapt it to suit your needs.

Available to order from our online shop
**www.disabilityrightsuk.org**

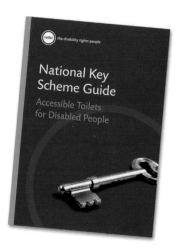

## National Key Scheme Guide

Updated every year, this guide lists the location of 9,000 NKS toilets around the UK. It shows opening times, provider name and whether the toilet is unisex.

Available to order from our online shop
**www.disabilityrightsuk.org**

# Advocacy and decision making

**There are ways in which we can be supported, and protect our interests if we need help to manage day-to-day affairs, if it becomes difficult to make decisions about our care or welfare, if we need to fight for what we want, or if, because of our mental state, we are unable to make decisions affecting our care. This chapter looks at: advocacy, which can help us deal with different bodies to get what we want; Powers of Attorney, which allow someone we trust to act on our behalf and make some, or all, decisions for us; and living wills, or advance directives, which ensure that our views and needs are acted upon in our best interests.**

## Advocacy

Sometimes the social care, benefits, welfare rights or healthcare systems can seem an impenetrable maze, especially if we are new to it all. Sometimes we may feel powerless in dealing with professionals or feel unable to challenge them.

However, many disabled people have been through various systems and understand how it works. Some disabled people, who have fought hard to understand and exercise their rights, have formed organisations to support others who are struggling to manage their affairs (largely through lack of knowledge and experience). The support these groups offer is often referred to as 'advocacy'.

We use the term advocacy to describe a way of helping disabled people to get what they want and what they are entitled to, and to represent their interests so they can retain or re-gain an independent life or receive the care or services they need.

Advocacy is about helping people whose ability to exercise choice or represent their own interests is limited. An advocate can be with you as you work your way through statutory systems or even, if you choose, speak on your behalf.

The best way to access an advocate or an advocacy service is to contact your local Centre for Independent Living or user-led organisation through your local authority. They should be able to put you in touch. Alternatively, a national impairment or subject-related charity that's relevant to you may know of an appropriate advocacy service.

Examples include Age UK, the MS Society, Action for Hearing Loss, RNIB or MIND. Contact details can be found in the 'Useful contacts' section at the back of this book.

### Advocacy schemes
National or local advocacy schemes might be concerned with specific clusters of needs or they may be more general. Information about advocacy schemes is available from:

### Action for Advocacy
The Oasis Centre, 75 Westminster Bridge Road, London SE1 7HS
T 020 7921 4395
E info@actionforadvocacy.org.uk
W www.actionforadvocacy.org.uk
Helps people find an advocate and helps people become advocates themselves. It also has useful reading material on its website.

### Independent Advocacy
Avenue M, Stoneleigh Park, Warwickshire CV8 2LG
T 024 7669 7443
E office@independentadvocacy.org
W www.independentadvocacy.org
Provides a comprehensive range of specialist advocacy and related services in Warwickshire, Coventry, Solihull and surrounding areas.

### Scottish Independent Advocacy Alliance
69a George Street, Edinburgh EH2 2JG
T 0131 260 5380
W www.siaa.org.uk

# Powers of attorney

There may come a time when we're struggling to manage our day-to-day affairs. We may want to have help from someone we trust by giving them a legal Power of Attorney.

Or, it may happen that at some point we are unable or unwilling to make decisions affecting our life or our affairs.

The 2005 Mental Capacity Act stipulates that people we deal with must always assume we have the capacity to make a decision unless they can definitely prove otherwise. Therefore, it's very important to have a Power of Attorney in place to ensure that our views are taken into account and that decisions are made in our best interests.

## POWER OF ATTORNEY

A Power of Attorney is a legal document that gives another person the authority to act on our behalf in certain specific circumstances.

This is generally for managing some or all of our financial affairs. We name the person and limit what they can deal with – for example, they might manage our bank account but not our property or healthcare.

A Power of Attorney is valid as long as we have the mental capacity to make decisions.

*Powers of attorney: Help with making decisions about your health, welfare or finances,* published by Age UK, describes in detail powers of attorney and lasting powers of attorney, the meaning of mental capacity, living wills, etc. It includes points to consider and where to get further advice and help. It is available to download from their website: www.ageuk.org.uk.

## A LASTING POWER OF ATTORNEY

A Lasting Power of Attorney (LPA) is a legal document that allows us to name someone to make decisions on our behalf at a time in the future when we no longer wish to make decisions for ourselves or lack the mental capacity to do so.

You can write an LPA well in advance of ever needing to use it. You might never need to use it, but you can rest assured that if necessary someone who you trust completely will be able to manage your affairs or make decisions in your best interests.

What follows is a very brief overview of what is an extremely complex area of law. It's possible to write most of a Lasting Power of Attorney yourself, but it's best to consult your solicitor or an advocacy group.

There are two types of LPA:
- a Personal Welfare LPA
- a Property and Affairs LPA.

Anyone aged 18 or over, with the capacity to do so, can make an LPA, appointing one or more people to make decisions on their behalf. You cannot make an LPA jointly with another person; each person must make their own LPA.

An LPA can only be used if it has been registered with the Office of the Public Guardian (OPG). The OPG ensures that people's best interests are always guarded. The OPG website has more information and publications on LPAs.

**Office of the Public Guardian**
PO Box 16185, Birmingham B2 2WH
☎ 0300 456 0300
Ⓦ www.publicguardian.gov.uk

The people involved in making an LPA are legally known as the donor, the attorney, a named person, a certificate provider and a witness.

### The donor
This is the person who makes the Lasting Power of Attorney – that is, you. You appoint someone to make decisions about your personal welfare or your property and affairs – or both.

### The attorney
This is the person or people you choose and appoint, using an LPA form, to make decisions on your behalf about either your personal welfare or your property and affairs, or both.

It is an important role and one that the person chosen must understand and agree to take on. If you were to register the LPA in the future, depending on which type it is, your attorney could, for instance, pay bills from your personal bank account on your behalf; they could negotiate and agree a direct payment with your local authority social care department; or they could agree, or not, to medical or surgical intervention. They must always act in your best interests and will be held to account by the Office of the Public Guardian.

### A named person

This is someone chosen by you (the donor) to be notified when an application is made to register your LPA. The named person has the right to object to the registration of the LPA if they have concerns about the registration. The named person is specified in the LPA form. Selecting someone to be informed about an application to register is a key safeguard to protect you.

### A certificate provider

This is a person that you, the donor, select to complete a Part B Certificate in the LPA form.

That certificate confirms that you understand the LPA and that you are not under any pressure to make it. The certificate provider is another important safeguard.

### A witness

This is someone who signs your LPA form to confirm that they witnessed:

- the donor (the person making the LPA) signing and dating the LPA form; or
- the attorney(s) (the person appointed by the donor) signing and dating the LPA form.

The witness acts as a further safeguard.

> **To summarise:**
> - Making an LPA is always a good idea.
> - You should always involve someone trained or qualified to advise you.
> - Making an LPA does not mean it is immediately active – you need never use it if you so choose.
> - An LPA must be registered with the Office of the Public Guardian before it can be acted on.

## Living wills/advance directives

Most of us are aware of the importance of having a will, which typically states how our property and money should be dealt with after our death, and perhaps also our wishes regarding funeral and burial arrangements. But it might be important for us to also consider having a 'living will' – officially known as an 'advance directive'.

Concerns about mental capacity and consent for treatment have become more of an issue with medical advancements and interventions such as cardiopulmonary resuscitation, artificial ventilation and intravenous hydration and nutrition. You may be concerned about the prospect of having treatment when you are incapable of refusing it or when you are unable to consent to it. However, you can make a living will or advance directive to the effect that in certain circumstances you do not wish to be subjected to medical treatment or intervention.

The creation of an advance directive – a living will – with a focus on the denial of medical intervention in certain situations is an extremely serious decision to make and should not be treated lightly. Writing an advance directive can provide a useful opportunity to discuss current or future illnesses with your family and friends.

> **Will Aid** is a special partnership between the legal profession and nine UK charities. Each November, participating solicitors waive their fee for writing a basic will; instead, clients are invited to make a donation to Will Aid. As well as gaining peace of mind by writing your will, you can help fund life-changing charity work at the same time. For more information visit www.willaid.org.uk, ring 0300 0300 013 or write to Roundham House, Oxen Road, Crewkerne, Somerset TA18 7HN.

If you write an advance directive, you should do so without any pressure or encouragement. Once you sign an advance directive, it falls within the 2005 Mental Capacity Act – so there is legal protection for a directive's authenticity, how and when it was signed, and so on.

If you decide to write an advance directive, it's very important that your friends and family are aware of it so that if it needs to be invoked, they will be able to show a copy to the relevant clinicians and ensure that your wishes are followed.

It is now generally accepted that an advance directive falls within common law and that medical staff should abide by your advance directive.

> For more information about living wills, read *Powers of attorney: Help with making decisions about your health, welfare or finances* published by Age UK. It can be downloaded from www.ageuk.org.uk.
>
> For discussions on advance directives, visit www.patient.co.uk and search for 'advance directives'.

# Public transport

**Transport and travel systems are gradually changing so that they will be more accessible to us, whatever our impairment. Transport regulations under UK and EC law come into effect, but progress is patchy geographically and between different forms of transport. This chapter covers some of the regulations regarding disabled people and transport and provides sources of advice and help for planning journeys on all types of transport.**

## Travel planning

If you're thinking of travelling, it's best to do some advance planning. If you think you'll need help at any point in your journey, for example getting on or off a train, you usually need to give advance notice.

Your first point of call for any transport enquiry across the UK should be Traveline.

**Traveline**
T 0871 200 2233; textphone 0870 241 2216
W www.traveline.org.uk

Nationally, general information on transport services and timetables is available through the following agencies.

ENGLAND
In most of England, county and unitary councils have responsibilities for public transport and have a public transport information officer. Some publish specific information for disabled passengers. Elsewhere, in the major conurbations, this responsibility is carried out by passenger transport executives and in London, by Transport for London. Contact details are below.

**Centro/Network West Midlands**
Centro House, 16 Summer Lane, Birmingham B19 3SD
T 0121 200 2787
W www.centro.org.uk

**MerseyTravel**
PO Box 1976, Liverpool L69 3HN
T 0151 227 5181; textphone 0151 330 1087
W www.merseytravel.gov.uk

**Nexus**
Nexus House, St James Boulevard, Newcastle upon Tyne NE1 4AX
T 0191 202 0747
W www.nexus.org.uk

**Transport for Greater Manchester**
2 Piccadilly Place, Manchester M1 3BG
T 0161 244 1000
W www.tfgm.com

**Transport for London**
Travel Information, 55 Broadway, London SW1H 0BD
T 020 7222 1234; textphone 020 7918 3015
E travinfo@tfl.gov.uk
W www.tfl.gov.uk

**Travel South Yorkshire**
11 Broad Street West, Sheffield S1 2BQ
T 01709 51 51 51
W www.travelsouthyorkshire.com

**West Yorkshire Metro**
Wellington House, 40-50 Wellington Street, Leeds LS1 2DE
T 0113 254 7676
W www.wymetro.com

**www.transportdirect.info** is a travel planning website that includes options for using all types of public transport and private motoring for point-to-point journeys in Great Britain. It includes information about car parking and cycle routes as well as travel tips and live travel news.

**Bridgend County Borough Council**
Passenger Transport
Co-ordination Unit

If visiting Bridgend by public transport, Bridgend Bus Station is staffed and able to provide assistance to travellers. All areas are accessible and toilets accept RADAR keys. If you require assistance please ring 01656 642591 to discuss your public transport requirements or for queries about the Welsh Government's Free Concessionary Travel Scheme. For timetable enquiries please contact Traveline Cymru 0871 200 22 33.

Should you require a little more help then why not make a booking with our Shopmobility team who can be contacted by telephone 01656 667992. Car owners with Blue Badges enjoy free parking at all Bridgend car parks.

If you intend to arrive by train, information on assistance can be obtained from Arriva Trains Wales, tel: 0845 6061 660 or
e-mail: customer.services@arrivatrainswales.co.uk

**www.bridgend.gov.uk**

At Manchester Airport our aim is to ease our customer journey and make it a unique and positive experience.

With this in mind we have developed a comprehensive guide with DisabledGo, which provides disabled customers and those with reduced mobility, with all the information required to plan their journey through one of the UK's busiest airports.

**For our online access guide visit: www.disabledgo.com and type 'Manchester Airport' into the search field**

**Or visit manchesterairport.co.uk**

manchesterairport.co.uk

Speciality Brandy Snaps

**SHARP & NICKLESS LTD**

College Street,
Long Eaton
Nottingham NG10 4NN

Tel & fax 0115 973 2169

## North West Trading Co

Buyers and suppliers of marine and offshore equipment

69 Portsoy Crescent,
Ellon, Aberdeenshire,
AB41 8AL

Tel:    01358 729884
Fax:    01358 729885
Email: nwtandco@btconnect.com
Web:  www.nwtandco.com

# Accessibility as standard

**The fully accessible TX series offers:**

- Hearing induction loop
- Integral ramp and intermediate step
- Wheelchair retention system
- Unique swivel seat for passengers with reduced mobility
- Adjustable centre rear seat belt harness for children
- Contrasting grab handles and seat edge for partially-sighted passengers
- Floor, roof and door handle lights
- Voice intercom, speaker and microphone

Choose the only taxi that is built for purpose, with accessibility features fitted as standard. **Choose a London Taxi.**

www.london-taxis.co.uk

IF ONLY I'D KNOWN THAT A YEAR AGO ...

NORTHERN IRELAND

In Northern Ireland, rail and bus services are overseen by:

**Translink**

Central Station, Belfast BT1 3PB

📞 028 9066 6630; textphone 028 9035 4007

🌐 www.translink.co.uk

SCOTLAND

In Scotland, the national transport agency liaises with seven regional transport partnerships and has a range of executive functions including administering fare concessions and the Blue Badge scheme.

**Transport Scotland**

Buchanan House, 58 Port Dundas Road, Glasgow G4 0HF

📞 0141 272 7100

🌐 www.transportscotland.gov.uk

WALES

In Wales transport planning is undertaken by four regional transport consortia:

**South East Wales Transport Alliance (SEWTA)**

Pencarn Avenue, Imperial Park, Coedkernew, Newport NP10 8AR

📞 0163 365 1028

🌐 www.sewta.gov.uk

**South West Wales Integrated Transport Consortium (SWWITCH)**

c/o Penllergaer Offices, City & County of Swansea, Penllergaer, Swansea SA4 9GJ

📞 01792 63 7644

🌐 www.swwitch.net

**Taith**

Taith Office, Flint Station, Market Square, Flint CH6 5NW

📞 01352 70 4561

🌐 www.taith.gov.uk

**TraCC**

Canolfan Rheidol, Rhondga Padern, Llanbadarn Fawr, Aberystwyth SY23 3HE

🌐 www.tracc.gov.uk

> *Wheels Within Wheels* is a guide to using a wheelchair on public transport. Published by **Ricability**: www.ricability.org.uk; Unit G03, Wenlock Business Centre, 50-56 Wharf Road, London N1 7EU. Telephone 020 7427 2460, textphone 020 7427 2469.

# Air travel

Because air travel is an international industry, we can encounter some attitudes and practices that are now outdated in the UK. Factors that can make air travel more complicated for disabled passengers can arise from security requirements, design and safety features of aircraft, the size of airports, and for many people, unfamiliarity with the environment.

YOUR RIGHTS

Under EC Regulation 1107/206 it is illegal for an airline, travel agent or tour operator to refuse a booking on the grounds of disability or refuse to allow a disabled person with a valid ticket and reservation to board an aircraft.

Airport managers are required to organise the services necessary to enable disabled passengers to board, disembark and transit between flights. Each airline is responsible for services onboard its aircraft. You cannot be charged extra for any of these services.

In Britain, if you are refused boarding on the grounds of disability or reduced mobility or don't get the services you requested and need, you can raise the issue initially with the Equality Advisory Support Service (see 'Useful contacts' below). They will advise you on your rights and may refer the matter to the Civil Aviation Authority, which has the power to prosecute. An airline found guilty of discrimination could face an unlimited fine.

## ASSISTANCE FOR DISABLED PASSENGERS

### Medical clearance

Airlines generally have procedures for assisting disabled passengers. Most disabled people, particularly those with permanent and stable conditions, won't require medical clearance before travelling. However, the rules vary between airlines. For certain conditions you will generally need clearance for flying even if you don't normally need treatment. It is important to check when you book what, if any, medical information will be required.

### Special assistance

Most airports are physically accessible and have introduced facilities and services to make it easier for disabled people to use them. They may provide these services themselves or have contracts with other organisations to do so. However, many airport terminals are large, complex premises so finding facilities and assistance may be difficult. Some people, who normally manage independently, may need help. Airports often have information for disabled people on their website and some publish access guides.

Wheelchair users should be able to use their own wheelchairs until boarding the plane. Other people may be given a wheelchair to reach the aircraft door. Depending on the airline and the size of the aircraft, there may be an on-board wheelchair to help you transfer to your seat.

You may be able to request a seat in a particular area, say near a toilet or with extra legroom. However, for safety reasons airlines allocate seats beside emergency exits (which do have more space) to people who are perceived as having the necessary dexterity and strength to open the doors.

Most pieces of equipment required by a disabled passenger are carried free of charge. Larger items (including wheelchairs) are carried in the hold, but smaller items can be taken into the cabin. Ask the airline about carriage of your equipment – particularly if you might need it during the flight and, especially, if you intend carrying liquid medicine on board.

### Advance planning

Ask in advance for any assistance or service that you might need in connection with your flight. Air travel often involves more organisations or other forms of transport, particularly if you are flying on a charter flight as part of a holiday package. If plans go wrong it is often the result of a failure in the communication chain. So it is advisable to check that appropriate messages have been passed on and to emphasise the importance of your requests.

> *Your Rights to Fly – What you need to know,* was issued by the Equality and Human Rights Commission in 2011. It can be downloaded from www.equalityhumanrights.com.

# Channel Tunnel

As an alternative to ferries or planes, the Channel Tunnel offers a useful route to continental Europe. There are two services:

### Eurostar

T 01233 617 575
W www.eurostar.com

Eurostar operates train services from London St Pancras International, Ebbsfleet and Ashford to Brussels, Lille and Paris. It offers a limited number of reduced-rate tickets for passengers using wheelchairs and their companion. As spaces are limited, it's worth booking well in advance. Assistance is available on request at check-in; you are asked to arrive as early as possible.

### Eurotunnel

T 01303 282 061
W www.eurotunnel.co.uk

Eurotunnel operates vehicle-carrying shuttle trains between Folkestone and Calais. Disabled drivers or disabled passengers are asked to make themselves known at check-in so that they can park at the front of the shuttle. A maximum of five vehicles carrying disabled drivers or passengers (who may need assistance in an emergency evacuation) can be carried in any shuttle. Terminals are accessible and have toilets for disabled people. There is no need for people to get out of their vehicles if they do not wish to.

# Bus and coach travel

Buses are becoming more accessible. Regulations now require all new buses to be equipped with lifts or ramps with a level floor to an area for any passenger using a wheelchair. Also required are features such as colour-contrasted handrails and easy-to-operate bell-pushes. Older vehicles will, unfortunately, continue to be in use for some years.

Information on routes normally served by accessible buses should be available from a public transport information office or from the individual bus company.

The boarding features of a modern bus generally work well at bus stations or other dedicated bus stands. But there can be problems at roadside bus stops if there isn't a footpath, or if the vehicle does not pull in close enough to the footpath because of road works or parked cars.

There has been slower progress in making scheduled long-distance coach travel accessible to wheelchair users, although since 2005 new coaches have been equipped with lifts and improvements are becoming significant. The key companies and support available are listed below:

## Goldline

Ⓦ www.translink.co.uk/goldline

Goldline is an express coach service between towns and cities in Northern Ireland. It uses wheelchair accessible coaches on an increasing number of its services.

## Megabus

Ⓣ 0141 332 9644

Ⓦ uk.megabus.com

Megabus has an increasing number of vehicles with a wheelchair lift. Wheelchair users should phone to make a booking so that a bus with a lift or ramp is made available.

## National Express

Ⓣ 0871 781 8179; textphone 0121 455 9986

Ⓔ dpth@nationalexpress.com

Ⓦ www.nationalexpress.com

National Express has introduced a new vehicle in which a lift is incorporated at the main entrance and there is a dedicated space for a passenger using a wheelchair. This type of vehicle should be in use across their network by the end of 2012. On other services, folded manual wheelchairs can be carried and assistance offered if you give 24-hours advance notice. They also offer a Disabled Coachcard which offers discounts to disabled travellers.

## Oxford Tube

Ⓣ 01865 77 2250

Ⓦ www.oxfordtube.com

Oxford Tube runs scheduled services between Oxford and London using low-floor buses, each of which has one space for a passenger using a wheelchair.

## Scottish City Link

Ⓣ 0141 332 9644

Ⓦ www.citylink.co.uk

Scottish City Link has wheelchair accessible coaches on its regular service between Edinburgh and Glasgow and on its services between Glasgow and London, run in partnership with Megabus.

## Victoria Coach Station

Ⓣ 020 7027 2520

Ⓦ www.tfl.gov.uk

Victoria is the terminus for most coach services in and out of London and an important station at which connections can be made. There is a mobility lounge where disabled people can wait and from which assistance can be provided. To book assistance call the number above.

Information on firms with accessible coaches available for private hire, for group trips and other purposes, should be available from a public transport information office or passenger transport executive.

## Door-to-door and community transport

Some areas have special transport schemes for people who are not able to use public transport. They include: Dial-a-Ride and Ring-and-Ride. This type of service allows you to book an adapted vehicle to carry you on a door-to-door journey. Demand for these services is likely to exceed the resources available so you may find a variety of restrictions in place, for example limits on the number of journeys you can book in any given period and travel may be restricted to a particular administrative area.

There are some general community transport schemes where no public transport is available, often, but not, exclusively in rural areas. Vehicles used for community transport are often accessible to disabled passengers.

Special transport schemes are locally run according to local priorities. You should be able to get information on schemes in your area from the relevant public transport information office.

For details of community transport schemes:
Ⓦ www.a2binfo.net.

**Community Transport Association UK**
Highbank, Halton Street, Hyde, Cheshire SK14 2NY
Ⓣ 0161 351 1475
Ⓦ www.ctauk.org
Community Transport Association gives advice and support on establishing and improving community transport schemes and provides training.

**British Red Cross**
44 Moorfields, London EC2Y 9AL
Ⓣ 020 7138 7900; textphone 020 7562 2050
Ⓦ www.redcross.org.uk
British Red Cross branches offer a transport service for people who cannot get about easily or use public transport. It helps people to get to medical appointments, go shopping or just get out of the house. Ring or visit the website for details of local branches.

## Ferries

Large, modern ships used on international journeys may have lifts between decks, toilets designed for disabled people, and adapted cabins. Much simpler vessels on estuary crossings with open car decks generally have few special facilities and may not be accessible.

If you are planning to travel by ferry, you need to remember that in tidal waters the gradient of any boarding ramp will vary according to the tide.

This is the case even in places like London due to river tides. At low tide, ramps may be very steep.

If you need assistance or information, get in touch with the ferry operator in advance. Contact details and other information can be obtained from the public transport information points or motoring organisations.

## Rail travel

Since 1998 all new trains have had to incorporate access features for disabled people, including spaces for passengers using manual wheelchairs, appropriate toilets and signage. Many older trains also have spaces for passengers using wheelchairs. Older rolling stock is being phased out but some is still in use. Very few trains can accommodate the larger models of scooters.

Accessibility for disabled passengers at train stations is variable. Many premises have been adapted, but this has mostly been at larger stations and those where modernisation was already planned. Many smaller stations still have steps to one or more platforms.

## PLANNING YOUR JOURNEY

Sometimes you can take through-services across major population centres rather than changing trains. Information on services and disruptions can be obtained from:

**National Rail Enquiries**
☎ 08457 484950; textphone 0845 605 0600
Ⓦ www.nationalrail.co.uk

The National Rail website also has 'Stations Made Easy' pages showing the layout of stations. This can be useful when planning a journey through a station you aren't familiar with.

Despite continuing improvements, many disabled passengers will need help at some points of their rail journey. If you think you might need assistance, it helps to give at least 24 hours' notice if possible. If you will be travelling on more than one train line, you should get information and assistance from the train operating company responsible for the first leg of your journey:

**Arriva Trains Wales**
☎ 0845 300 3005; textphone 0845 758 5469
**C2C**
☎ 01702 357 640
**Chiltern Railways**
☎ 0845 600 5165; textphone 0845 707 8051
**Cross Country Trains**
☎ 0844 811 0124; textphone 0844 811 0125
**East Coast**
☎ 0845 722 5225
**East Midlands Trains**
☎ 0845 712 5678
**First Capital Connect**
☎ 0800 058 2844; textphone 0800 975 1052
**First Great Western**
☎ 0800 197 1329
**First Hull Trains**
☎ 0845 071 0222
**First TransPennine Express**
☎ 0800 107 2149; textphone 0800 107 2061
**Grand Central Railway**
☎ 0844 811 0072; textphone 0845 305 6815
**Greater Anglia**
☎ 0800 028 2878
**Heathrow Express**
☎ 0845 600 1515

**London Midland**
☎ 0800 092 4260; textphone 0844 811 0134
**London Overground**
☎ 0845 601 4867
**Merseyrail**
☎ 0800 027 7347 (also textphone)
**Northern Rail**
☎ 0808 156 1606; textphone 0845 604 5608
**ScotRail**
☎ 0800 912 2901
**SouthEastern**
☎ 0800 783 4524; textphone 0800 783 4548
**South West Trains**
☎ 0800 528 2100; textphone 0800 692 0792
**Southern Railway**
☎ 0800 138 1016; textphone 0800 138 1018
**Virgin Trains**
☎ 0845 744 3366; textphone 0845 744 3367

**Passenger Focus**
Freepost (RRRE-ETTC-LEET), PO Box 4257, Manchester M60 3AR
☎ 0300 123 2350
Ⓔ info@passengerfocus.org.uk
Ⓦ www.passengerfocus.org.uk
Passenger Focus is the national watchdog for passengers. It can assist with complaints about rail travel where the response from an initial approach to the train operator has been unsatisfactory.

The **Disabled Persons Railcard** gives one-third off many rail fares for the cardholder and an adult travelling companion. A list of qualifying criteria and an application form are in the leaflet *Rail travel made easy*, available from travel centres and staffed stations. It takes up to two weeks to obtain a new or renewed railcard, so applications should be made ahead of any planned journeys.

A one-year railcard currently costs £20 and a three-year one is available for £54. The Disabled Persons Railcard application helpline is 0845 605 0525; textphone 0845 601 0132; email disability@atoc.org or go to www. disabledpersons-railcard.co.uk.

Application forms should be sent to: Disabled Persons Railcard Office, PO Box 11631, Laurencekirk AB30 9AA.

## Taxis

In London, all licensed taxis must be able to carry a passenger using a standard wheelchair. So all London black cabs manufactured since 1989 must have space to carry a passenger using a manual wheelchair and either carry or be equipped with a ramp.

> **www.traintaxi.co.uk** is a database giving information on the availability of taxis at stations and tram stops throughout Britain. It includes telephone numbers for up to three taxi companies for advanced bookings and indicates which ones say they have accessible vehicles. Before booking, you should check whether the company can meet your requirements.

Black cabs now also feature a hidden step into the cab which the driver can simply swing out from the chassis and are fitted with swivel seats that can be rotated through 90 degrees, enabling the passenger to take their seat outside of the taxi and then swivel into the vehicle.

Similar rules have been introduced by local authorities responsible for regulating taxis in other areas.

In some areas price concession systems are available to disabled people for journeys by taxi and/or private hire cars. This may be as part of a more general concession scheme or a separate system. On a local basis, other specialist taxi services may exist for disabled people.

## Trams and underground networks

Trams and other light rail systems developed over recent years in a number of places, including Blackpool, Croydon, Greater Manchester, Nottingham, Sheffield and the West Midlands, have been designed to be accessible.

The Tyne Wear Metro and the Docklands Light Railway in East London, are fairly accessible to wheelchair users but you may need to be accompanied. Access for disabled passengers is still limited on the older underground networks in London and Glasgow.

In London, new developments, such as the Jubilee Line extension between Westminster and Stratford, are designed to be accessible.

Transport for London is running a programme to create step-free routes to the platforms and other access improvements at almost 100 stations. You can find up-to-date information on Underground maps published by Transport for London and available at www.tfl.gov.uk.

## Travel training

In some areas, travel training is available to help disabled people use accessible buses and other forms of public transport independently.

> *Doing Transport Differently* includes information and travellers' tales to encourage all people to use public transport. To order or download a copy, visit the Disability Rights UK online shop at www.disabilityrightsuk.org.

This can help you gain confidence, particularly if you are used to using specialist transport. Contact your local authority to find out about schemes in your area.

There are considerable variations both in the extent of this provision and how it is organised – those who may be involved include local authority social care and education departments, health organisations, transport companies and voluntary bodies.

# Motoring

**Being independently mobile may mean having a vehicle to use as a driver or a passenger. Because of developments in technology and vehicle design, it has become easier to find cars that can be adapted to meet our needs. This chapter provides information on driving, purchasing or leasing cars, and on parking, tax and insurance concessions for disabled drivers.**

## Getting started

### DRIVING LICENCES

All applicants for a licence must declare to the Driver and Vehicle Licensing Agency (DVLA) any existing disability or medical condition affecting their fitness to drive. If your disability is stable and non-progressive, your licence will normally be valid until you are 70; otherwise, a licence may be restricted to one, two or three years. You can apply to renew a restricted licence when it expires. Renewal is usually conditional on some form of assessment.

If you receive the higher rate mobility component of disability living allowance (DLA), you can get a provisional driving licence from the age of 16.

Existing licence holders are legally required to inform the DVLA if they become disabled in some way or if there is a deterioration or change in any existing disability or medical condition.

Modern adaptations mean it is possible for disabled people with more substantial impairments to drive. So if you are struggling to drive your current car it's well worth having an assessment at your local mobility centre (see 'Useful contacts' below) to find out if there are adaptations that could make it easier (and safer) for you to drive.

Some medical conditions can lead to you being judged unfit to drive.

These are:

- epilepsy, unless you have been free of seizures for a year, or for the previous three years have only had seizures when asleep
- severe mental disorder
- liability to sudden attacks of giddiness or fainting
- insulin dependent diabetes where you have had two non-symptomatic hypoglycaemic attacks in the past year
- inability to read a number plate at a distance of 20m (new style number plate) or 20.5 metres (old style number plate) in good daylight, with the aid of spectacles or contact lenses if usually worn
- persistent drug or alcohol misuse (substance abuse is excluded from discrimination law and is not classed as a disability)
- any other disability likely to cause you to be a danger to the public while driving.

For further information about driving licences contact:

For England, Scotland and Wales:
**Drivers Medical Group**
DVLA, Swansea SA99 1TU
☎ 0300 790 6806; textphone 0300 123 1278
✉ eftd@dvla.gsi.gov.uk
🌐 www.dvla.gov.uk

For Northern Ireland:
**DVLNI**
Driver Licensing Division, County Hall, Castlerock Road, Coleraine BT51 3TB
☎ 0845 402 4000; textphone 028 7034 1380
✉ dvlni@doeni.gov.uk
🌐 www.dvlni.gov.uk

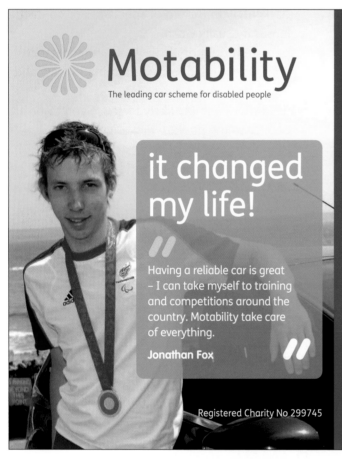
IF ONLY I'D KNOWN THAT A YEAR AGO ...

## DRIVING LESSONS

All new drivers are advised to have professional driving lessons at least at the start of their learning period. Many driving instructors have training in and experience of teaching disabled people. They will know about techniques for transferring between a car and a wheelchair, operating adapted controls, etc. Disability motoring organisations and mobility centres can provide details of appropriately trained instructors.

Some driving schools have cars fitted with basic adaptations such as simple hand controls, or you can have lessons in your own adapted vehicle.

If you intend to get a car through the Motability Scheme (see below), grants towards the cost of driving lessons may be available if you are under the age of 25.

If someone takes you out who is not a driving instructor, they must be over 21 and have held a valid, full driving licence for a minimum of three years in the relevant vehicle category.

> For information about driving tests or to book the theory or practical test, visit www.gov.uk.

## DRIVING TESTS

There are two parts to the driving test: theory and practical.

### The theory test

The theory test can be taken as soon as you have your provisional licence; it is taken at a test centre. Virtually all test centres are accessible, but if there is a reason why you cannot get in, arrangements can be made for you to take the test at another venue.

For the theory test you need to use a touch-screen computer and a mouse. If you cannot do this, you should inform the test centre in advance, preferably when you book the test. The theory test is made up of two parts: a multiple-choice test and a hazard perception test. You need to pass both parts. The test is available in 21 languages and British Sign Language (BSL).

### The practical test

Disabled people are given priority when booking the practical test. Additional time is allotted so the examiner can be informed of the nature and function of any adaptations, to allow you extra time to get in and out of the car, or for any other reason. If you are deaf, you can take an interpreter with you. The interpreter must be over 16 and not a driving instructor. The Driving Standards Agency asks anyone with a disability that may affect their driving or their taking of the test to let them know when booking.

## Adaptations and accessories for your car

### MOBILITY CENTRES

There are a wide range of accessories and adaptations to help us use vehicles. As well as adaptations to driving controls, there is equipment to enable us to drive the car seated in a wheelchair, swivel seats to make it easier to get in and out of the car, and hoists for loading a wheelchair into the boot.

It's worth checking what is available before spending money on adaptations you might not need. The best place to get advice on what might help you is a mobility centre.

The Forum of Mobility Centres is a network of 17 independent organisations covering England, Scotland, Wales and Northern Ireland (see 'Useful contacts' at the end of this chapter).

They offer advice and assessments to people who have a medical condition or who are recovering from an accident or injury that may affect their ability to drive, or to get in or out of a motor vehicle. You can attend whichever centre is most convenient. Some centres have satellite offices so you don't always need to travel to their main office.

Working with our **COMMUNITY** for **A Better Tomorrow**

## TOYOTA

TOYOTA (GB) PLC

IF ONLY I'D KNOWN THAT A YEAR AGO ...

An assessment at a mobility centre for a driver referring him or herself costs £50 to £130 (depending on the centre). In Scotland, the assessment is free if you are referred by a GP. Assessment as a passenger costs less – generally £20 to £50. Motability customers may qualify for a free assessment under the New Deal scheme.

## MOBILITY ROADSHOW

The annual Mobility Roadshow provides an opportunity to view and test drive a wide range of adapted cars and other vehicles, see mobility products and talk to voluntary organisations. The roadshow takes place every summer.

**Mobility Roadshow**
Telford International Centre
27-29 June 2013
W www.mobilityroadshow.co.uk

Disability Rights UK's guide *Get Motoring* provides comprehensive practical guidance for disabled motorists on how to find, finance, adapt and maintain a suitable car. The guide is available from Disability Rights UK, telephone 020 7250 3222 or download it for free from www.disabilityrightsuk.org.

## Finance

### MOTABILITY

The Motability Scheme is a car leasing scheme designed for disabled people. You are eligible if you receive the higher rate mobility component of disability living allowance (DLA), the enhanced rate of personal independence payment (see the 'Benefits' chapter) or the war pensioners mobility supplement.

Motability provides a car for three years (or every five years if the car is heavily adapted or is a wheelchair accessible vehicle), fully maintained, insured and with breakdown cover for the duration of the lease. They will fit some simple driving adaptations free of charge. You sign over your relevant component of DLA, personal independence payment or war pensioners mobility supplement to Motability for the period of the lease. For some cars, you may be required to make an additional 'advance payment'.

Motability has charitable funds that can help with advance payments and more expensive adaptations.

You don't need to be a driver to use Motability. You can nominate another person to drive at no extra cost or, if you can't drive you can nominate two people to drive for you. A third driver can be added at an additional cost. Only one named driver can be under the age of 21.

**Motability Operations**
City Gate House, 22 Southwark Bridge Road, London SE1 9HB
T 0845 456 4566; textphone 0845 675 0009
W www.motability.co.uk

### CHARITIES

If you don't qualify for the Motability Scheme, you may be able to get help from a charity that gives grants to individuals. Your local library should be able to help you find sources, for example the Round Table, Rotary or Lions Club and other local charities. Your local Community Foundation may know of local charities that give grants to individuals (see 'Useful contacts'). Disability organisations appropriate to your condition may know of sources of help.

### VAT

Some specialist vehicles and adaptations to vehicles can be zero-rated for VAT when provided for disabled people. The circumstances under which this applies are carefully defined and adaptations have to be made when the vehicle is bought. You cannot re-claim VAT retrospectively, so it's important that your dealer understands the regulations.

For more information see *VAT Notice 701/7*, available from HM Revenue and Customs (www.hmrc.gov.uk).

IF ONLY I'D KNOWN THAT A YEAR AGO ...

# Tax, insurance and other matters

### ROAD TAX

People who receive the higher rate mobility component of DLA or war pensioners mobility supplement are eligible to apply for exemption from vehicle excise duty (road tax).

If you are on the Motability Scheme your tax disc will be sent directly to you free of charge.

If you have your own vehicle you need to contact the Disability Living Allowance Unit (see 'Useful contacts) for a certificate of entitlement to DLA. You need this to get your free tax disc.

For more information see 'vehicles exempt from vehicle tax' section at www.gov.uk.

### INSURANCE

Insurers cannot charge higher premiums for disabled motorists unless the extra charge is based on factual, statistical data or there are other relevant factors to indicate there is a higher risk. A number of brokers and insurance companies specialise in motor insurance for disabled drivers. Information about these brokers can be obtained from disability motoring organisations (see 'Useful contacts').

### CONCESSIONARY TOLLS

As disabled people, we often qualify for exemptions or reductions in tolls payable on roads, bridges and tunnels and the central London Congestion Charge. You will need to check in advance to find out whether you qualify. Generally, presentation of your Blue Badge is sufficient to prove your eligibility, but sometimes additional evidence is required, and you may need to apply for your concession in advance.

# Parking: the Blue Badge scheme

The Blue Badge scheme is a national system of on-street parking concessions for people with severe mobility problems.

### WHO IS ELIGIBLE?

The Blue Badge is available to anyone over the age of 2 years who:
- receives the higher rate mobility component of disability living allowance (DLA)
- receives the war pensioners mobility supplement, or
- is a registered blind person.

In addition, you could be eligible if you:
- have a permanent and substantial disability that causes inability to walk or very considerable difficulty in walking
- have a severe disability in both upper limbs, regularly drive a car and are unable to use a parking meter or have great difficulty in doing so, or
- are aged under 2 and need to travel with bulky medical equipment or be close to a vehicle for medical treatment.

If you're the parent of a child under 3 years old, you can apply for a Blue Badge if your child must always be accompanied by bulky medical equipment that is very difficult to carry around and/or which needs to be kept near a vehicle at all times to get emergency treatment for a condition when necessary.

### MAKING AN APPLICATION

Blue Badges are issued by local authorities, who are responsible for assessing whether you are eligible. The quickest and easiest way to apply for a badge is online at www.gov.uk. But you can also apply by contacting your local authority directly.

The cost of the Blue Badge varies, depending on where you live. The maximum you can be charged in England is £10, in Scotland £20, in Northern Ireland £2. In Wales it is free.

IF ONLY I'D KNOWN THAT A YEAR AGO ...

## WHERE YOU CAN PARK?

Blue Badge holders can park without charge at parking meters and in pay-and-display bays. They are exempt from time limits imposed on others and may park for up to three hours on double and single yellow lines, except where loading or other restrictions apply. This time limit does not apply in Scotland.

The scheme does not apply in parts of central London where four local authorities have their own schemes, although there are some parking spaces provided for Blue Badge holders visiting the area.

A Blue Badge does not always entitle you to free parking in off-street car parks, even if it is run by the local council. Always check the signs to find out if you need to pay. If you have difficulty using the parking machine or need extra time over the permitted limit, ring the parking operator (the number will be on the sign) to avoid being issued with a penalty charge.

Although the Blue Badge scheme does not apply to off-street car parks, it is often used as the basis for concessions and to indicate that designated disabled parking bays are being used correctly.

If you are visiting an unfamiliar local authority area it's worth checking their website to find out their policy on charging Blue Badge holders, and to see if they provide information on the location of parking bays reserved for badge holders.

**Parking in other European countries**

Blue Badges are recognised in 29 European countries. When driving in another European country, you are entitled to the same concessions as those granted to the disabled citizens of that country. Concessions vary from one country to another so check before you travel.

Outside the European Union, it will be a matter of local policy whether countries recognise the Blue Badge. Some countries may award a short-term badge. Always check before you use your badge. If you incur a fine that you don't pay, you could be refused entry next time you want to visit that country.

> A **Department for Transport** guide to parking concessions can be downloaded from: www.dft.gov.uk.

## Useful contacts

**Blue Badge Network**
198 Wolverhampton Street, Dudley DY1 1DZ
📞 07964 59 0060
📧 headoffice@bluebadgenetwork.org.uk
🌐 www.bluebadgenetwork.org.uk
A membership organisation which aims to help disabled people overcome access and mobility problems and to maintain the integrity and validity of the concessionary parking permit by the prevention of fraud and misuse.

**National Blue Badge Helpline**
📞 0844 463 0213
Can help with delays in applications. Use this number to report lost, stolen or misused badges.

> For worldwide information on local rules for using a disabled parking card, visit: www.fiadisabledtravellers.com, www.theaa.com or www.adviceguide.org.uk.

## Get Motoring

A practical guide for disabled motorists to help find and finance a car. New 2012 edition.

Available to order from our online shop
**www.disabilityrightsuk.org**

IF ONLY I'D KNOWN THAT A YEAR AGO ...

**Disability Living Allowance Unit**

Warbreck House, Warbreck Hill, Blackpool FY2 0YE

T 0845 712 3456; textphone 0845 722 4433

In Northern Ireland call:

T 02890 906 812

**Disabled Motoring UK**

National Headquarters, Ashwellthorpe, Norwich NR16 1EX

T 01508 48 9449

E info@disabledmotoring.org

W www.disabledmotoring.org

A national membership charity that campaigns on behalf of all disabled motorists, passengers and Blue Badge holders and provides information on all matters related to motoring, mobility and Blue Badges. Members receive a free monthly magazine, travel concessions and advice and information from trained information officers.

**Forum of Mobility Centres**

T 0800 559 3636

W www.mobility-centres.org.uk

**Mobility Choice**

Crowthorne House, Nine Mile Ride, Wokingham RG40 3GA

T 0845 241 0390 / 01344 75 0400

W www.mobilityroadshow.co.uk

**National Association for Bikers with a Disability (NABD)**

Unit 20, The Bridgewater Centre, Robson Avenue, Urmston, Manchester M41 7TE

T 0844 415 4849

E office@thenabd.org.uk

W www.nabd.org.uk

Provides a range of services for its members including advice and help on training, licensing, adaptations, insurance and the costs of adaptations. It has a network of local representatives and produces a quarterly magazine.

---

**Ricability** publications have information on equipment to help disabled motorists and passengers. It has a list of over 600 models of cars with information such as the width of door opening, height of the seat and size of the boot, and a list of companies and organisations providing services and products.

For more information contact Ricability at Unit G03, Wenlock Business Centre, 50-56 Wharf Road, London N1 7EU, 020 7427 2460, textphone 020 7427 2469, www.ricability.org.uk.

IF ONLY I'D KNOWN THAT A YEAR AGO ...

# Holidays

**It can sometimes be difficult and time consuming for us to find appropriate holiday accommodation, transport, travel insurance or essential information about travelling. However, many holiday providers have specialist facilities and some are committed to ensuring accessibility. Some disability organisations arrange, or advise on holiday travel. This chapter provides information on holidays, whether you're travelling independently or with a group.**

## General information

It's useful to find out about the area you're thinking of visiting before you book. Some guide books, the travel sections of newspapers and travel blogs on the internet provide specific information for disabled visitors. Some hotel websites include accessibility information.

You can find details via national and local tourist board websites or at:
- Ⓦ www.openbritain.net
- Ⓦ www.disabledgo.com

When considering booking a specific hotel, it's best to ask for their 'access statement'. This will explain access and facilities for disabled people in their hotel. You should make this request in writing so that you have evidence of what you asked and were told.

Some towns in Britain have access guides. You can get information from a tourist information centre or disability organisation in the area.

**Tourism for All**
7a Pixel Mill, 44 Appleby Road, Kendal LA9 6ES
Ⓣ 0845 124 9971
Ⓦ www.tourismforall.org.uk

Tourism for All is a central source of holiday and travel information for disabled people, older people and carers. It provides information on accessible accommodation, visitor attractions and transport in the UK and for some overseas destinations. It can also help identify sources of funding for disabled people on low incomes. Tourism for All works with all sectors of the tourism industry to improve accessibility and carries out inspections under the National Accessible Scheme.

Disability Rights UK's publication *Holidays in the British Isles: a guide for disabled people* is packed with information on taking a holiday and contains resources such as places to stay and things to do throughout the British Isles. To order a copy, go to our website and click on shop (www.disabilityrightsuk.org).

## Your specific requirements

Whether you book your holiday independently, directly with an accommodation provider or through a tour operator or travel agent, it is advisable to disclose your requirements when you make enquiries and when booking. The more information you give the better, but how much you disclose is up to you. Some accommodation providers might assume things about you if you are disabled. But remember that it is never acceptable for anyone to discriminate against you because of your disability or health condition. It can be helpful to prepare a list of facilities you would like to have at your destination – both essential and desirable. Think about the physical accessibility of the premises and surroundings, and the availability of equipment, appropriate transport and assistance, or other services.

You may need to arrange transport for part of your journey, for example, to and from the airport or your accommodation. See the 'Public transport' chapter for more information.

# JUST IN CASE
## YOU'RE TRAVELLING ABROAD...

- Ensure you have comprehensive travel insurance which takes into account your personal circumstances and medical history
- Research your destination and the facilities and support available there
- Check our travel advice at **www.fco.gov.uk/travel** for the latest in-country situation
- Check which vaccinations and health precautions you may need by visiting your GP or by visiting **www.fitfortravel.nhs.uk**
- Check if you need permission to take your prescribed medicines with you. Take your prescription with you and ensure you have enough to cover emergencies
- **For more information and to order our free Disabled Travellers leaflet go to www.fco.gov.uk/publications or call 08444 777 399.**

Foreign &
Commonwealth
Office

IF ONLY I'D KNOWN THAT A YEAR AGO ...

# Travelling abroad

Attitudes, services and legislation relating to disability will be different in other countries. Many organisations dealing with specific conditions can advise their members on overseas travel.

## MEDICAL TREATMENT

If you become ill or have an accident abroad, you will probably have to pay for all or part of your treatment. This is a major reason to have travel insurance for the full period of your holiday.

*Health Advice for Travellers*, issued by the Department of Health and available from Post Offices and other information points, gives information on health and medical treatment in other countries. It contains a form to get a European Health Insurance Card (EHIC), which you must have to make use of reciprocal health agreements the UK has with European Union and some other countries. The EHIC is valid for five years, so remember to check the expiry date of your card before you travel.

## REGULAR MEDICATION

If you use, or are likely to require, any regularly prescribed medicines, make sure you take an adequate supply with you, including enough for any unforeseen delays.

These items should be packed in hand luggage so that they are available during the journey and can readily be explained to Customs or Immigration officials. It may be useful to carry a note from your GP explaining your need for them. Any liquids or gels should be in their original packaging. This is especially important if you are flying.

## PASSPORTS

The Identity & Passport Service (IPS) offers assistance with passport applications, both paper or online. It provides Braille and audio information. Regional and other offices used for face-to-face interviews with new passport applicants are accessible and have staff on hand who can use sign language. For more information contact:

**IPS Passport Adviceline**
☎ 0300 222 0000; textphone 0300 222 0222
Ⓦ www.ips.gov.uk

> **The Foreign & Commonwealth Office** publishes a guide for disabled people intending to travel abroad. *Disabled Travellers* can be downloaded from their website at www.fco.gov.uk/en/travel-and-living-abroad/publications.

# Insurance

Taking out insurance is recommended. Your trip might get cancelled or you could be ill and unable to go. Without insurance, there is little you can do to get your money back. Make sure you get appropriate insurance for your type of trip, particularly if planning an activity holiday.

## YOUR RIGHTS AS A DISABLED PERSON

All companies have a legal duty to ensure that they do not treat disabled customers in a less favourable way than they would treat other customers. The Equality Act 2010 places duties on service providers, which includes insurance and travel companies providing services within the UK.

For example, a company must not refuse to provide a service to a disabled person that they offer to other members of the public unless this can be justified (see below). And they must not provide the service on terms or standards that are worse than those they would give to any other customer.

However, the law does allow insurers to apply special conditions or extra charges to disabled people in certain circumstances. For example, they can charge a disabled person a higher premium if they can show that a disabled person is at a greater risk and therefore more likely to make a claim.

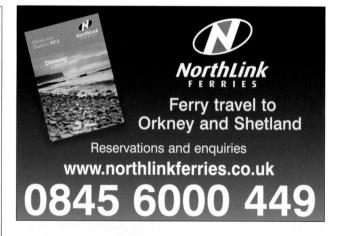

IF ONLY I'D KNOWN THAT A YEAR AGO ...

An insurance company can only justify different treatment for a disabled person if:

- the decision is based on information that is relevant to the assessment of the risk being insured
- the information (such as statistical data or a medical report) is from a source on which it is reasonable to rely
- the less favourable treatment is reasonable when this information and all other relevant factors are taken into account.

It is worth checking whether a standard policy offered by a travel company suits your situation – does it, for example, cover any equipment you have to take? Some voluntary organisations can assist their members, or people with the condition with which they are concerned, to get appropriate insurance cover that would otherwise be difficult to obtain.

Some companies have insurance packages specifically for disabled people, for example:

**All Clear Travel Insurance**
All Clear House, 1 Redwing Court, Ashton Road, Romford, Essex RM3 8QQ
📞 0845 250 5350
🌐 www.allcleartravel.co.uk

**Chartwell Insurance**
East Winch Hall, East Winch, King's Lynn, Norfolk PE32 1HN
📞 0800 089 0146
✉ info@chartwellinsurance.co.uk
🌐 www.chartwellinsurance.co.uk

**En Route Insurance**
5th Floor, Cavendish House, Breeds Place, Hastings, East Sussex TN34 3AA
📞 0800 783 7245
✉ info@enrouteinsurance.co.uk
🌐 www.enrouteinsurance.co.uk

**Free Spirit**
P J Hayman & Company Ltd, Stansted House, Rowlands Castle, Hampshire PO9 6DX
📞 0845 230 5000
✉ contact@freespirittravelinsurance.com
🌐 www.freespirittravelinsurance.com

**Travelbility**
J & M Insurance Services, Peregrine House, Bakers Lane, Epping CM16 5DQ
📞 0845 338 1638
🌐 www.jmi.co.uk

## Useful contacts

### CHARITABLE ORGANISATIONS

Many voluntary organisations that deal with specific disabilities or operate on a local basis give advice on holidays and/or arrange holidays for their members. Some, including Action for Blind People, have their own holiday accommodation. In addition, the following organisations make holiday provision more widely for disabled people.

**Action for Blind People**
Vision Hotels Central Office, 14-16 Verney Road, London SE16 3DZ
📞 0845 603 0051
✉ enquiries@visionhotels.co.uk
🌐 www.visionhotels.co.uk

**3H Fund (Helping Hands for Holidays)**
Unit 2B, Speldhurst Business Park, Langdon Road, Tunbridge Wells, Kent TN1 2RA
📞 01892 86 0207
✉ info@3hfund.org.uk
🌐 www.3hfund.org.uk
3H provide subsidised group holidays for physically disabled people aged 11 years upwards, who would otherwise be unable to take a break. Travel, accommodation and experienced volunteer and nursing staff are provided. The programme includes hotel-based and activity holidays.

# Tameside Markets

People you know selling things that you want

## Ashton
### Farmer's Market

**Multi Award Winning**

Selling local produce
**Last Sunday of every month**

## Ashton Market

**Market Hall**
9am - 5.30pm Monday to Saturday
**Market Ground**
Open 7 days a week with over 150 stalls
**Tuesday**
The biggest Flea Market in the region
**Sunday**
Giant Table-Top Sale and Market

**Tameside**
Metropolitan Borough
*Great lives, excellent services*

For further information **www.tameside.gov.uk/markets**
**www.shopatashton.com** or call **0161 342 3268/9**

IF ONLY I'D KNOWN THAT A YEAR AGO ...

## BREAK

Davison House, 1 Montague Road, Sheringham NR26 8WN

☎ 01263 82 2161

✉ office@break-charity.org

🌐 www.break-charity.org

Break has a house in Norfolk providing inclusive holidays and short breaks with 24-hour care for children and adults with learning disabilities, associated disabilities and high-level care needs. They also have two self-catering chalets in North Devon for independent holidays.

## Calvert Trust

🌐 www.calvert-trust.org.uk

Calvert Trust has activity centres in the Lake District, Northumbria and Exmoor equipped for disabled people and their companions. The centres offer a wide range of outdoor adventure activities.

## Holiday Homes Trust

Gilwell Park, Chingford, London E4 7QW

☎ 020 8433 7290

✉ scout.holiday.homes@scout.org.uk

🌐 www.holidayhomestrust.org

Holiday Homes Trust offers low-cost self-catering holidays in six-berth chalets and caravans with some adaptations at a number of holiday parks around England and Wales. They welcome any family with a disabled member. The season is generally from Easter to October and bookings are taken from the previous October.

## Holidays with Help

4 Pebblecombe, Adelaide Road, Surbiton, Surrey KT4 6LL

☎ 01772 739 144

✉ hwhholidays@btinternet.com

🌐 www.holidayswithhelp.org.uk

Holidays with Help run respite holidays for disabled people and their carers at holiday centres in England. They arrange activities and outings. Experienced helpers and medical personnel are available. Applications are accepted from groups, families and individuals. Application forms can be downloaded from the website.

## Livability Holidays

50 Scrutton Street, London EC2A 4XQ

☎ 020 7452 2000

✉ info@livability.org.uk

🌐 www.livability.org.uk

Livability offer a range of holiday accommodation including hotels at Minehead and Llandudno and self-catering units, houses and flats around England and Wales including units at holiday parks and self-contained houses and flats equipped for disabled people.

## Vitalise

Short Break Bookings Team, Business Design Centre, 52 Upper Street, London N1 0QH

☎ 0303 303 0145

🌐 www.vitalise.org.uk

Vitalise provide respite breaks for disabled people at accessible centres with 24-hour care and personal support, in Essex, Southport and Southampton. There are themed weeks for specific interests and age groups. They run holidays for visually impaired people accompanied by volunteer sighted companions and can arrange overseas holidays for disabled people at accessible hotels.

## COMMERCIAL ORGANISATIONS

The following organisations specialise in offering holidays and related services to disabled people.

## Access at Last Ltd

18 Hazel Grove, Tarleton, Preston PR4 6DQ

☎ 01772 81 4555

🌐 www.accessatlast.com

Founded by a wheelchair user, this website gives information on wheelchair accessible hotels and self-catering accommodation in many countries.

## Accessible Travel & Leisure

Avionics House, Kingsway Business Park, Naas Lane, Quedgeley, Gloucester GL2 2SN

☎ 01452 72 9739

✉ info@accessibletravel.co.uk

🌐 www.accessibletravel.co.uk

A specialist travel service that offers a wide range of holidays and related services for disabled people – including Mediterranean holidays, cruises and tours in South Africa and Egypt. Accessible villas, apartments and hotels are offered as well as accessible transfers or car hire, local representatives and insurance.

IF ONLY I'D KNOWN THAT A YEAR AGO ...

## Can Be Done Ltd

Can Be Done Ltd, Congress House, 14 Lyon road, Harrow HA1 2EN

📞 020 8907 2400

✉ holidays@canbedone.co.uk

🌐 www.canbedone.co.uk

Founded by a wheelchair user, this tour operator offers holidays for people with access or mobility problems. Their programme includes a range of destinations around the world. Tailor-made holidays and tours can be arranged.

## Chalfont Line

4 Providence Road, West Drayton UB7 8HJ

📞 01895 45 9540

✉ holidays@chalfont-line.co.uk

🌐 www.chalfont-line.co.uk

Chalfont Line is an adapted-coach hire company with a programme of leisurely paced holidays in Britain and overseas for wheelchair users and people with impaired mobility. They can provide a door-to-door service and personal assistance.

## Diana's Supported Holidays

📞 0844 800 9373

✉ enquiries@dsh.org.uk

🌐 www.dsh.org.uk

Diana's provide holidays with support for people with learning disabilities in Britain and abroad. Groups are of at least six with a qualified leader and support staff. One-to-one support can be arranged although a lower ratio is normally provided. In addition to the programmed holidays, other destinations can be arranged for groups.

## Enable Holidays Ltd

39 Station Street, Walsall, West Midlands WS2 9JT

📞 0871 222 4939

✉ info@enableholidays.com

🌐 www.enableholidays.com

Enable Holidays offer package holidays at selected resorts in the Mediterranean, the Canaries, Florida and European cities at accessible hotels. Powered wheelchairs and other equipment can be booked and adapted vehicles arranged for transfers and outings in many locations.

## HOMELEIGH COUNTRY COTTAGES

Our self-catering holiday cottages are situated in the peaceful Pembrokeshire countryside, a few minutes drive from many blue flag beaches including Amroth, Saundersfoot and Tenby. We offer a warm welcome to guests who need a little extra help to make their holiday perfect. Facilities include extra-wide level entry doors, wet room style showers, shower chairs, electric beds, hoists and commodes.

For more information:
Email: enquiries@homeleigh.org
Phone: 01834 831765
Homeleigh Country Cottages, Red Roses, Whitland, Carmarthenshire SA34 0PN

**www.homeleigh.org**

## Traveleyes

PO Box 511, Leeds LS5 3JT

📞 0844 804 0221

🌐 www.traveleyes.co.uk

A travel company organising small group holidays for visually impaired and sighted people, with the latter acting as guides in exchange for a discounted price. Holidays have included walking trips in southern Spain and the Atlas Mountains, visits to Malta and Morocco, and activity breaks in southern Africa. Groups are kept to around 15 and the air holidays are ATOL protected.

## Wings on Wheels

8 Cornfields, Church Lane, Tydd St Giles, Wisbech PE13 5LX

📞 01945 87 1111

🌐 www.wingsonwheels.co.uk

Offers a programme of escorted holidays for disabled and non-disabled people to destinations in Europe and further afield.

We have 14 public toilets across the City of Belfast, with disabled access available at 12 of these.

For more information call us on 0800 032 8100

www.belfastcity.gov.uk/waste

... contributing towards an overall improvement in physical and mental wellbeing

# MID SUSSEX
## DISTRICT COUNCIL

To find out more information about public toilets in our area please contact us on 01444 458166 or visit www.midsussex.gov.uk

**Blaenau Gwent**

For more information on public facilities and access at many attractions, why not telephone before you travel?

Please telephone for all enquiries:

**01495 311 556**

*Best wishes from*

# CRAWLEY
## BOROUGH COUNCIL

# mencap
**The voice of learning disability**

Member of the Changing Places Consortium

Available to order from our online shop
www.disabilityrightsuk.org

# Chichester
# District Council

For information on toilet facilities and access to local attractions, please visit our website
**www.chichester.gov.uk**
before you travel.

Alternatively please telephone
**01243 785166**

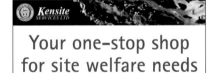

# Public toilets

**This chapter looks at public toilet provision and describes Disability Rights UK's National Key Scheme for accessible toilets. It also explores the accessibility of other public toilet facilities and the Changing Places Scheme.**

## Public toilet provision

Traditionally, local authorities have provided public toilets, and in many areas features for disabled people have been included for years. There are however, still a large number of inaccessible public toilets.

In recent years, there have been significant changes in the ways that toilets in public places are provided and managed.

- Many local authorities have contracted out the cleaning and maintenance of public toilets. Pre-built, self-cleaning toilets (sometimes called 'automatic' or 'superloos') have been installed in an increasing number of locations and are maintained by the supplier.
- In some areas, responsibility for public conveniences has been handed over to other bodies such as parish councils, or to private companies that are responsible for managing elements of town centre public spaces.

- Community Toilet Schemes have been established in some areas to provide public access to toilets in some privately owned places such as pubs and cafes.
- Toilets inside the growing number of shopping centres and other semi-public areas are usually the responsibility of the owners or managers of the premises.

Overall, there has been a reduction in the number of traditional public conveniences, including some unisex units for disabled people, operated by local authorities. Recently, however, as a result of greater awareness and the impact of building regulations and anti-discrimination law, appropriately designed toilets have become more common in privately owned buildings used by the public, such as large shops, restaurants and bars and also in public premises, including parks and libraries.

## National Key Scheme for toilets for disabled people

The National Key Scheme (NKS), also known as the Radar key scheme, is widely used throughout the UK. It was introduced over 30 years ago because an increasing number of local authorities and other bodies were locking their toilets for disabled people to counter vandalism and misuse, or delaying the provision of new toilets until a security system was available. The scheme has now been adopted by over 400 local authorities.

### HOW THE SCHEME WORKS

If toilets have to be locked, providers are asked to fit the standard NKS lock and make keys available to disabled people in their area. Whenever possible a key should be held nearby for disabled people who do not have one with them.

The NKS lock has also been fitted to toilets provided by a wide range of other organisations including transport companies, pubs, visitor attractions, shops, educational establishments and community organisations.

> **The NKS guide to accessible toilets**
> Disability Rights UK maintains a regularly updated list of the toilets fitted with an NKS lock. Our annually published *National Key Scheme Guide* currently includes the location details of over 9,000 toilets. You can order the latest edition of the guide from our online shop. The guide is also available as a iphone app, price £4.99 from Applestore.

IF ONLY I'D KNOWN THAT A YEAR AGO ...

## TO GET A KEY

You can order a key online from Disability Rights UK by visiting www.disabilityrightsuk.org or by sending us a cheque for £4, with a statement explaining why you need the key (for example, details of your disability or health condition).

## TRAVELLING ABROAD

There are similar schemes in other countries. Each country tends to use a different type of key or locking mechanism.

B&BF's **Just Can't Wait** toilet card is for people who may need to use a toilet quickly when a public one is not available. The card is shown in a shop or other establishment as a request to use a staff or other toilet. It does not guarantee access to a toilet, but most places will be willing to help. For details, contact the Bladder & Bowel Foundation (see 'Useful contacts' at the back of this book).

# Changing Places toilets

Some disabled people need facilities additional to those found in a standard toilet for disabled people.

Changing Places toilets have:
- a height adjustable, adult-sized changing table;
- a tracking hoist system or a mobile hoist;
- enough space for assistants on both sides of the WC.

Entry may be limited according to when the premises in which they are situated are open.

There are over 400 Changing Places toilets around the country. For details of current and planned Changing Places toilets locations, visit their website.

**Changing Places**
- 📞 020 7696 6019
  (England, Wales and Northern Ireland)
- 📞 01382 385 154 (Scotland)
- 🌐 www.changing-places.org

## THE CHANGING PLACES CAMPAIGN

Across the UK, many disabled people and their families are denied the right to do everyday things because of a lack of suitable public toilets. Instead, families have to change their disabled family members on dirty floors or are forced to stay at home.

Over 230,000 people living in the UK need personal assistance to use the toilet or change continence pads. Standard accessible toilets do not meet their needs. They need Changing Places toilets – which provide enough space and the right equipment – in a safe, clean environment.

*Changing Places Consortium* is campaigning for Changing Places toilets to be installed in all big public places – like city centres, shopping centres, arts venues, hospitals, motorway service stations, leisure complexes, large railway stations and airports.

We want Changing Places toilets to be provided in addition to standard accessible toilets.

To find out more about installing a Changing Places toilet in your venue call the Changing Places consortium on 020 7696 6019 or visit:

**www.changing-places.org**

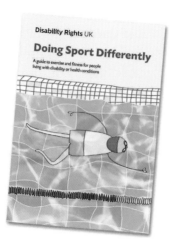

## Doing Sport Differently

This guide will support and encourage people with lived experience of disability or health conditions to participate in or become involved in fitness and sport.

Available to order from our online shop
**www.disabilityrightsuk.org**

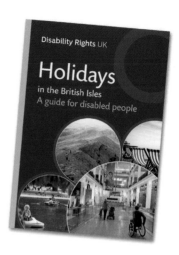

## Holiday Guide

Practical information to help you plan and book a holiday, advice on travelling around, listings of national and local resources and a selection of accessible accommodation.

Available to order from our online shop
**www.disabilityrightsuk.org**

## Get Caravanning

A guide to exploring caravanning from a disabled person's point of view. It provides all the information you need to start or resume this popular leisure activity.

Available to order from our online shop
**www.disabilityrightsuk.org**

## Doing Transport Differently

This guide includes information and travellers' tales to help and inspire people with lived experience of disability or health conditions to use public transport.

Available to order from our online shop
**www.disabilityrightsuk.org**

# Leisure activities

**There are opportunities for us to take part in a range of leisure activities depending on our interests. It's possible to take part in most activities that anyone else enjoys, perhaps just with some adapted equipment or a change in activity times or environment. This chapter provides information about organisations, activities and places that may be of interest.**

## Choosing your activity

A local library and the internet are good places to find ideas and information. Organisations in your area or local disability organisations may be able to put you in touch with special interest groups.

Below we look at a selection of activities that may be of interest to you, but there will be many more where provision will be made for disabled people.

## Reading

### AUDIO BOOKS

Enjoying books can be difficult for some of us who, for whatever reason, cannot use printed material. Audio books are increasingly available in libraries, bookshops and online. The organisations below may also be able to help.

**Bag Books**
1 Stewart's Court, 218-220 Stewart's Road, London SW8 4UB
📞 020 7627 0444
📧 office@bagbooks.org
🌐 www.bagbooks.org
Bag Books produces multi-sensory story packs for people with profound learning disabilities. Originally designed for children, the range now includes titles suitable for teenagers and adults.

**Calibre Audio Library**
Aylesbury HP22 5XQ
📞 01296 43 2339
📧 enquiries@calibre.org.uk
🌐 www.calibre.org.uk
Calibre, a national charity, has a wide range of unabridged books on cassette or MP3 disc for adults and children who are visually impaired or cannot use printed books. Members can order items to borrow either by post or on the internet.

**ClearVision**
Linden Lodge School, 61 Princes Way, London SW19 6JB
📞 020 8789 9575
🌐 www.clearvisionproject.org
ClearVision provides mainstream children's books incorporating Braille, print and pictures that can be shared by visually impaired children and sighted children and adults. Over 13,000 books are available. They are suitable for children learning Braille, or who may do so in the future, but not for partially sighted children learning to read print. Membership is free to families.

**Isis Publishing Ltd**
7 Centremead, Osney Mead, Oxford OX2 0ES
📞 0800 731 5637
📧 sales@isis-publishing.co.uk
🌐 www.isis-publishing.co.uk
Isis is a major audio publisher of unabridged titles on cassette, CD and MP3 formats to direct and internet customers.

**Listening Books**
12 Lant Street, London SE1 1QH
📞 020 7407 9417
📧 info@listening-books.org.uk
🌐 www.listening-books.org.uk
Listening Books offers an audio book service to people for whom holding a book, turning a page or reading in the usual way is not possible.

## Doing Life Differently

Packed with practical advice about ways to do everyday things differently.

Available for free download:
**www.disabilityrightsuk.org**

**RNIB National Library Service**
PO Box 173, Peterborough PE2 6WS
T 0303 123 9999
E library@rnib.org.uk
W www.rnib.org.uk

The Library Service aims to ensure that visually impaired people have the same access to library facilities as sighted people. It offers a lending service with many titles available in electronic form as well as more traditional aural and tactile formats.

## Arts

You can get information on taking part or visiting arts-related activities from a wide range of organisations, some of which are listed below. The internet, radio, local newspapers and notice boards are also good sources of information.

**Arts Council of England**
14 Great Peter Street, London SW1P 3NQ
T 0845 300 6200; textphone 020 7973 6564
W www.artscouncil.org.uk
The Arts Council is responsible for arts funding and development in England and provides information and advice to artists and arts organisations including specific information on access for disabled people.

Elsewhere in the UK contact:
**Arts Council of Northern Ireland**
77 Malone Road, Belfast BT9 6AQ
T 028 9038 5200
E info@artscouncil-ni.org
W www.artscouncil-ni.org

**Creative Scotland**
Waverley Gate, 2-4 Waterloo Place, Edinburgh EH1 3EG
T 0845 603 6000
E enquiries@creativescotland.com
W www.creativescotland.com

**Arts Council of Wales**
Bute Place, Cardiff CF10 5AL
T 0845 873 4900; textphone 029 2045 0123
E info@artswales.org.uk
W www.artswales.org

**Artsline**
c/o 21 Pine Court, Wood Lodge Gardens, Bromley BR1 2WA
T 020 7388 2227 (also textphone)
W www.artsline.org.uk
Artsline provides online information for disabled people on arts and events and activities in and around London. Full access details for London arts and entertainment venues and events are provided.

**Attitude is Everything**
54 Chalton Street, London NW1 1HS
T 020 7383 7979
W www.attitudeiseverything.org.uk
This organisation works with audiences, artists and the music industry to improve deaf and disabled people's access to live music. It promotes a *Charter of Best Practice* to venues and festivals throughout the country.

**Disabled Photographers' Society**
PO Box 85, Longfield, Kent DA3 9BA
E enquiriesw@disabledphotographers.co.uk
W www.disabledphotographers.co.uk
The Society provides information on how you can adapt cameras and other photographic equipment and has access to engineers who can help. It arranges an annual exhibition of members' work and organises occasional photographic holidays and events. They have links with mainstream photographic bodies.

**MAGIC Deaf Arts** is a grouping of 16 of the major museums and art galleries in London. Each provides events and facilities for deaf and hard-of-hearing visitors, including specialist tours and employing sign-language interpreters at public talks and lectures. Visit their website www.magicdeaf.org.uk for a calendar of events.

### Music and the Deaf
The Media Centre, 7 Northumberland Street, Huddersfield HD1 1RL
T 01484 48 3115; textphone 01484 48 3117
W www.matd.org.uk
Music and the Deaf helps deaf people of all ages access music and the performing arts. It provides talks, signed theatre performances and workshops. In West Yorkshire it runs after-school clubs and a Deaf Youth Orchestra. Music and the Deaf also runs training days and collaborative projects with orchestras, opera, theatre and dance companies, and is one of the five lead organisations in Sing-up, a project to promote singing in schools.

### National Theatre
South Bank, London SE1 9PX
T 020 7452 3000
E access@nationaltheatre.org.uk
W www.nationaltheatre.org.uk
The National Theatre aims to be accessible and welcoming to all. Its three auditoriums have allocated wheelchair spaces and assistance dogs are welcome. Blind and visually impaired people can attend audio-described performances and touch tours, and get synopses notes and cast lists on CD or in Braille. Deaf and hearing impaired people can attend captioned performances.

### Nordoff Robbins
2 Lissenden Gardens, London NW5 1PQ
T 020 7267 4496
E musicservices@nordoff-robbins.org.uk
W www.nordoff-robbins.org.uk
A national organisation that seeks to use the power of music to transform the lives of children and adults living with illness, disability, trauma or in isolation. Their trained practitioners work in a range of settings including music therapy, music and health projects and community music schemes as well as the organisation's own centres.

### Shape
Deane House Studios, 27 Greenwood Place, London NW5 1LB
T 020 7424 7330; textphone 020 7424 7368
W www.shapearts.org.uk
Shape offers a range of activities to enable disabled and deaf people to participate and enjoy arts and cultural activities, mainly in the London area.

Shape Tickets is a service offering its members tickets, often at reduced prices, at venues throughout London coupled with access assistance and transport if required.

### Signed Performances In Theatre (SPIT)
6 Thirlmere Drive, Lymm, Cheshire WA13 9PE
W www.spit.org.uk
SPIT promotes BSL interpreted performances in mainstream theatre and provides a link between arts organisations and the Deaf community. Its website includes a directory of signed and captioned performances nationwide.

### STAGETEXT
1st floor, 54 Commercial Street, London E1 6LT
T 020 7377 0540; textphone 020 7247 7801
W www.stagetext.org
STAGETEXT provides access to the theatre for deaf and hard-of-hearing people through captioning. The full text, together with character names, sound effects and off-stage noises, is shown on LED displays as the words are spoken or sung. Around 200 productions are captioned each year in over 80 venues across the UK. Information on forthcoming performances is given on its website.

### VocalEyes
1st floor, 54 Commercial Street, London E1 6LT
T 020 7375 1043
E enquiries@vocaleyes.co.uk
W www.vocaleyes.co.uk
VocalEyes is a national organisation established to provide audio descriptions for performances in the theatre. It now also works in museums, galleries and architectural heritage sites. A programme of forthcoming events is published in print, Braille and on tape as well as on their website.

### Zinc Arts
Great Stony, High Street, Chipping Ongar, Essex CM5 0AD
T 01277 36 5626; textphone 01277 36 5003
E email info@zincarts.org.uk
W www.zincarts.org.uk.
Zinc Arts aims to advance and promote the creativity, culture and heritage of disabled people and other socially excluded groups in Essex and Hertfordshire. It arranges a wide range of programmes.

# Cinemas

Cinemas are becoming more accessible to people with impaired mobility, hearing or sight. The wide scale development of new cinema buildings means improvements with respect to physical access, with at least some screens in multiplexes having spaces for wheelchair users.

A programme is now underway to substantially increase both the number of cinemas equipped to show films with digital subtitles and audio description and the number of films available. Film and venue information can be found at:
Ⓦ www.yourlocalcinema.com

If you are registered blind, receiving disability living allowance or attendance allowance, the Cinema Exhibitors' Association (CEA) offers a national card verifying entitlement to a free ticket for a person accompanying you to the cinema. There is a £5.50 administration charge and the card has to be renewed each year. Application forms are available from participating cinemas or from www.ceacard.co.uk. The CEA card is administered and run by The Card Network, Network House, St Ives Way, Sandycroft CH5 2QS. Telephone 0845 123 1292; textphone 0845 123 1297; email info@ceacard.co.uk.

# Days out

While most modern tourist attractions should be able to cater for all of us, it is advisable to check in advance if you have any specific requirements, if the attraction is large or for particular events.

Sites with a conservation aim, including historic buildings, nature reserves, forests and industrial heritage displays, may have limited access for some of us. However, several organisations have worked to improve facilities for disabled visitors. The following organisations have specialist publications and web pages about their facilities:

**Cadw: Welsh Historic Monuments**
Plas Carew, Unit 5/7 Cefn Coed, Parc Nantgarw, Cardiff CF15 7QQ
Ⓣ 01443 33 6000
Ⓔ cadw@wales.gsi.gov.uk
Ⓦ www.cadw.wales.gov.uk

**English Heritage**
Customer Services Department, Kemble Drive, PO Box 567, Swindon SN2 2YP
Ⓣ 0870 333 1181; textphone 0800 015 0516
Ⓔ customers@english-heritage.org.uk
Ⓦ www.english-heritage.org.uk

**Historic Scotland**
Longmore House, Salisbury Place, Edinburgh EH9 1SH
Ⓣ 0131 668 8600
Ⓦ www.historic-scotland.gov.uk

**The National Trust**
Membership Department, PO Box 39, Warrington WA5 7WD
Ⓣ 0844 800 1895; textphone 0844 800 4410
Ⓔ enquiries@nationaltrust.org.uk
Ⓦ www.nationaltrust.org.uk

**National Trust for Scotland**
Hermiston Quay, 5 Cultins Road, Edinburgh EH11 4DF
Ⓣ 0131 458 0303
Ⓔ information@nts.org.uk
Ⓦ www.nts.org.uk

**Royal Society for the Protection of Birds**
The Lodge, Potton Road, Sandy, Bedfordshire SG19 2DL
Ⓣ 01767 68 0551
Ⓦ www.rspb.org.uk

> www.disabledgo.com provides online access guides including detailed information gathered by personal inspections around the UK at a wide range of entertainment venues, places to visit, restaurants and shops.

## ENJOY AN ACCESSIBLE HOLIDAY IN ENGLAND

England is a country of impressive diversity and variety. From the rolling hills of the Cotswolds and bustling city life of Manchester, to the charms of sleepy Cornish villages and the dramatic coastal splendour of the northeast.

Importantly, England's tourism businesses are making it a top priority to ensure that their facilities and services are more accessible to their visitors. That means that holidays in England, with its plethora of exciting attractions and rich variety of accommodation, are becoming easier for everyone.

VisitEngland's National Accessible Scheme (NAS) is a way of highlighting those accommodation providers that have improved their accessibility, making England that much easier for everyone to enjoy. Scheme participant Hoe Grange Holidays is a group of beautiful Four Star Gold self-catering cabins on the edge of the Peak District National Park whose owners are dedicated to making their accommodation not only accessible but also horse friendly!

Other venues we commend for their excellent accessibility include Sandcastle Waterpark in Blackpool, which has ramps, wide gangways, lifts, induction loops, showerchairs and even pool accessible wheelchairs, so you can get busy making a splash!

The Leicester Theatre Trust create awe-inspiring theatre for all. A variety of assisted performances are staged at The Curve theatre, where touch tours, care for assistance dogs and audio guides are just some of the services provided.

Finally, at the Great North Museum: Hancock you'll find an interactive model of Hadrian's Wall, dinosaur replicas, Egyptian mummies, a planetarium and much more! Notably, the museum's redevelopment has allowed for excellent physical access and excellent services for hearing and visually impaired visitors.

All of VisitEngland's star-rated accommodation and quality-assured attractions can provide visitors with information about their facilities and services in the form of an Access Statement to help you 'know before you go'. So if you're hoping to know a bit more about the availability of subtitles on televisions or the number of steps to the front door, feel free to ask to see the access statement before you travel.

You can discover accessible accommodation, places to go and find information on transport, accessible toilets and more on:

www.visitengland.com/
accessforall

VisitEngland

## Shopping

While some people find going to the shops a chore, for many going shopping or looking round the shops is a leisure activity. The growth of purpose-built shopping centres has made things easier for many of us.

Shopmobility Schemes provide wheelchairs and scooters for hire and use in many shopping, leisure and commercial facilities throughout the UK. Some schemes provide children's wheelchairs, escorts or special services for people visiting their area.

You can find your nearest Shopmobility scheme on their online directory. You will need to contact a specific scheme to make equipment bookings or find out detailed information.

**National Federation of Shopmobility**
PO Box 6641, Christchurch BH23 9DQ
📞 0844 414 1850
📧 info@shopmobilityuk.org
🌐 www.shopmobilityuk.org

IF ONLY I'D KNOWN THAT A YEAR AGO ...

# Adult education

You may want to learn more about a subject for your own personal interest or to attain or improve vocational skills.

Day or evening courses are offered in specialist adult education centres, schools, colleges or other community premises.

There are courses specifically for disabled students but it is increasingly possible to participate in mainstream courses. Prospectuses provide basic information for disabled people and a named contact if you want to know more.

Most adult courses are organised by adult education colleges but there are a variety of other providers including university extra-mural departments.

## Adult Residential Colleges Association (ARCA)
6 Bath Road, Felixstowe IP11 7JW
Ⓦ www.arca.uk.net
This association of small colleges specialises in short-stay residential courses for the general public. Each college has its own programme of weekend, midweek and day courses, and some offer summer schools and courses leading to recognised qualifications. A range of accommodation is available and most dietary needs can be catered for. Many of the colleges have facilities for disabled people. Check individual requirements before booking.

## University of the Third Age (U3A)
Old Municipal Buildings, 19 East Street, Bromley BR1 1QE
Ⓣ 020 8466 6139
Ⓦ www.u3a.org.uk
U3A promotes autonomous local learning groups for people no longer in full-time employment. There are almost 750 independent local U3A groups in the UK with over 259,000 members.

## Workers' Educational Association (WEA)
4 Luke Street, London EC2A 4XW
Ⓣ 020 7426 3450
Ⓔ national@wea.org.uk
Ⓦ www.wea.org.uk
The WEA is a major national voluntary adult education organisation providing over 10,000 courses a year, mainly arranged through local branches.

Around the UK contact:

## WEA Northern Ireland
3 Fitzwilliam Street, Belfast BT9 6AW
Ⓣ 028 9032 9718
Ⓦ www.wea-ni.com

## WEA Scottish Association
Riddles Court, 322 Lawnmarket, Edinburgh EH1 2PG
Ⓣ 0131 226 3456
Ⓔ hq@weascotland.org.uk
Ⓦ www.weascotland.org.uk

## WEA South Wales
7 Coopers Yard, Curren Road, Cardiff CF10 5NB
Ⓣ 029 2023 5277
Ⓔ weasw@weascotland.org.uk
Ⓦ www.weasouthwales.org.uk

## WEA North Wales
Coleg Harlech, Harlech, Gwynedd LL46 2PU
Ⓣ Residential courses 01766 78 1900
   Community courses 01248 35 3254
Ⓦ www.harlech.ac.uk

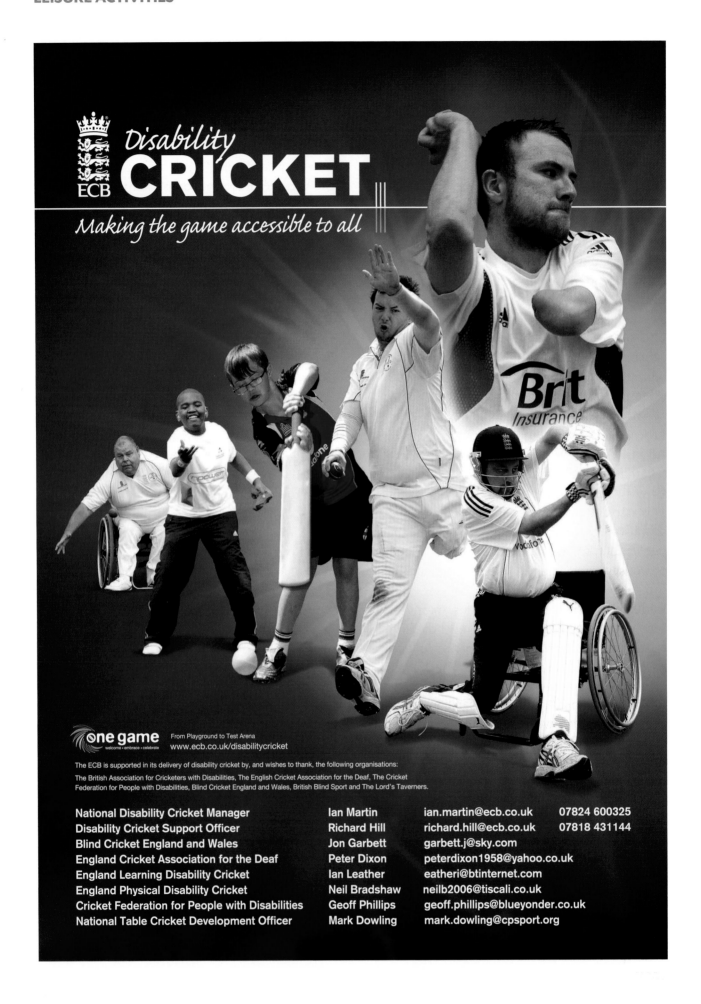

Disability **CRICKET**

*Making the game accessible to all*

**one game**
welcome • embrace • celebrate
From Playground to Test Arena
www.ecb.co.uk/disabilitycricket

The ECB is supported in its delivery of disability cricket by, and wishes to thank, the following organisations:

The British Association for Cricketers with Disabilities, The English Cricket Association for the Deaf, The Cricket Federation for People with Disabilities, Blind Cricket England and Wales, British Blind Sport and The Lord's Taverners.

| | | | |
|---|---|---|---|
| **National Disability Cricket Manager** | **Ian Martin** | ian.martin@ecb.co.uk | **07824 600325** |
| **Disability Cricket Support Officer** | **Richard Hill** | richard.hill@ecb.co.uk | **07818 431144** |
| **Blind Cricket England and Wales** | **Jon Garbett** | garbett.j@sky.com | |
| **England Cricket Association for the Deaf** | **Peter Dixon** | peterdixon1958@yahoo.co.uk | |
| **England Learning Disability Cricket** | **Ian Leather** | eatheri@btinternet.com | |
| **England Physical Disability Cricket** | **Neil Bradshaw** | neilb2006@tiscali.co.uk | |
| **Cricket Federation for People with Disabilities** | **Geoff Phillips** | geoff.phillips@blueyonder.co.uk | |
| **National Table Cricket Development Officer** | **Mark Dowling** | mark.dowling@cpsport.org | |

IF ONLY I'D KNOWN THAT A YEAR AGO ...

# Sport

There are a multitude of organisations concerned with sporting provision for disabled people. They may be local or national, concerned with one sport or many, cater solely for disabled people or be involved with promoting inclusive activities.

In some areas local organisations have been formed to provide a range of sporting and other recreational activities for disabled people. They may use premises owned by the local council or other bodies but a number have their own purpose-built centres.

Specialist organisations often have an important role in introducing people to sport and for those wishing to be involved in competitions. 'Taster' sessions, which give us an opportunity to try a range of activities, are often arranged locally at local sports or leisure centres.

## GENERAL INFORMATION

For information on facilities and sporting groups in your local area, contact the local authority sports or leisure department. The following organisations may also be able to point you in the right direction.

**English Federation of Disability Sport (EFDS)**
Sport Park, Loughborough University, 3 Oakwood Drive, Loughborough LE11 3QF
☏ 01509 22 7750
Ⓦ www.efds.co.uk
EFDS is an umbrella group of disability sports organisations that works with policy makers and mainstream sports governing bodies to develop opportunities for disabled people to become more involved as competitors, recreational participants, administrators, officials and coaches. It seeks to create greater co-operation between disability sports organisations and works with the following national disability sports organisations that are recognised by Sport England: BALASA (British Amputee & Les Autres Sports Association), British Blind Sport, CP Sport, Dwarf Athletics, Mencap Sport, Special Olympics, UK Deaf Sport and WheelPower – British Wheelchair Sport.

**British Paralympics Association (BPA)**
60 Charlotte Street, London W1T 2NU
☏ 020 7842 5789
Ⓔ info@paralympics.org.uk
Ⓦ www.paralympics.org.uk
Aside from being the representative organisation for elite paralympians, the BPA also provides Parasport, which has been designed to inspire, educate, inform and signpost disabled people, and those interested in disability sport, to high-quality opportunities. Parasport aims to help us find our personal best. You can access it via the website.

**www.activeplaces.com** is a database giving details of over 50,000 public and private sports facilities in England including activities available, charges, membership and accessibility for disabled people.

**Disability Sport Northern Ireland,**
Adelaide House, Falcon Road, Belfast BT12 6SJ
☏ 028 9038 7062; textphone 028 9038 7064
Ⓦ www.dsni.co.uk

**Scottish Disability Sport**
Caledonia House, South Gyle, Edinburgh EH12 9DQ
☏ 0131 317 1130
Ⓔ admin@scottishdisabilitysport.com
Ⓦ www.scottishdisabilitysport.com

**Disability Sport Wales**
Sport Wales National Centre, Sophia Gardens, Cardiff CF11 9SW
☏ 0845 846 0021
Ⓔ office@fdsw.org.uk
Ⓦ www.disabilitysportwales.org

For more information, read Disability Rights UK's guide *Doing Sport Differently*, a comprehensive guide to accessing sporting and leisure activities. Generously sponsored by VISA, the guide covers a wide range of sport and fitness activities from rambling to archery. Visit www.disabilityrightsuk.org to download a free copy.

# SportsAble

The Disability Sports Club in Maidenhead, Berkshire

SportsAble is a unique sports disability charity, dedicated to the promotion of awareness of disability through sport and recreational activity – and the integration of disabled and able-bodied people.

Find out more at www.sportsable.co.uk

IF ONLY I'D KNOWN THAT A YEAR AGO ...

## Sportsable

Braywick Sports Ground, Maidenhead SL6 1BN

**T** 01628 62 7690

**E** info@sportsable.co.uk

Sportsable promotes awareness of disability through sport and recreation and integration of disabled and non-disabled people. They run a sports club providing facilities for disabled people in Maidenhead. They also introduce sport to disabled people in the community through outreach programmes with schools, sports and social clubs.

## SPECIFIC SPORTING ACTIVITIES

The following are just some of the organisations and projects concerned with helping us take part in specific sporting activities.

### British Disabled Angling Association (BDAA)

9 Yew Tree Road, Delves, Walsall WS5 4NQ

**T** 01922 86 0912

**W** www.bdaa.co.uk

Represents disabled anglers across UK, including coarse, sea, specimen and game fishing. Services include: courses, group development, access audits of fishing areas, training people to coach disabled people and disability awareness training.

### Disability Snowsport UK

Glenmore Grounds, Aviemore PH22 1RB

**T** 01479 86 1272

**E** admin@disabilitysnowsport.org.uk

**W** www.disabilitysnowsport.org.uk

Offers ski instruction at a purpose-built adaptive ski school at Cairngorm and at ski slopes around the country. Activity weeks are held in Europe and North America.

### Inclusive Fitness Initiative (IFI)

Sport Park, Loughborough University, 3 Oakwood Drive, Loughborough LE11 3QF

**T** 01509 22 7750

**E** ifi@efds.co.uk

**W** www.efds.co.uk

Launched by the English Federation for Disability Sport, IFI promotes the provision and management of integrated facilities for disabled people in general fitness centres. It accredits venues that provide accessible facilities, inclusive fitness equipment, appropriate staff straining and inclusive marketing.

## RYA Sailability

RYA House, Ensign Way, Hamble, Southampton SO31 4YA

**T** 0844 556 9550

**E** sailability@rya.org.uk

**W** www.rya.org.uk/sailability

RYA Sailability promotes and co-ordinates participation by disabled people in the sailing community. It provides information to individuals on where they can sail and supports sailing centres and clubs in improving opportunities for disabled people.

## SPECTATOR FACILITIES

The creation of new and enlarged stadiums, the greater awareness of the needs of our access needs and the impact of regulations has led to improved facilities for disabled spectators in many places. At many football grounds for example, audio commentary is available for visually impaired supporters and many race courses now have raised platforms for wheelchair users.

There are still, however, limitations so it is always worth contacting venues in advance to find out about accessible facilities or to ask about a particular facility or service. Access information for many venues can also be found by contacting:

### Event Mobility Charitable Trust

8 Bayliss Road, Kemerton, Tewkesbury GL20 7JH

**T** 01386 72 5391

**E** info@eventmobility.org.uk

**W** www.eventmobility.org.uk

Some events are problematic for us to attend because they extend over a large area or the facilities for spectators are temporary. Event Mobility provides powered scooters and wheelchairs at a range of events including agricultural and countryside shows, major golf championships and horse shows. Bookings need to be made in advance. A donation is requested (£18 for scooters and £10 for manual wheelchairs). Visit the website for a list of events that will provide the service or send a stamped addressed envelope to the address above.

IF ONLY I'D KNOWN THAT A YEAR AGO ...

**Level Playing Field**
The Meridian, 4 Copthall House, Station Square, Coventry CV1 2FL
☏ 0845 230 6237
📧 info@levelplayingfield.org.uk
🌐 www.levelplayingfield.org.uk

Level Playing Field promotes good facilities for disabled spectators at sports grounds. They have links with Disabled Supporters Associations at many clubs and their website includes information on facilities for disabled fans at grounds around the country.

## Other activities

It would be hard to find any form of leisure activity that does not have an organisation dedicated to it. Many are devoted to encouraging the participation of disabled people:

**Motorsport Endeavour**
123 Ealing Village, London W5 2EB
☏ 020 8991 2358
📧 info@motorsportendeavour.com
🌐 www.motorsportendeavour.com
Motorsport Endeavour runs events involving disabled people in all forms of motorsport. A wide-ranging programme includes rallies, karting and visits to motorsport venues. The club is open to drivers as well as people wishing to take other roles such as navigators, marshals, timekeepers and spectators. Motorsport Endeavour is also establishing links for disabled people who are seeking employment in the motorsport industry.

**Thrive**
The Geoffrey Udall Centre, Beech Hill, Reading RG7 2AT
☏ 0118 988 5688
📧 info@thrive.org.uk
🌐 www.thrive.org.uk
Thrive's aim is to improve the lives of elderly and disabled people through gardening and horticulture. It runs demonstration gardens, supports a network of community and therapeutic gardening projects and runs an extensive programme of training courses. It runs the **Blind Gardeners' Club** and produces publications and factsheets offering practical advice on many gardening topics. Their website (www.carryongardening.co.uk) provides information about equipment and techniques to make gardening easier.

www.accessiblegardens.org.uk, which launched in April 2011 has a directory of gardens with accessibility reviews written by people with disabilities. The site also has articles about people, organisations and schools involved with gardens.

**The Wheelyboat Trust**
North Lodge, Burton Park, Petworth GU28 0JT
☏ 01798 34 2222
📧 info@wheelyboats.org
🌐 www.wheelyboats.org
The Trust places specially designed Wheelyboats on lakes and other waters in all parts of the British Isles where they can be used for fishing, bird-watching or other activities. The boats have a bow door which lowers to form a boarding ramp and the open level deck provides access throughout. For a list of locations, ring or visit the website.

### MOUNTAIN TRIKE

**The all-terrain wheelchair company**
With a conventional wheelchair, the smallest everyday journey or outdoor activity can seem daunting. The Mountain Trike gives riders the freedom to go to places that were previously inaccessible, whilst maintaining the function and versatility of a standard wheelchair. Venture out around town, into the countryside, to the beach, down muddy tracks, over grass or along cobbled streets, gravel driveways and even through snow.

Email: info@mountaintrike.co.uk
Tel: 07969 097 166 or 07816 955 945

**www.mountaintrike.co.uk**

IF ONLY I'D KNOWN THAT A YEAR AGO ...

# Health services

**We need to use health services just like everyone else – for anything from flu to advice on quitting smoking. We may also need to use the health service for specific impairments – for instance, we may use a spinal injury unit or we might need radiotherapy for cancer. This chapter describes how to access health services and explains upcoming changes.**

## General information

### PLANNED CHANGES

The government is making radical changes to the way the NHS works. These changes are embodied in the Health and Social Care Act 2012. The changes will directly affect the provision of NHS services to patients. Part of the government's plan will see teams of local general practitioners (GPs) take over the commissioning of healthcare; that means they will hold a budget and purchase most health services for their patients. For details visit:
Ⓦ www.dh.gov.uk

### YOUR RIGHTS

Health service providers have responsibilities under the Equality Act 2010. We have the right to ask for and receive, without question, any particular provision that we need for impairment-related reasons, such as:

- large print information about medicines, surgical intervention, treatments, etc
- a longer appointment time to help you fully understand what's under discussion
- fully accessible premises for your appointment or treatment
- equal access – for example, as much access to regular screening services as anyone else.

The NHS Constitution sets out our rights as an NHS patient. These rights cover how we access health services, the quality of care we receive, the treatments and programmes available to us, confidentiality, information and our right to complain if things go wrong. For more information or to download a copy of the Constitution, go to:
Ⓦ www.nhs.uk/choiceinthenhs/
  rightsandpledges/nhsconstitution/
  pages/overview.aspx

### LOCAL HEALTH SERVICES

**Primary care services**

Primary care services are managed by local primary care trusts, which work with local authorities and other agencies that provide health and social care. NHS walk-in centres and the NHS Direct telephone service are also part of primary care.

For information about all these services, visit the NHS Choices website:
Ⓦ www.nhs.uk

Primary care trusts are to be abolished from April 2013 and information about primary care services will then be held by local offices of the NHS Commissioning Board.

**General practitioners (GPs)**

GP surgeries provide a wide range of family health services, including:

- advice on health problems
- vaccinations
- examinations and treatment
- prescriptions for medicines
- referrals to hospital and other healthcare and social services.

Your surgery should be able to offer you an appointment to see a GP or other healthcare professional quickly if necessary. However, if it's more convenient, you should also be able to book appointments in advance.

You can ask for a home visit if you are unable to get to the surgery for a medical reason.

You can register with any GP practice that will accept you and you can change GP practice without giving a reason. In England, a list of GP practices in your area can be obtained from your primary care trust or online at NHS Choices by entering your postcode:

Ⓦ www.nhs.uk/servicedirectories/
   Pages/ServiceSearch.aspx?ServiceType=GP

If you have difficulty finding a GP or if you have been refused entry to a GP list or been removed from a list you should contact your primary care trust. In Scotland and Wales, you should contact your local health board.

In some areas, GP practices work from larger health centres that offer a wider range of services. A GP may refer patients to other services provided in the community including health visitors, community nurses, occupational health practitioners, physiotherapists or, in some practices, employment advisers. Health visitors are specialist nurses employed to give advice and assistance on family and infant health and associated issues. Community nurses visit people at home to give nursing care, such as changing dressings, and to assist with the provision of home nursing equipment.

Employment advice is increasingly being offered in primary care to people who are out of work because of ill-health and who need support and advice to get back into employment.

If you are off work, your GP will write a 'fit note' saying when you will be fit for work and what work you can do. The fit note allows your GP to provide more information on how your condition affects your ability to work. This will help your employer to understand how they might help you return to work sooner or stay in work. More information is on the NHS Choices website:

Ⓦ www.nhs.uk/chq/Pages/2584.aspx

Your GP can refer you for 'talking treatment' (free on the NHS). This will usually be a short course of counselling or a set number of sessions of cognitive behavioural therapy (CBT), which can be helpful for depression and other mental health issues. If counselling or CBT are not available at the surgery, your GP can refer you to a local counsellor or therapist for NHS treatment.

### NHS walk-in centres

These 90 or so centres offer a range of treatments for minor illnesses and injuries. You don't need an appointment and many are open 365 days a year and outside office hours. They are not designed for treating long-term conditions or immediately life-threatening problems. Many centres provide a face-to-face service similar to NHS Direct.

You can find the location of walk-in centres at NHS Choices:

Ⓦ www.nhs.uk

There are minor injuries units in some areas to treat non-serious injuries such as sprains, breaks, cuts, burns and bites. Accident and Emergency departments deal with more immediately life-threatening conditions.

### NHS Direct

NHS Direct is a 24-hour nurse-led advice and information service. It provides information on:

- what to do if you or a member of your family feel ill
- particular health conditions
- local healthcare services including doctors, dentists and late opening pharmacies
- self-help and support organisations.

NHS Direct is currently rebranding and becoming NHS 111. The number is freephone and now active in most parts of the UK – just dial 111. If your area has not switched to 111 yet, call:

### NHS Direct for England and Wales
Ⓣ Helpline 0845 4647
   Textphone 0845 606 4647
Ⓦ www.nhsdirect.nhs.uk

### NHS24 for Scotland
Ⓣ 0845 424 2424
Ⓦ www.nhs24.com

### Wales
Ⓦ www.wales.nhs.uk

### Northern Ireland
Ⓦ www.hscni.net

# Advice, information and involvement in health services

## ACCESS TO HEALTH RECORDS

You have the right to see your health records (except in highly unusual circumstances), under the Access to Health Records Act 1990 and the Data Protection Act 1998. If you do wish to see them, ask your doctor.

Sometimes your clinician will share information with other health professionals who need to know in order to be involved in your healthcare. But otherwise, information about your health is confidential and no one involved in your care and treatment should pass on information without your consent.

In very rare circumstances, doctors may be required by law to share information with the police or other public bodies, for instance if there is a major risk to someone's life or health.

## SHARED DECISION-MAKING

When you talk to a doctor, nurse or other health professional about your health or care, any decision about what to do should be shared. What that means is:

* sharing information: what you know about your own condition, what the professional knows about the condition and about what's possible
* agreeing what to do – not just being told
* writing down what's going to happen next.

> **The King's Fund** publication *Making shared decision-making a reality: No decision about me, without me* describes what shared decision-making means in practice. Download or order a printed copy from: www.kingsfund.org.uk/publications/nhs_decisionmaking.html

## USEFUL CONTACTS

**NHS Choices**

Ⓦ www.nhs.uk

The NHS Choices website provides information on many different health conditions and services. It is designed to give people as much information as possible to make health choices.

**Patient Advocacy and Liaison Service (PALS)**

Ⓦ www.pals.nhs.uk

In England, each NHS Trust area or hospital has a PALS unit that can advise and support you with any concerns you have about local health services. For information on your local PALS ask your GP, health centre, clinic or hospital, ring NHS Direct or visit their website.

**The King's Fund**

11-13 Cavendish Square, London W1G 0AN

Ⓣ 020 7307 2400

Ⓔ enquiry@kingsfund.org.uk

Ⓦ www.kingsfund.org.uk

The King's Fund seeks to understand how the health system in England can be improved. It helps to shape policy, transform services and bring about behaviour change. Its work includes research, analysis, leadership development and service improvement. It organises conferences and events and produces a wide range of resources to help everyone working in health to share knowledge, learning and ideas.

**Local Involvement Networks (LINks)**

Ⓦ www.nhs.uk

If you want to get involved in helping to shape local health and social care services you can contact LINks. These organisations, independent of both the NHS and local authorities, bring together people from disability and community groups and residents of the area to feed into the planning of health and social care. You can find contacts for the LINks in your area on the NHS Choices website.

LINks will progressively be replaced over the next few years by local Health Watch organisations, run in partnership with the NHS and local authorities. Some Health Watch bodies are already up and running, for example, in Kent.

**The Patients Association**

Ⓣ 0845 608 4455

Ⓔ helpline@patients-association.com

The Patients Association helpline informs patients and gathers their views. They also produce booklets and guides for patients.

## Complaints

If you want to complain about healthcare you have been given, you should first give the provider – eg the GP, the hospital, the community provider – the opportunity to resolve your complaint. Disputes can often be settled amicably.

All NHS organisations should have an official complaints procedure. Information will be available from the appropriate PALS office, a local Citizens Advice Bureau or ICAS (Independent Complaints Advocacy Service).

If you go through the procedure but still don't feel your complaint has been properly dealt with, you can contact the Parliamentary and Health Service Ombudsman. The Ombudsman is independent of both the government and the NHS.

**Parliamentary and Health Service Ombudsman**
📞 0345 015 4033
🌐 www.ombudsman.org.uk
If you think an NHS practitioner or social care employee has been guilty of professional misconduct, you can complain to their professional or regulatory body.

The purpose of the professional regulators is to protect and promote the safety of the public. They do this by setting standards of behaviour, education and ethics that health professionals must meet.

Regulators register health professionals who are fit to practise in the UK, and can remove a professional from the register and stop them from practising if it's in the interests of public safety. They deal with concerns about professionals who are unfit to practise due to poor health, misconduct or poor performance.

Details of how to contact the 13 health and social care professional regulators are available from the General Medical Council (available in English and 12 other languages).

**General Medical Council**
Regent's Place, 350 Euston Road, London NW1 3JN
📞 0845 357 3456
✉ gmc@gmc-uk.org
🌐 www.gmc-uk.org

## Help with costs

Some aspects of healthcare that are normally charged for, such as prescriptions (see a more in-depth discussion later in this chapter) and eyesight or dental examinations, are free for certain groups including: children, people over 60, people with certain medical conditions, pregnant women, people with a war disablement pension and people receiving some income-related benefits.

The NHS Low Income Scheme provides help to people who are not exempt from charges but who may be entitled to full or partial help if they have a low income, or if they are waiting for a benefit claim to be decided. You can claim for an exemption certificate before you need treatment and so can budget accordingly.

However, if you've already paid for something, you can apply for a refund at the same time as you apply for a certificate. You will need to fill in form HC11, which is available from a Jobcentre Plus office or hospital or online.

Full details are given in the NHS booklet *Help with health costs*, which is widely available.

The NHS Low Income Scheme covers:
- NHS prescriptions
- NHS dental treatment
- sight tests, glasses and contact lenses
- travel to receive NHS treatment
- NHS wigs and fabric supports.

# Continuing healthcare

Many of us living with ill-health, injury or disability get a direct payment from our local authority to pay for the care we need. With direct payments, we can manage our own care needs and become more independent.

People who do not get direct payments, continue to rely on social care to provide services directly.

If health-related needs become paramount, the local authority may ask the NHS to support or take over your care package. This is known as 'continuing care'. It's provided by your local primary care trust (PCT). PCTs will employ a lead manager responsible for providing and managing your care package.

You will need an assessment to migrate from a local authority package to NHS care. The assessment determines what proportion of your care needs should be met by the NHS.

Care provided by the NHS is free at the point of delivery and unlike local authority care, NHS care is not means tested. So there may be a financial advantage in moving to continuing care if it's appropriate for you.

Changes being piloted in the NHS will allow recipients of direct payments to migrate their current package of care across to continuing care if the care is assessed as wholly health related. For information see the 'Social care' chapter.

# Going into and leaving hospital

## BENEFITS

Going into hospital as an inpatient may affect your benefits. Some benefits (for example, attendance allowance or disability living allowance) can be stopped after you've been in hospital for a few weeks, while other means-tested benefits may be reduced. Let the offices dealing with your benefits know if you are going into hospital and how long you are likely to stay.

## ONGOING CARE AND SUPPORT

If you need ongoing care and support, you shouldn't be discharged from hospital until proper arrangements and a care plan are in place to ensure you can return home safely without being put at risk of harm. Discharge planning should start early and should involve you and, if you want, your family and carers. The NHS and local authorities should work together to ensure this happens. Don't agree to be discharged unless you're happy with the care plan in place.

In some areas there are voluntary services that provide practical support to people coming home from hospital. Ask your hospital or healthcare professional what might be available.

Don't agree to go into a residential home, if this is suggested, if you're not happy to. It can sometimes be difficult for people to get out of a care home once they've gone in.

If you have been kept in a psychiatric hospital under the Mental Health Act you are entitled to free aftercare and support when you leave.

### Short periods of support
If you need a short period of intensive support and rehabilitation to regain your independence on leaving hospital you may get 'intermediate care' (called 'six-week support for vulnerable people' in Wales). Intermediate care is free and can last up to six weeks. You should have an assessment to see what ongoing support you need.

### Longer periods of care
If you need care for a longer period, or indefinitely, the NHS may put in place a care package for you. This is similar to care packages provided by social services through a local authority and is called 'continuing care' (see above). This care could be provided directly or you may be given an individual budget (see the 'Social care' chapter) which enables you to make your own decisions about your support and services.

# àdams
## neuro physio

Your resource for Experienced Community-Based
Neuro Physiotherapists

Contact the Director, Nikki Adams

On **0795 2273521**

www.adamsneurophysio.org.uk
n.adams@blueyonder.co.uk

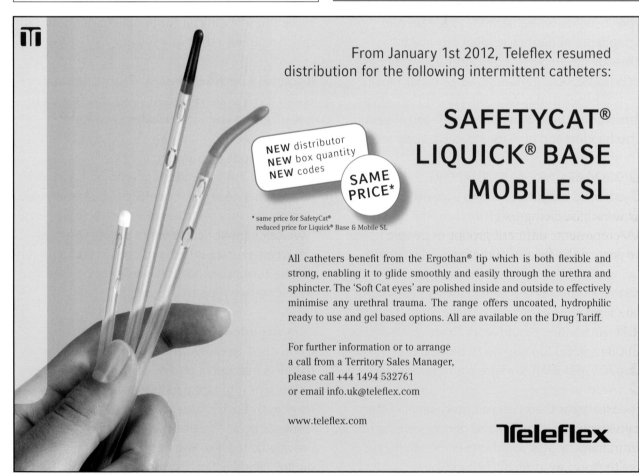

# Other therapies and treatment services

### AUDIOLOGY AND HEARING AID SERVICES

Hearing therapists provide advice, support and help to anyone with a hearing problem. They can show people how to get the best from their remaining hearing. Referrals are often made after attending an ear, nose and throat department (ENT) or Hearing Aid Clinic.

The NHS hearing aid service is free and includes testing, fitting and servicing. Your GP can refer you to a hospital ENT or an audiology department. After you have been assessed, an appropriate hearing aid is chosen and you will be given advice on how to use it most effectively.

Hearing aids can be bought privately from a registered hearing aid dispenser. This may be quicker and more convenient, although more expensive, than using the NHS.

A simple five-minute hearing check is available online at the **Action on Hearing Loss** website (www.actiononhearingloss.org.uk) or by ringing 0844 800 3838. Or you can talk to one of the Action on Hearing Loss help team on 0808 808 0123.

**British Academy of Audiology (BAA)**
Chester House, 68 Chestergate, Macclesfield, Cheshire SK11 6DY
☎ 01625 66 4545
✉ admin@baaudiology.org
🌐 www.baaudiology.org
BAA represents different groups of people working in the field of audiology.

**Health & Care Professions Council**
Park House, 184 Kennington Park Road, London SE11 4BU
☎ 0845 300 6184
🖶 020 7820 9684
🌐 www.hpc-uk.org
The Health & Care Professions Council keeps a register of professionals who meet its standards for training, professional skills, behaviour and health. You can complain to the Council about hearing aid dispensers or other health and care professionals on the register.

### CHIROPODY

Chiropody (also called podiatry) concerns the care of feet. People with conditions such as poor circulation or diabetes frequently need foot care. Elderly people can find their mobility enhanced by treatment, as can people with foot deformities. Disabled people, children, pregnant women and pensioners are entitled to free treatment under the NHS. Most chiropodists/podiatrists will treat people at home if they are unable to get to a clinic.

Chiropody is available privately but if you want NHS treatment, first see your GP, practice nurse or health visitor. They can refer you to an NHS chiropodist. Chiropody is available on the NHS free of charge in most parts of the UK, although whether or not you receive free treatment will depend on how serious your condition is and how quickly it needs to be treated.

**The Society of Chiropodists and Podiatrists**
1 Fellmonger's Path, Tower Bridge Road, London SE1 3LY
☎ 020 7234 8620
🌐 www.feetforlife.org
This professional body can advise on finding a chiropodist in your area. Its website provides information on foot care.

### PRESCRIPTION FOOTWEAR

We offer sophisticated video gait analysis and bio-mechanical assessments, including plantar pressure mapping and electronic in-shoe pressure measurement. This supports the existing footwear and lower limb orthotic service for people with conditions such as arthritis, diabetes, foot deformities and general conditions related to ageing. A full podiatry/chiropody service is also available.

For more information or to book an appointment ring 01243 55 4407 or email info@prescriptionfootwear.co.uk.

**www.prescriptionfootwear.co.uk**

## TELEFLEX

Teleflex is a global provider of medical devices used in hospital and home care. We serve healthcare providers in more than 130 countries with specialty devices for vascular access, general/regional anaesthesia, urology, respiratory, cardiac, surgery and the home care environment. Teleflex also provides products and services for device manufacturers.

### Continence care solutions

Teleflex is committed to making life easier and more manageable for people who use intermittent and Foley catheters as their method of bladder control. We have developed a broad portfolio of urinary catheters and collection products to meet patient needs and to offer clinical solutions. For specific information on intermittent catheters or to order your free samples go to www.intermittent-catheters.co.uk.

### Homecare delivery solution

In addition to quality products, we offer a discreet, complimentary and confidential delivery service, delivering your prescription items directly to your home at a time that is convenient to you. This service is provided by an independent organisation with experience and expertise spanning many different clinical and product areas. So they understand your needs, which, in turn, means they will provide you with an excellent home service.

For more information go to the following website and click on the Home Delivery tab: **www.intermittent-catheters.co.uk**.

To contact Teleflex in relation to any of our products and services, call our friendly customer service team on 01494 532 761 or email info.uk@teleflex.com.

Teleflex, St Mary's Court,
Old Amersham,
Bucks HP7 0UT.

**www.teleflex.com**

**Teleflex**

## CONTINENCE

It has been estimated that nearly three-quarters of us will have bladder or bowel problems at some stage in our lives.

There are many causes of incontinence. Most areas have a continence service with specialist advisers. Your GP can advise about diagnosis and treatment and if necessary refer you to a specialist.

There are many straightforward ways of managing incontinence. A continence adviser or community nurse can talk to you about options. The availability of equipment on the NHS varies from area to area: some equipment may be free, some available on prescription and some may have to be bought privately. A laundry service or waste collection service for disposable products may be available.

Advice and support is also available from:

**Bladder and Bowel Foundation (B&BF)**
SATRA Innovation Park, Rockingham Road, Kettering NN16 9JH
☎ 0870 770 3246 or 0800 011 4623
✉ info@bladderandbowelfoundation.org
🌐 www.bladderandbowelfoundation.org

**ERIC (Education and Resources for Improving Childhood continence)**
34 Old School House, Britannia Road, Kingswood, Bristol BS15 8DB
☎ 0117 301 2100 or 0845 370 8008
✉ info@eric.org.uk
🌐 www.eric.org.uk

**www.lofric.co.uk** is a useful resource for people with urinary problems and bladder disorders. Developed by Astra Tech, it provides information and advice on intermittent self-catheterisation.

**PromoCon Information Service**
Redbank House, St Chad's Street, Cheetham, Manchester M8 8QA
☎ 0161 607 8219
✉ Promocon@disabledliving.co.uk
🌐 www.promocon.co.uk

**The Cystitis & Overactive Bladder Foundation**
946 Bristol Road South, Northfield, Birmingham
B31 2LQ
☎ 0121 702 0820
🅔 info@cobfoundation.org
🅦 www.cobfoundation.org

DENTAL SERVICES
All treatment that is necessary in your dentist's opinion to protect and maintain good oral health is available on the NHS. This means the NHS provides any treatment you need to keep your mouth, teeth and gums healthy and free of pain, including dentures, crowns and bridges.

Dental implants and orthodontic treatment, such as braces, are available on the NHS, but only if there's a medical need for the treatment.

Everyone should be able to access NHS dental services. There is no need to register with a dentist. Simply find a practice that's convenient for you, whether it's near your home or work, and ring them to see if any appointments are available. Remember to ask if the practice provides NHS services.

To find a dentist, you can:
• search on NHS Choices for a dentist near you
• text 'dentist' to 64746 or NHSGO from your mobile phone – you will be sent up to three text messages with details of dentists near you
• ring NHS Direct on 0845 4647.

If the dental practice you first contact is full or does not provide NHS treatment, this doesn't mean that NHS dental care is not available locally. Contact your local primary care trust and ask for the dental access helpline. They are required to commission services to meet the needs of their local population, for both urgent and routine dental care.

There is a high demand for NHS dentists in some areas, and you may have to join a waiting list. You can do that by contacting the primary care trust. You'll be contacted as soon as an appointment is available.

If you are unable to visit a dentist, some general dental practitioners will treat you at home. Community dental services should provide treatment for people who cannot use general dental services. Information can be obtained from your local primary care trust.

Dentistry is one of very few NHS services you usually have to pay for. Depending on what you need to have done, you should only ever be asked to pay one charge for each complete course of treatment, even if you need to visit your dentist more than once to finish it. You will not be charged for individual items within the course of treatment.

There are three standard charges for all NHS dental treatments:
• **Band 1** – £17.50
  This course of treatment covers an examination, diagnosis (including x-rays), advice on how to prevent future problems, a scale and polish if needed, and application of fluoride varnish or fissure sealant.
• **Band 2**– £48
  This course of treatment covers everything listed in Band 1 above, plus further treatment such as fillings, root canal work or removal of teeth.
• **Band 3**– £209
  This course of treatment covers everything listed in Bands 1 and 2 above, plus crowns, dentures and bridges.

If your dentist says you need a particular type of treatment, you should not be asked to pay for it privately. You can find out what's available on the NHS on the NHS Choices website.

You do not have to pay for NHS dental treatment if, when the treatment starts, you are:
• aged under 18
• under 19 and in full-time education
• pregnant or have had a baby in the previous 12 months
• staying in an NHS hospital and your treatment is carried out by the hospital dentist
• an NHS hospital dental service outpatient (however, you may have to pay for dentures or bridges).

You also do not have to pay if, when the treatment starts, any of the following situations apply:
- you are receiving income support, income-related employment and support allowance, income-based jobseeker's allowance or guarantee pension credit
- you are named on a valid NHS tax credit exemption certificate or you are entitled to an NHS tax credit exemption certificate
- you are named on a valid HC2 certificate.

## OCCUPATIONAL THERAPY
Occupational therapists (OTs) provide practical advice and support on maintaining your independence. They can assess your ability to undertake everyday activities such as bathing, dressing and getting around, and can advise on suitable home adaptations and equipment. OTs can also help you participate in social and other activities. You may be referred to an OT by a hospital consultant or GP or you can refer yourself to the social care department.

**British Association/College of Occupational Therapists**
College of Occupational Therapists, 106-114 Borough High Street, London SE1 1LB
☎ 020 7357 6480
Ⓦ www.baot.co.uk
This is the professional and representative body for occupational therapists. It can provide information about OTs in private practice.

## OPTICAL SERVICES
NHS eye tests check your vision and will normally examine your eyes for early signs of other sight problems and some other conditions such as diabetes. You qualify for a free NHS sight test if you are:
- under 16
- under 19 and in full-time education
- 60 or over
- registered as blind or partially sighted
- diagnosed with diabetes or glaucoma
- 40 or over, and your mother, father, brother, sister, son or daughter has been diagnosed with glaucoma
- advised by an ophthalmologist (eye doctor) that you're at risk of glaucoma
- a prisoner on leave from prison

- eligible for an NHS complex lens voucher; your optometrist (optician) can advise you about your entitlement.

You are also entitled to a free NHS sight test if you:
- receive income support
- receive income-based jobseeker's allowance
- receive guarantee pension credit
- receive income-related employment and support allowance
- are entitled to, or named on, a valid NHS tax credit exemption certificate
- are named on a valid NHS certificate for full help with health costs (HC2).

If you're named on an NHS certificate for partial help with health costs (HC3), you may get some help towards the cost of your sight test.

If you qualify for a free NHS sight test you may be entitled to an NHS-funded mobile sight test, where the optometrist comes to visit you:
- in your own home
- at a residential or care home
- at a day centre.

This may be carried out or arranged through a local optician or by self-referral to a specialist organisation.

**The Outside Clinic** provides a national, domiciliary optician service which is offered on NHS terms. Its opticians make home visits by appointment and are equipped to detect glaucoma, cataracts and other potential problems. They can test your eyesight and advise on the choice of spectacles. They also offer appointments to deliver and fit glasses, aftercare service and repeat appointments.

For further information contact The Outside Clinic, Old Town Court, 10-14 High Street, Swindon SN1 3EP. Telephone 0800 854 477, email info@outsideclinic.com or visit www.outsideclinic.com.

### General Optical Council (GOC)

41 Harley Street, London W1G 8DJ

**T** 020 7580 3898

**E** goc@optical.org

**W** www.optical.org

The General Optical Council is the statutory body that regulates the optical professions in the UK. It maintains a register of people who have adequate training, practical experience and qualifications to practise as dispensing opticians and optometrists and manages matters relating to optical training and examinations. Complaints from members of the public about members of the optical profession are considered by the Council's disciplinary system, and can lead to removal from the register.

### Federation of Ophthalmic and Dispensing Opticians (FODO)

199 Gloucester Terrace, London W2 6LD

**T** 020 7298 5151

**E** optics@fodo.com

**W** www.fodo.com

FODO represents opticians in their business interests whether as individuals, family firms or chains. It issues guidance to its members on how they can improve facilities and services for disabled people and it hosts the Domiciliary Eye Care Committee.

### PHARMACY AND PRESCRIPTIONS

In addition to dispensing prescribed drugs and selling medicines that do not require a prescription, pharmacists or chemists are a useful source of information on a range of health matters including drug interactions, stopping smoking and sexual health.

Repeat prescription and delivery services are often available locally and it may be more convenient to go to the pharmacy rather than to your GP.

You can reduce the cost of prescriptions if you don't qualify for free prescriptions. If you have an average of two or more prescriptions each month, it will almost certainly be cheaper to buy a prescription prepayment certificate. This enables you to pay a set (reduced) fee for three or 12 months. Ask your pharmacist for details.

Some people with particular long-term or other conditions now qualify for free prescriptions – for example, people with cancer and people with a physical condition that makes it impossible to attend the pharmacy. Your GP or pharmacist can tell you more. The back of a prescription form also describes all the exemptions from charges – and you may have to sign the declaration at the bottom of the form to confirm your own exemption.

### Royal Pharmaceutical Society of GB

1 Lambeth High Street, London SE1 7JN

**T** 020 7572 2737

**E** enquiries@rpsgb.org

**W** www.rpsgb.org.uk

The professional and regulatory body for pharmacists in England, Scotland and Wales.

### PHYSIOTHERAPY

Physiotherapy aims to improve movement, strength and function by using a range of treatments including exercise, manipulation, heat, light and sound. Physiotherapists work widely in hospitals and in community settings, often as part of a multidisciplinary rehabilitation team. They can help people living with a disability or health condition to function as well as possible. Some areas have domiciliary physiotherapists who make home visits.

Physiotherapy is available free on the NHS, usually on referral by your GP. In some areas, self-referral systems are in place, allowing you to access physiotherapy directly. To find out whether self-referral is available in your area contact the reception staff at your GP surgery, or ask at your local NHS hospital. It is sometimes possible to access physiotherapy treatment through other routes, such as charities and the voluntary sector.

Many physiotherapists work privately, some of them providing specialist services, for example treatment for sports injuries. If you see a physiotherapist privately you will have to pay for treatment. If you decide to see a private physiotherapist, make sure they are a fully qualified member of a recognised professional body, such as the Chartered Society of Physiotherapy.

## ADAMS NEURO PHYSIOTHERAPY LTD

Neurological physiotherapy is the treatment of patients with a neurological disorder (those affecting the brain, spinal cord and nerves, such as stroke, brain injury, cerebral palsy, MS and Parkinson's disease).

**Getting and continuing neuro physiotherapy once you are back home**
Ask your GP about what is provided locally. Find out about the Long Term Conditions Team. Check what's going on at your leisure centre – many now provide supported leisure activity schemes you may be able to join.

Once discharged from NHS care, you might still feel that you could benefit from specialist guidance from a neuro physiotherapist on how best to continue your rehabilitation programme. This is particularly the case if you are still worried about falling, or if any movements still hurt or need a lot of effort to do. Your family may also appreciate advice on how best to help you.

Think about whose services will help you most. Ask about the neurological experience of the therapist and check they are registered with the Health Professions Council. Clinic visits can be a useful focus for activity but you will need to build the activities into your daily routine. Setting up a home programme can be far more cost effective and less tiring for you in the long run, and can include home-based advice about you and how/where you sit, stand and rest.

*Advice from Nikki Adams, Neuro Physiotherapist at Adams Neuro Physio*

**www.adamsneurophysio.org.uk**

### Chartered Society of Physiotherapy
14 Bedford Row, London WC1R 4ED
**T** 020 7306 6666
**W** www.csp.org.uk
This is the professional organisation for physiotherapists with a recognised qualification. Physiotherapists in private practice can be found on the 'Physio2u' pages of its website.

### SPEECH AND LANGUAGE THERAPY
Speech and language therapists treat children and adults with communication difficulties. After an assessment, the therapist will advise on a programme to maximise communication skills, if necessary using methods such as signing or technological aids. Help with certain swallowing and feeding problems may also be available.

If you think that you, your child or a relative needs to see a speech and language therapist ask your GP, district nurse, health visitor, or your child's nursery staff or teacher for a referral.

### Association of Speech & Language Therapists in Independent Practice
Coleheath Bottom, Speen, Princes Risborough, Bucks HP27 0SZ
**T** 01494 488 306
**W** www.helpwithtalking.com
Provides information on independent speech and language therapy across the UK. Contact the Association or search their online database to find a local, private therapist.

### Royal College of Speech & Language Therapists
2 White Hart Yard, London SE1 1NX
**T** 020 7378 1200
**W** www.rcslt.org
The professional body for speech and language therapists.

# Mental health and wellbeing

**Looking after our mental – as well as physical health is important for everyone. Things that are positive for mental wellbeing include having control in your own life, supportive friendships and relationships, employment or other activity where you are contributing (from parenting to public life) and physical wellbeing (particularly exercise and being free of drug and alcohol problems).**

## Mental health and mental health problems

About one in four of the UK population will experience mental health problems at some point – and millions each year get through it. Life may change as a result, but it is possible to get through the difficult times and get your life back. Just think of all the people who have experienced mental health difficulties – from Winston Churchill to Stephen Fry, as well as millions we've never heard of. Some say the experience of mental distress gives them new understandings and empathy.

At first, the shock of a mental health crisis or difficulty may leave you with feelings of loss and confusion, but recovery is possible. You can find your own path to the life you want – a life that is meaningful and fulfilling.

For some of us, the problems may be temporary. For others, they continue or recur. In either case, a good life is possible and has been achieved by many people – through discovering our inner-resources, making sense of what has happened and finding good sources of support, especially from others who have experienced it too. There are many stories of recovery on the Scottish Recovery Network website (www.scottishrecovery.net), as well as helpful resources. And there are many support groups and services that can help.

"Recovery is ... a personal journey of discovery: making sense of, and finding meaning in, what has happened; discovering your own resources, resourcefulness and possibilities; building a new sense of self, meaning and purpose in life; growing within and beyond what has happened to you; and pursuing your dreams and ambitions. The challenge for services is to assist people in their journey." (Perkins 2012)

SEEKING SUPPORT

Developing a mental health problem can be scary. You may have frightening thoughts or feel unable to do things you can normally do.

It can be particularly helpful to look for support from people who have experienced similar problems or challenges – through self-help or user-led organisations: the National Survivor and User Network has contacts with self-help groups around the country. There are also organisations bringing people together who share particular experiences (for instance, Depression Alliance, MDF the bipolar organisation and the Hearing Voices network).The Expert Patient Programme also has peer support groups in different parts of the country.

Self-help groups can offer you ways to live through the experience – and you don't have to do it alone. They can also help with 'self-management' – learning ways of managing your own mental health condition in ways that work for you. There are a number of toolkits and booklets to help you.

You can get information and advice from national helplines and publications provided by charities like Mind or Rethink.

> **Disability Rights UK Wellbeing Programme**
> Disability Rights UK has developed an approach to supporting employees and employers together to enhance wellbeing at work. For more information about our Wellbeing Programme, email sarah.cosby@disabilityrightsuk.org.

It can be difficult to ask for help. You may feel inhibited because of prejudice. As it says on the Rethink website: "No one is expected to be able to overcome mental health problems without support. Asking for help is not a sign of weakness. On the contrary, it takes courage."

### Seeking help through your GP

Your GP may be able to offer treatment or support directly – for instance, through medication, counselling or a talking therapy such as cognitive behavioural therapy – or may refer you to someone who can help with your problem. There are many different types of medication – for instance, anti-depressants, anti-psychotic drugs and mood stabilisers.

You might be referred to a psychiatrist or to a community mental health team (which includes people from different professions, like social work, nursing, psychology, occupational therapy, psychiatry) or to an early intervention team (for people with early experiences of mental health problems). You may be given a diagnosis such as depression, bipolar disorder (or manic depression), schizophrenia, anxiety, obsessive compulsive disorder or personality difficulties. A stay in hospital may be suggested if you are very unwell.

### Information and choice

Having information can help a lot when it comes to understanding what professionals are offering and planning what you want to do. Remember – except in very rare circumstances (see 'Mental health crises' below) it is your decision which treatments and support to choose. It's your life: you choose.

Advocacy can be helpful – someone to support you in trying to get what you want. You might get a friend, a family member or advocacy service to help you. See the chapter on 'Advocacy and decision making' for more about this.

### PLANNING FOR RECOVERY

One of the things that makes the most difference when you are experiencing mental health problems is maintaining your normal activities and relationships where you can – or taking some time out while you are really unwell, but leaving the door open to return.

Keeping your job or college place will support your recovery – the longer you are out, the harder it can be to get back. Similarly, with important relationships and friendships – you may not want to see people for a while, but keeping some contact so you can resume contact later can make a real difference.

It can be good to start your activities gradually at first, with some support if you need it. But you don't need to be fully well to start working or seeing friends. Try to keep your commitments where you feel that you can.

As you think about your own recovery journey, you may decide to make some changes in your life, which could be an opportunity to grow and develop. Doing it with support from others – perhaps family or friends, peer support, or maybe professional support – can help.

### DISCRIMINATION

Unfortunately, some people are prejudiced when it comes to people who are experiencing or have experienced mental health problems. Some employers, for example, may discriminate by not employing someone because they have had psychiatric treatment. Such discrimination is against the law (the Equality Act) and is being actively challenged. A group of mental health charities are running a major campaign called *Time to Change*, to tackle discrimination on mental health grounds.

If you have mental health problems that affect your day-to-day activities over time, you have rights and protections under the Equality Act ('disability' is the overarching term used in the Act to cover all mental and physical health conditions and disabilities). You should not be treated unfavourably – that is, discriminated against because you have a mental health condition.

Also, if you require a 'reasonable adjustment' in order to work, go to school/college or use any type of services (from shops to travel) the Act requires that such adjustments must be made as long as they are reasonable for the business offering them.

For instance, you might need to start working again gradually (part-time at first), work a different shift pattern, take time off for medical appointments or to have phone contact with a mental health support worker from work when needed.

If you do face discrimination, contact the Equality Advisory Support Service or the Disability Law Service (see the chapter on 'Discrimination').

Remember: it is against the law for employers to use pre-employment health screening questionnaires – you should not be asked by an employer, during a recruitment process, whether you have experienced mental ill-health. The best employers simply ask everyone, once they have been offered the job whether there is anything they need to perform to their best (see the chapter on 'Work').

PRACTICAL HELP

If you have longer-term mental health problems you may qualify for a scheme or initiative aimed at supporting disabled people (anyone living with a long-term health condition or impairment that affects their day-to-day activities).

There are programmes designed to give disabled people more choice and control over the services we use – like individual budgets and direct payments. These enable you to manage your own care and support if you wish (see the chapter on 'Social care').

There are schemes to help people get back into work – for example, Access to Work and Work Choice. Your local Jobcentre Plus office can give you details.

You may be entitled to disability benefits such as disability living allowance (to help with extra costs of disability) – soon to be replaced by the new personal independence payment, or to employment and support allowance. For more information see the chapter on 'Benefits' and check for up-to-date details on benefits at:
Ⓦ www.disabilityrightsuk.org:
Ⓦ www.gov.uk

> By arming yourself with information, you can improve your quality of life and find the best route to your own unique recovery.

MENTAL HEALTH CRISIS

If you – or a family member or friend – has a mental health crisis, there should be a local crisis number to call. Seek information from Mind or Rethink. Some areas have 'crisis houses', where people can take time out with support.

In rare circumstances if there are risks of harm to you or to others, or a serious risk to your health, it is possible that you could be placed in a hospital and/or treated against your will. If this happens, you have the right to appeal to a Mental Health Review Tribunal. Mind and Rethink have information on your rights and can put you in touch with legal advisers. See 'Useful contacts' below.

## Useful contacts

Some organisations that may be able to help include the following:

> **Disability Rights UK** provides information for people with mental health problems, including the *Surviving and Thriving toolkit* to support employee wellbeing. For details email enquiries@disabilityrights.org

**BiPolar UK**
11 Belgrave Road, London SW1V 1RB
Ⓣ 020 7931 6480
Ⓦ www.bipolaruk.org.uk
BiPolar UK works to enable people affected by bipolar disorder (manic depression) to take control of their lives. Services include publications, support and development of self-help opportunities and an eCommunity to communicate with others on bipolar related topics.

### Depression Alliance

20 Great Dover Street, London SE1 4LX

**T** 0845 123 2320

**E** information@depressionalliance.org

**W** www.depressionalliance.org

Depression Alliance is a UK charity that focuses on relieving and preventing depression. It provides help and information through publications, supporter services and a network of self-help groups for people affected by depression.

### Jobcentre Plus

**W** www.jobcentreplus.com

Jobcentre Plus offers a range of services for disabled people, people with health conditions and carers. A key feature of most of these services is the network of disability employment advisers who provide advice on finding and keeping a job. Disability employment advisers can also provide the entry to Access to Work funds, enabling your employer to make reasonable adjustments at a relatively low cost or indeed no cost at all. Contact details for local Jobcentre Plus offices are listed on their website.

### Mind

15-19 Broadway, Stratford, London E15 4BQ

**T** Mindinfoline 0300 123 3393

**E** info@mind.org.uk

**W** www.mind.org.uk

Mind is the leading mental health charity in England and Wales, providing support through over 180 local associations. It provides training for health professionals and the public and campaigns for improved services and better legislation.

### National Survivor User Network

27-29 Vauxhall Grove, London SW8 1SY

**T** 020 7820 8982

**E** info@nsun.org.uk

**W** www.nsun.org.uk

A user-led initiative that brings together groups and organisations in England, run by users and survivors of mental health services. Membership is open to service users and survivors, organisations and groups led by them and any ally of these organisations and groups. The network provides information and access to other forms of support to members by working in partnership with other organisations that have similar aims and objectives.

### Rethink

89 Albert Embankment, London SE1 7TP

**T** 0300 500 0927

**E** info@rethink.org

**W** www.rethink.org

Rethink works to help everyone affected by severe mental illness recover a better quality of life. It provides support with information, advice, services, groups, campaigns and research.

### SANE

1st Floor, Cityside House, 40 Adler Street, London E1 1EE

**T** 020 7375 1002; helpline 0845 767 8000

**E** info@sane.org.uk

**W** www.sane.org.uk

SANE raises awareness of mental illness, campaigns to improve services, and initiates and funds research into the causes of serious mental illness. It also provides information and support to those experiencing mental health problems.

### Stand to Reason

**E** info@standtoreason.org.uk

**W** www.standtoreason.org.uk

A service-user led organisation working with and for people with mental health problems. It aims to raise the profile, fight prejudice, establish rights and achieve equality for people who have experience of mental distress and ill-health.

### The UK Advocacy Network (UKAN)

Volserve House, 14-18 West Bar Green, Sheffield S1 2DA

**E** office@u-kan.co.uk

**W** www.u-kan.co.uk

UKAN is a user-controlled national federation of advocacy projects, patients' councils, user forums and self-help and support groups working in the field of mental health. UKAN offers information, training and support on the improvement of mental health services.

### Time To Change

15-19 Broadway, London E15 4BQ

**E** info@time-to-change.org.uk

**W** www.time-to-change.org.uk

A partnership of organisations to end mental health discrimination. The programme is run by Mind and Rethink and evaluated by the Institute of Psychiatry at King's College.

# Further information

This section lists organisations providing general or condition-specific information and further information on the wide range of support offered by Disability Rights UK. It includes organisations that can help you locate local advice services, as well as regulatory bodies and places you can complain to if you have any issues. It also covers details of nationwide Disabled/Independent Living Centres and Mobility Centres.

## Disability Rights UK

We are the leading charity in the UK run by and for disabled people and offer support across many areas to anyone with lived experience of disability or health conditions, regardless of impairment type.

### RESOURCES

We provide a comprehensive range of resources, available to download free of charge from our website. These include factsheets on welfare benefits and tax credits and practical guides written by and for disabled people including our *Doing Life Differently* series that covers subjects ranging from sport to transport and careers.

To download our free publications:
- W www.disabilityrightsuk.org/factsheets
  www.disabilityrightsuk.org/publications

### HELPLINES

Disability Rights UK's helplines provide information and advice on a variety of issues.

### Disabled Students Helpline

- T 0800 328 5050
- E skill4disabledstudents@disabilityrightsuk.org

Provides advice to disabled students on post-16 education and training, the Equality Act, welfare benefits and access to Higher Education. Also provides advice to professionals working with disabled students.

### Independent Living Advice Line

- T 0845 026 4748
- E independentliving@disabilityrightsuk.org

Provides advice on getting direct payments, personal budgets and getting funding from social services in relation to care needs.

### Member Organisations Welfare Rights Advice Service

- T 020 7566 0113
- E ken.butler@disabilityrightsuk.org

Provides advice to our member organisations on social security benefit and tax credit issues.

### Tribunal Support Unit

- T 020 7566 0117
- E tribunalsupportunit@disabilityrightsuk.org

Provides support to advice agencies on complex welfare benefit cases.

### Equality Advisory Support Service

- T 0800 444 205; textphone 0800 444 206

In 2012, Disability Rights UK began co-delivering this Helpline, taking over the baton from the Equality and Human Rights Commission Helpline. The Helpline is for individuals who think they may have experienced discrimination of any kind. The service aims to support individuals referred from local organisations, advisory groups, faith-based organisations and other groups working within the community that support people experiencing discrimination and provides advice and information on discrimination and human rights issues.

# General disability advice

The organisations and information sources listed here can provide general information, advice and guidance to disabled people, depending on where in the UK you are.

### United Kingdom's Disabled People's Council (UKDPC)

Stratford Advice Arcade, 107-109 The Grove, Stratford, London E15 1HP

- ☏ 020 8522 7433
- ✉ corrie.pegg@ukdpc.net
- ⓦ www.ukdpc.net

Members are organisations run by disabled people. Information on campaigns and a wide range of matters can be found on their website.

In Northern Ireland:

### Disability Action

Portside Business Park, 189 Airport Road West, Belfast BT3 9ED

- ☏ 028 9029 7880; textphone 028 9029 7882
- ✉ hq@disabilityaction.org
- ⓦ www.disabilityaction.org

A pan-disability organisation providing information on services for disabled people in Northern Ireland. It has offices in Belfast, Londonderry, Dungannon and Carrickfergus.

In Scotland

### Advice Service Capability Scotland

11 Ellersly Road, Edinburgh EH12 6HY

- ☏ 0131 337 9876; textphone 0131 346 2529
- ✉ ascs@capability-scotland.org.uk
- ⓦ www.capability-scotland.org.uk

Organisation providing general advice on disability issues.

### UPDATE

Hays Business Centre, 4 Hay Avenue, Edinburgh EH16 4AQ

- ☏ 0131 669 1600
- ✉ info@update.org.uk
- ⓦ www.update.org.uk

Scotland's national disability information organisation provides a public helpline service on the above telephone number, although people may be referred to organisations that are more appropriate whether geographically or because they have more specialised knowledge.

In Wales:

### Disability Wales/Anabledd Cymru

Bridge House, Caerphilly Business Park, Van Road, Caerphilly CF83 3GW

- ☏ 029 2088 7325
- ✉ info@disabilitywales.org
- ⓦ www.disabilitywales.org

A national association of disability groups in Wales promoting rights, inclusion, equality and support of all disabled people. It publishes leaflets and provides an information service.

### GOV.UK

- ⓦ www.gov.uk

The government's new online information service (formerly DirectGov) providing information on public services with links to government departments and agencies and a wide range of other organisations.

# Specific advice

The organisations and helpline details provided here can offer advice or support on specific issues relating to their own areas of knowledge and expertise. Often it is a particular group of people that they support, for example older people, ex servicemen or families, or a certain area of expertise that they offer advice on, such as independent living. Organisations that provide advice and support on specific disabilities or impairments are listed later in this section.

England and UK-wide:

### Assist UK
Redbank House, 4 St Chad's Street, Manchester M8 8QA
T 0161 834 1044; textphone 0870 770 5813
W www.assist-uk.org
National membership organisation leading a network of disabled and independent living centres and services.

### Barnardo's
Tanners Lane, Barkingside, Essex IG6 1QG
T 020 8550 8822
W www.barnardos.org.uk
Advise and in some areas directly provide social care and educational services for disabled children, young people and their families.

### Bradnet
Noor House, 11 Bradford Lane, Laisterdyke, Bradford BD3 8LP
T 01274 224444; textphone 01274 201860
W www.bradnet.org.uk
A user-led organisation that promotes the equality and inclusion of disabled people by empowering disabled people to live the life they choose. They do this through providing outreach and advocacy services, help in education and employment and advice on independent living.

### Care and Repair England
The Renewal Trust Business Centre,
3 Hawksworth Street, Nottingham NG3 2EG
T 0115 950 6500
W www.careandrepair-england.org.uk
Charity offering advice and support on housing and other living condition issues for disabled and older people.

### Carers UK
20 Great Dover Street, London SE1 4LX
T 020 7378 4999; adviceline 0808 808 7777
W www.carersuk.org
Provides information and advice on benefits, services and other support available to carers.

### Child Poverty Action Group (CPAG)
94 White Lion Street, London N1 9PF
T 020 7837 7979
E info@cpag.org.uk
W www.cpag.org.uk
Produce benefits and tax credit handbooks and guides for claimants and advisers; consultancy and training for advisers; policy work and lobbying for the abolition of child poverty in the UK.

### Contact a Family
209-211 City Road, London EC1V 1JN
T 020 7608 8700; textphone 0808 808 3556
   Helpline 0808 808 3555
W www.cafamily.org.uk
Offer advice and support for families caring for disabled children, including those with rare disorders.

### Disabled Motorists Federation
c/o Chester-Le-Street District CVS Volunteer Centre, Clarence Terrace, Chester-Le-Street, County Durham DH3 3DQ
T 0151 648 3457
W www.disabledmotoristsfederation.org.uk
Charity who provide information for disabled people and their carers on travel in general and motoring in particular.

### Disabled Parents Network
Poynters House, Poynters Road, Dunstable, Bedfordshire LU5 4TP
T 0300 330 0639
W www.disabledparentsnetwork.org.uk
Provide information, advice, advocacy and support, including peer support, for disabled parents, their families and supporters. Membership and online forum available.

### Independent Age

6 Avonmore Road, London W14 8RL

T 0207 605 4200; helpline 0845 262 1863

E advice@independentage.org

W www.independentage.org

Provide advice on all aspects of care and welfare benefits for older people, their families and their carers. Also offer a befriending service.

### Leonard Cheshire Disability

66 South Lambeth Road, Vauxhall, London SW8 1RL

T 020 3242 0200

E info@lcdisability.org

W www.lcdisability.org

National charity offering a wide range of support services for disabled people throughout the UK.

### Livability

50 Scrutton Street, London EC2A 4XQ

T 020 7452 2000

W www.livability.org.uk

Charity offering residential care services, supported living, holidays, housing, training and brain injury rehabilitation.

### Motability

Motability Operations, City Gate House, 22 Southwark Bridge Road, London SE1 9HB

T 0845 456 4566; textphone 0845 675 0009

W www.motability.co.uk

Offer contract car, wheelchair or scooter hire or hire purchase schemes designed to help people with disabilities improve their mobility.

### Ricability

Unit G03, The Wenlock, Wharf Road, London N1 7EU

T 020 7427 2460; textphone 020 7247 2469

W www.ricability.org.uk

Consumer research charity providing information and practical advice for people with disabilities.

### Scope

6 Market Road, London N7 9PW

T 0808 800 3333

E response@scope.org.uk

W www.scope.org.uk

National charity offering advice and support on any aspect of living with a disability.

### Shelter

88 Old Street, London EC1V 9HU

T 0300 330 1234; helpline 0808 800 4444

W www.shelter.org.uk

Charity working to alleviate the distress caused by homelessness and bad housing. Provides advice, information and advocacy. Their website contains a wide range of information sheets and guides.

### The Royal British Legion

Haig House, 199 Borough High Street, London SE1 1AA

T 020 3207 2100; helpline 0845 772 5725

W www.britishlegion.org.uk

Organisation supporting ex-servicemen by offering advice and support in a number of areas including war pensions, benefits, debt advice, care homes, resettlement training, employment and remembrance travel.

### Transport for All

336 Brixton Road, London SW9 7AA

T 020 7737 2339

E contactus@transportforall.org.uk

W www.transportforall.org.uk

London based charity campaigning for a fully accessible transport network. Provide information, advice and advocacy on travel for disabled and elderly people. Also offer travel training to service users and access advice to transport providers.

### Tourism for All

7A Pixel Mill, 44 Appleby Road, Kendal, Cumbria LA9 6ES

T 0845 124 9971

E info@tourismforall.org.uk

W www.tourismforall.org.uk

National Charity dedicated to securing standards of tourism that are equal to all. Provide information via their helpline to older and disabled people on how their specific access needs can be met and their rights when travelling or on holiday.

# Local advice

Advice on services available to us, and support to obtain them often needs to be sourced locally. In addition, there may be times when seeing someone face-to face locally will be the best option to ensure we get the best advice. A wide range of local organisations exist including those specifically related to disability and those offering more general advice services.

## Citizens Advice Bureaux (CAB)

Myddelton House, 115-123 Pentonville Road, London N1 9LZ

T 020 7833 2181
Advice is not available on this number
W www.citizensadvice.org.uk

The Citizens Advice Service helps people resolve legal, financial and other problems by providing free information and advice from over 3,500 locations in England and Wales.

**Face-to-face advice** is available from Citizens Advice Bureaux. To locate your local Bureau, visit:
W www.citizensadvice.org.uk/index/getadvice

**For online advice**, self-help information and a selection of factsheets and guides, (covering the law in England, Scotland, Wales and Northern Ireland) visit:
W www.adviceguide.org.uk

**Over-the-phone advice** is also available from every CAB. In addition, Citizens Advice are in the process of developing a national phone service that will become operational in different parts of the UK over the next two years. It is now fully operational in Wales. In England the service is currently being rolled out area by area. If it is not yet available in your area, you will hear options for recorded information:

## Citizens Advice National Phone Service
For England
08444 111 444; textphone 08444 111 445
For Wales
08444 772 020; textphone 08444 111 445

Around the UK:
## Citizens Advice Northern Ireland
46 Donegall Pass, Belfast BT7 1BS
E info@citizensadvice.co.uk
W www.citizensadvice.co.uk

## Citizens Advice Scotland
1st Floor, Spectrum House, 2 Powderhall Road, Edinburgh EH7 4GB
T 0808 800 9060
W www.cas.org.uk

## DIAL
PO Box 833, Milton Keynes, Buckinghamshire MK12 5NY
T 01302 310 123
E informationenquiries@dialuk.org.uk
W www.scope.org.uk/dial

A national network of over 80 disability information and advice line services run by disabled people providing free, impartial and confidential information services for disabled people and their families and advisors mainly by telephone. Some also offer additional services. Scope has now taken over DIAL services. A full list of local DIALs and a search facility for finding a DIAL near you can be found on the website listed above.

# Disabled Living Centres

Disabled Living Centres provide information about equipment to help with daily living. Assist UK leads the UK network of local Centres and the Disabled Living Foundation also provide a central point of contact for advice on equipment (see London below). At the Centres you can see and try products and professional staff can offer information and advice about suitability. Centres are a valuable source of information relating to access, design and equipment for daily living. This can be useful to carers, older people and healthcare workers, students and manufacturers.

## ASSIST UK'S DISABLED LIVING CENTRES

**Bexley:** Inspire Community Trust
T 020 3045 5100; textphone 0132 334 716
W www.inspirecommunitytrust.org

**Birmingham:** Assist Birmingham Centre (ABC)
T 0121 464 4942; textphone 0121 464 7565
E assist.birminghamcentre@birmingham.gov.uk

**Boston:** Disabled Living Centre
T 0845 054 7171
E imclean@redcross.org.uk
W www.redcross.org.uk

**Brighton & Hove:** Daily Living Centre
T 01273 29 6132
E dlc@brighton-hove.gov.uk
W www.brighton-hove.gov.uk

**Bristol:** Living
T 0117 965 3651 (also textphone)
W www.thisisliving.org.uk

**Castleford:** Ability Centre
T 01977 723 922
E SC_CCabilitycentre@wakefield.gov.uk

**Croydon:** Access Ability Centre
T 020 8664 8860
E glenn.bartlett@croydonpct.nhs.uk

**Doncaster:** South Yorkshire Centre for Inclusive Living (SYCIL)
T 01302 89 2949; textphone 01302 32 9788
W www.sycil.org.uk
E admin@sycil.org

**Dudley:** Assisted Living Centre
T 01384 813695
E helen.cartwright@dudley.gov.uk
W www.dudley.gov.uk

**Dundee:** Independent Living Centre
T 01382 307631
E dilc@dundeecity.gov.uk

**Dunstable:** The Disability Resource Centre
T 01582 470900
E information@drcbeds.org.uk
W www.drcbeds.org.uk

**Eastbourne:** East Sussex Disability Association
T 01323 51 4515; textphone 01323 51 4502
E info@esda.org.uk
W www.esda.org.uk

**Edinburgh:** Lothian Disabled Living Centre
T 0131 537 9190
E lothiandlc@nhslothian.scot.nhs.uk
W www.smart.scot.nhs.uk

**Elgin:** Independent Living Centre
T 01343 55 9461; textphone 01343 55 1376
E info.ilc@moray.gov.uk
W www.moray.gov.uk

**Ellesmere Port:** Poole Centre ILC
T 0151 337 6399

**Gainsborough:** BRC Disabled Living Centre
T 01427 81 6500
E george.thornhill@ipct.nhs.uk
W www.redcross.org.uk

**Grangemouth:** Dundas Resource Centre
T 01324 50 4311
W www.falkirk.gov.uk
E lindsay.russell@falkirk.gov.uk

**Grantham:** BRC – Disabled Living Centre
T 0845 054 7171
E granthamdlc@redcross.org.uk

**Halton:** Independent Living Centre
T 01928 56 3340
E sue.lightfoot@hsthpct.nhs.uk

## DISABLED LIVING CENTRES

**Handforth:** East Cheshire Independent Living Centre
- T 01625 37 4053

**Hartford:** Independent Living Centre
- T 1606 88 1980
- E jackie.waring@cheshirewestandchester.gov.uk

**Hillingdon:** Independent Living Centre
- T 01895 484 880
- E hil-pct.hcfil@nhs.net

**Leeds:** The William Merritt Disabled Living Centre
- T 0113 305 5332 (also textphone)
- E thewilliammerritt.dlc@nhs.net
- W www.williammerrittleeds.org

**Leicester:** BRC Disabled Living Centre
- T 0845 373 0217; textphone 0116 262 9465
- E dicinfo@redcross.org.uk
- W www.redcross.org.uk

**Lincoln:** Disabled Living Centre
- T 01522 545111
- E lincolndlc@redcross.org.uk
- W www.redcross.org.uk

**Liverpool:** Disabled Living Centre
- T 0151 296 7742; textphone 0151 296 7748
- E disabled.living.centre@liverpoolch.nhs.uk
- W www.liverpoollifehouse.org.uk

**London:** Disabled Living Foundation
- T 0845 130 9177; textphone 020 7432 8009
- E info@dlf.org.uk
- W www.dlf.org.uk

**Mablethorpe:** BRC Disabled Living Centre
- T 01507 47 8574; helpline 0845 054 7171
- E mablethorpeDLC@redcross.org.uk
- W www.redcoss.org.uk

**Manchester:** Burrows House
- T 0161 607 8200
- E info@disabledliving.co.uk
- W www.disabledliving.co.uk

**Middlesbrough:** Independent Living Centre
- T 01642 25 0749; textphone 01642 244718
- E ilc.middlesbrough.gov.uk

**Milton Keynes:** Centre for Integrated Living
- T 01908 23 1344; textphone 01908 23 1505
- E info@mkcil.org.uk
- W www.mkweb.co.uk/mk_disability

**Nottingham:** Disabilities Living Centre
- T 0115 985 5780
- E info@dlcnotts.co.uk
- W www.dlcnotts.co.uk

**Oxfordshire:** Guideposts Trust Independent Living Centre
- T 01993 89 9985
- E ilc@guidepoststrust.org.uk
- W www.guidepostsilc.org.uk

**Semington:** Independent Living Centre
- T 01380 87 1007
- E welcome.ilc.semington@googlemail.com
- W www.ilc.org.uk

**Stamford:** Disability Living Centre
- T 01780 48 0599
- E stamforddlc@redcross.org.uk
- W www.redcross.org.uk

**Suffolk:** AGA Mobility Systems Ltd
- T 01449 720 809
- E info@agamobilitysystems.co.uk
- W www.agamobilitysystems.co.uk

**Truro:** Tremorvah Industries
- T 01872 32 4340; textphone 01872 324364
- E enquiries@tremorvah.cornwall.gov.uk
- W www.tremorvah.co.uk

**Welwyn Garden City:** Hertfordshire Action on Disability
- T 01707 32 4581
- E info@hadnet.org.uk
- W www.hadnet.co.uk

**Wolverhampton:** The Neville Garrett Centre for Independent Living
- T 01902 55 3648; textphone 01902 55 1510
- E ssces@wolverhampton.gov.uk

# Mobility centres

Mobility centres offer practical, independent advice and assessment to disabled drivers, older people and carers. They assess your ability to drive and provide advice about suitable vehicles and adaptations. For more information contact:

**Forum of Mobility Centres**
- ☎ 0800 559 3636
- Ⓦ www.mobility-centres.org.uk

## MOBILITY CENTRES AROUND THE UK

### ENGLAND

**Bristol**: Mobility Service, Living (dlc), The Vassall Centre, Gill Avenue, Fishponds, Bristol BS16 2QQ
- ☎ 0117 965 9353
- Ⓔ mobserv@thisisliving.org.uk
- Ⓦ www.thisisliving.org.uk

**Cornwall**: Cornwall Mobility Centre, Tehidy House, Royal Cornwall Hospital, Truro, Cornwall TR1 3LJ
- ☎ 01872 25 4920
- Ⓔ mobility@rcht.cornwall.nhs.uk
- Ⓦ www.cornwallmobilitycentre.co.uk

**Derbyshire:** Derby DrivAbility (Derby Regional Mobility Centre), Kingsway Hospital, Kingsway, Derby DE22 3LZ
- ☎ 01332 37 1929
- Ⓔ driving@derbyhospitals.nhs.uk
- Ⓦ www.derbydrivability.com

**Hampshire:** Wessex DriveAbility, Leornain House, Kent Road, Portswood, Southampton SO17 2LJ
- ☎ 023 8051 2222
- Ⓔ enquiries@wessexdriveability.org.uk
- Ⓦ www.wessexdriveability.org.uk

**Hertfordshire:** Hertfordshire Action on Disability Mobility Centre, The Woodside Centre, The Commons, Welwyn Garden City, Hertfordshire AL7 4DD
- ☎ 01707 38 4581
- Ⓔ driving@hadnet.org.uk
- Ⓦ www.hadnet.org.uk

**Kent**: South East DriveAbility, Cobtree Ward, Preston Hall Hospital, London Road, Aylesford, Kent ME20 7NJ
- ☎ 01622 79 5719
- Ⓔ wk-pct.sedriveability@nhs.net

**Lancashire**: Wrightington Mobility Centre, Wrightington Hospital, Hall Lane, Appley Bridge, Wigan, Lancashire WN6 9EP
- ☎ 01257 25 6409
- Ⓔ mobility.centre@alwpct.nhs.uk

**Norfolk:** East Anglian DriveAbility, 2 Napier Place, Thetford, Norfolk IP24 3RL
- ☎ 01842 75 3029
- Ⓔ info@eastangliandriveability.org.uk
- Ⓦ www.eastangliandriveability.org.uk

**Oxfordshire**: Contact via West Midlands Regional Driving Assessment Centre (see below).

**Surrey**: Queen Elizabeth's Foundation Mobility Centre, Damson Way, Fountain Drive, Carshalton, Surrey SM5 4NR
- ☎ 020 8770 1151
- Ⓔ info@qef.org.uk
- Ⓦ www.qef.org.uk

**Tyne and Wear**: North East Drive Mobility, Walkergate Park, Centre for Neuro-rehabilitation and Neuro-psychiatry, Benfield Road, Newcastle upon Tyne NE6 4QD
- ☎ 0191 287 5090
- Ⓔ northeast.drivemobility@ntw.nhs.uk
- Ⓦ www.ntw.nhs.uk

**West Midlands:** Regional Driving Assessment Centre, Unit 11, Network Park, Duddeston Mill Road, Birmingham B8 1AU
- ☎ 0845 337 1540
- Ⓔ info@rdac.co.uk
- Ⓦ www.rdac.co.uk

**West Yorkshire:** The William Merritt Disabled Living Centre and Mobility Service, St Mary's Hospital, Green Hill Road, Leeds LS12 3QE
- ☎ 0113 305 5288
- Ⓔ mobility.service@nhs.net
- Ⓦ www.williammerrittleeds.org

IF ONLY I'D KNOWN THAT A YEAR AGO ...                    221

NORTHERN IRELAND

**Disability Action:** Portside Business Park, 189 Airport Road West, Belfast BT3 9ED

T 028 9029 7880

E mobilitycentre@disabilityaction.org

W www.disabilityaction.org

SCOTLAND

**Scottish Driving Assessment Service:** Astley Ainslie Hospital, 133 Grange Loan, Edinburgh EH9 2HL

T 0131 537 9192

E marlene.mackenzie@nhslothian.scot.nhs.uk

WALES

**North Wales Mobility and Driving Assessment Service:** Disability Resource Centre, Glan Clwyd Hospital, Bodelwyddan, Denbighshire LL18 5UJ

T 01745 58 4858

E mobilityinfo@btconnect.com

W www.wmdas.co.uk

**South Wales Mobility and Driving Assessment Service:** Rookwood Hospital, Fairwater Road, Llandaff, Cardiff CF5 2YN

T 029 2055 5130

E helen@wddac.co.uk

W www.wmdas.co.uk

## Disability-specific organisations

These organisations are concerned with specific conditions and disabilities. Some are mainly involved with research and/or medical treatment but many provide services, information and advice. Getting in touch with an organisation that specifically helps people with your disability or condition can be a great first port of call and many organisations run national and local support groups and online networking forums.

ARTHRITIS

**The Arthritic Association**

One Upperton Gardens, Eastbourne, East Sussex BN21 2AA

T 01323 416550; freephone 0800 652 3188

W www.arthriticassociation.org.uk

Supports people with arthritis through a self-help programme involving diet, physical therapy and the use of specific supplements.

**Arthritis Care**

18 Stephenson Way, London NW1 2HD

T 0808 800 4050

E info@arthritiscare.org.uk

W www.arthritiscare.org.uk

Provides information, workshops, courses and support to people of all ages through its regional offices and local groups.

Around the UK:

**Arthritis Care Northern Ireland**

The McCune Building, 1 Shore Road, Belfast BT15 3PG

T 028 9078 2940; helpline 0808 800 4050

E Nireland@arthritiscare.org.uk

W www.arthritiscare.org.uk/InyourArea/NorthernIreland

**Arthritis Care Scotland**

Unit 25A, Anniesland Business Park, Glasgow G13 1EU

T 0141 954 7776; helpline 0808 800 4050

E Scotland@arthritiscare.org.uk

W www.arthritiscare.org.uk/InyourArea/Scotland

**Arthritis Care Wales**

One Caspian Point, Pierhead Street, Cardiff Bay CF10 4DQ

T 02920 444 155; helpline 0808 800 4050

E Wales@arthritiscare.org.uk

W www.arthritiscare.org.uk/InyourArea/Wales

### Arthritis Research UK

Copeman House, St Mary's Gate, Chesterfield, Derbyshire S41 7TD

T 0300 790 0400

E enquiries@arthritisresearchuk.org

W www.arthritisresearchuk.org

Funds medical research and publishes free booklets and information sheets on all the different types of arthritis and musculoskeletal conditions covering drugs, symptoms and self-management.

### ASTHMA
### Asthma UK

Summit House, 70 Wilson Street, London EC2A 2DB

T 0800 121 62 55; helpline 0800 121 6244

E info@asthma.org.uk

W www.asthma.org.uk

Works to improve the lives of people with asthma by providing independent advice and information to everyone about asthma; providing teaching materials to schools; and funding community projects and medical research.

Around the UK:

### Asthma UK Cymru

3rd Floor, Eastgate House, 35-43 Newport Road, Cardiff CF24 0AB

T 029 2043 5400; helpline 0800 121 6244

E wales@asthma.org.uk

W www.asthma.org.uk

### Asthma UK Northern Ireland

Ground Floor, Unit 2, College house, City Link Business Park, Durham Street, Belfast BT12 4HQ

T 0800 151 3035; helpline 0800 121 6244

E ni@asthma.org.uk

W www.asthma.org.uk

### Asthma UK Scotland

4 Queen Street, Edinburgh EH2 1JE

T 0131 226 2544; helpline 0800 121 6244

E scotland@asthma.org.uk

W www.asthma.org.uk

### BLADDER AND BOWEL CONDITIONS
### Bladder & Bowel Foundation

SATRA Innovation Park, Rockingham Road, Kettering, Northamptonshire NN16 9JH

T 01536 53 3255; helpline 0845 345 0165

E info@bladderandbowelfoundation.org

W www.bladderandbowelfoundation.org

Campaigns for people with bowel and bladder control problems. It provides user-friendly booklets, a magazine, online support and information. It also runs local support groups.

### Crohn's and Colitis UK

4 Beaumont House, Sutton Road, St Albans, Hertfordshire AL1 5HH

T 0845 130 2233

   Information service 01727 73 4470

E info@CrohnsAndColitis.org

W www.nacc.org.uk

Offers educational meetings, financial support, counselling, information and support nationally and through local groups to people of all ages living with inflammatory bowel disease.

### Cystitis & Overactive Bladder Foundation

Kings Court, 17 School Road, Birmingham B28 8JG

T 0121 702 0820

E info@cobfoundation.org

W www.cobfoundation.org

A membership organisation providing information and support for people with cystitis and other overactive bladder conditions and their families through local support groups, educational materials and an online chat room.

### ERIC (Education & Resources for Improving Childhood Continence)

36 Old School House, Britannia Road, Kingswood, Bristol BS15 8DB

T 0845 370 8008 (24 hours – 7 days a week)

E info@eric.org.uk

W www.eric.org.uk

Provides information and support to children, teenagers, parents and professionals on all aspects of childhood wetting and soiling. It sells a range of products to help manage childhood continence problems. For a free catalogue, call 0117 301 2100 or visit www.ericshop.org.uk.

# DISABILITY-SPECIFIC ORGANISATIONS

## CANCER

**CancerHelp UK**
Angel Building, 407 St John Street, London EC1V 4AD
- T 020 7242 0200
  Supporter services 0300 123 1022
- W www.cancerhelp.org.uk

The information service on cancer and cancer services of Cancer Research UK. Information is provided by experts in an easy to use way.

**National Association of Laryngectomee Clubs**
Lower Ground Floor, 152 Buckingham Palace Road, London SW1W 9TR
- T 020 7730 8585
- W www.laryngectomy.org.uk

Provides information and support for people living with a laryngectomy and their families and carers through almost 100 local clubs.

**Macmillan Cancer Support**
89 Albert Embankment, London SE1 7UQ
- T 020 7840 7840; textphone 0808 808 0121
- W www.macmillan.org.uk

A major provider of cancer information and support, both emotional and practical. It has specialist cancer nurses who give information on any type of cancer or treatment, practical advice and details of local support groups and services; publishes over 70 publications; and has a vibrant online community.

**Prostate Cancer UK**
Cambridge House, 100 Cambridge Grove, London W6 0LE
- T 020 8222 7622; helpline 0800 074 8383
- E info@prostatecanceruk.org
- W www.prostatecanceruk.org

Raises awareness, supports research, and provides information and support to men with prostate cancer and their families through support groups, specialist nurses, and an online community.

**Prostate Cancer UK – Scotland**
Unit F22-24, Festival Business Centre, 150 Brand Street, Glasgow G51 1DH
- T 0141 314 0050
- E scotland@prostatecancer.org
- W www.scotland.prostate-cancer.org.uk

## DEMENTIA

**Alzheimer's Society**
Devon House, 58 St Katharine's Way, London E1W 1LB
- T 0845 300 0336
- E enquiries@alzheimers.org.uk
- W www.alzheimers.org.uk

Provides information and support for people with dementia and their families, through regional networks and a network of over 250 branches in England, Northern Ireland and Wales.

In Scotland similar services are provided by:
**Alzheimer Scotland**
22 Drumsheugh Gardens, Edinburgh EH3 7RN
- T 0808 808 3000 (24-hour dementia helpline)
- E helpline@alzscot.org
- W www.alzscot.org

**Dementia UK**
6 Camden High Street, London NW1 0JH
- T 020 7874 7200
- E info@dementiauk.org
- W www.dementiauk.org

Runs training courses for those caring for people with dementia and promotes Admiral Nursing, specialist mental health nurses who work with families affected by dementia. Admiral nurses can be contacted through their helpline 0845 257 9406 or via email on direct@dementiauk.org.

## DIABETES

**Diabetes UK**
Macleod House, 10 Parkway, London NW1 7AA
- T 020 7424 1000; helpline 0845 120 2960
- E info@diabetes.org.uk
- W www.diabetes.org.uk

Campaigns for the rights of people with diabetes, funds research and provides a range of support services, including family support weekends and children's support holidays.

**Insulin Dependent Diabetes Trust**

PO Box 294, Northampton NN1 4XS

T 01604 62 2837

E enquiries@iddtinternational.org

W www.iddtinternational.org

Run by people with insulin dependent diabetes and their relatives, this organisation campaigns for informed choice of treatment and the continued availability of animal insulin. It has launched the 'Hospital Passport' for use by diabetics to inform hospital staff about their diabetes and treatment.

## LEARNING DISABILITIES

**Down's Syndrome Association**

Langdon Down Centre, 2a Langdon Park, Teddington, Middlesex TW11 9PS

T 020 8614 5100

E info@downs-syndrome.org.uk

W www.downs-syndrome.org.uk

Provides information and support to people with Down's syndrome, their families and carers and professionals who work with them. The Association also champions the rights of people with Down's syndrome and strives to improve knowledge of the condition.

Around the UK:

**Ireland Office**

Unit 2 Marlborough House, 348 Lisburn Road, Belfast BT9 6GH

T 028 9066 5260

E enquiriesni@downs-syndrome.org.uk

W www.downs-syndrome.org.uk/about-us/northern-ireland.html

**Wales Office**

206 Whitchurch Road, Cardiff CF14 3NB

T 029 2052 2511

E wales@downs-syndrome.org.uk

W www.downs-syndrome.org.uk/about-us/wales.html

**Mencap**

123 Golden Lane, London EC1Y 0RT

T 020 7454 0454; helpline 0808 808 1111

E help@mencap.org.uk

W www.mencap.org.uk

Charity providing children and adults with learning disabilities, support and advice on benefits, independent living, housing, education, employment and leisure via 500 affiliated local societies.

Around the UK:

**Mencap Cymru**

31 Lambourne Crescent, Cardiff Business Park, Llanishen, Cardiff CF14 5GF

T 029 2074 7588; helpline 0808 808 1111

E helpline.wales@mencap.org.uk

W www.mencap.org.uk/wales

**Mencap Northern Ireland**

Segal House, 4 Annadale Avenue, Belfast BT7 3JH

T 028 9069 135; helpline 0808 808 1111

E helpline.ni@mencap.org.uk

W www.mencap.org.uk/northern-ireland

**The National Autistic Society (NAS)**

393 City Road, London EC1V 1NG

T 020 7833 2299; helpline 0808 800 4104

E nas@nas.org.uk

W www.autism.org.uk

A UK charity for people of all ages with autism (including Asperger syndrome) and their families. They provide information, support and pioneering services, through employment support, local groups, befriending schemes, and finding services in the community.

Around the UK:

**NAS Northern Ireland**

59 Malone Road, Belfast BT9 6SA

T 028 9068 7066

E northern.ireland@nas.org.uk

**NAS Scotland**

Central Chambers, 1st Floor, 109 Hope Street, Glasgow G2 6LL

T 0141 221 8090

E scotland@nas.org.uk

**NAS Cymru**

6/7 Village Way, Greenmeadow Springs Business Park, Tongwynlais, Cardiff CF15 7NE

T 029 2062 9312

E wales@nas.org.uk

# DISABILITY-SPECIFIC ORGANISATIONS

## MENTAL HEALTH

### Mind

15-19 Broadway, Stratford, London E15 4BQ;
Mind infoline, PO Box 277,
Manchester M60 3XN
- **T** 020 8519 2122; Mind infoline 030 0123 3393
- **E** info@mind.org.uk
- **W** www.mind.org.uk

Provides support through over 180 local associations; provides training for health professionals and the public; and campaigns for improved services and better legislation.

### Mind Legal Advice Service

PO Box 277, Manchester M60 3XN
- **T** 0300 466 6463
- **E** legal@mind.org.uk
- **W** www.mind.org.uk

Around the UK:
### Mind Cymru

3rd Floor, Quebec House, Castlebridge,
5-19 Cowbridge Road East, Cardiff CF11 9AB
- **T** 029 2039 5123; Mind infoline 0300 123 3393
- **E** contactwales@mind.org.uk
- **W** www.mind.org.uk/mind_cymru

The leading mental health charity in Wales.

In Scotland similar services are provided by:
### Scottish Association for Mental Health

Brunswick House, 51 Wilson Street, Glasgow, G1 1UZ
- **T** 0141 530 1000
- **E** info@samh.org.uk (mental health enquiries)
  enquire@samh.org.uk (general enquiries)
- **W** www.samh.org.uk

### Rethink

89 Albert Embankment, London SE1 7TP
- **T** 0300 500 0927
- **E** info@rethink.org; advice@rethink.org
- **W** www.rethink.org

Helps people affected by severe mental illness recover a better quality of life. Provides information and advice, local support groups and nearly 300 services including carer support, criminal justice, employment and training, respite and housing.

### SANE

First Floor Cityside House, 40 Adler Street,
London E1 1EE
- **T** 020 7375 1002
- **E** info@sane.org.uk
- **W** www.sane.org.uk

Works to raise mental health awareness and combat stigma; provide emotional support and information via phone, email and online forum; and initiate research into causes, treatments and experiences of mental illness.

Around the UK:
### Mindwise (Northern Ireland)

Wyndhurst, Knockbracken Healthcare Park,
Saintfield Road, Belfast BT8 8BH
- **T** 028 9040 2323
- **E** info@mindwisenv.org
- **W** www.mindwisenv.org

### Hafal (Wales)

Suite C2, William Knox House, Britannic Way,
Llandarcy, Neath SA10 6EL
- **T** 01792 81 6600
- **E** hafal@hafal.org
- **W** www.hafal.org

## SENSORY IMPAIRMENTS

### Action for Blind People

53 Sandgate Street, London SE15 1LE
- **T** 030 3123 9999
- **E** helpline@rnib.org.uk
- **W** www.actionforblindpeople.org.uk

Offers information and services, particularly in the fields of employment, housing, holidays, and sport to blind and partially sighted people of all ages. They have offices all over England.

### Action on Hearing Loss (formerly RNID: Royal National Institute for Deaf People)

19-23 Featherstone Street, London EC1Y 8SL
- **T** 0808 808 0123; textphone 0808 808 9000
- **E** informationline@hearingloss.org.uk
- **W** www.actiononhearingloss.org.uk

Aims to improve the quality of life for the nine million deaf and hard of hearing people in the UK through campaigning, supporting cutting-edge research, raising awareness, training in sign language and lipreading and providing information and services such as employment advice, communication support, and care services.

Around the UK:

**Action on Hearing Loss Northern Ireland**

Harvester House, 4-8 Adelaide Street, Belfast B2 8GA

- 📞 028 9023 9619; textphone 028 9024 9462
- ✉ information.nireland@rnid.org.uk
- 🌐 www.actiononhearingloss.org.uk/about-us/northern-ireland.aspx

**Action on Hearing Loss Scotland**

Empire House, 131 West Nile Street, Glasgow G1 2RX

- 📞 0141 341 5330; textphone 0141 341 5347
- ✉ scotland@hearingloss.org.uk
- 🌐 www.actiononhearingloss.org.uk/about-us/scotland.aspx

**Action on Hearing Loss Cymru**

16 Cathedral Road, Cardiff CF11 9LJ

- 📞 029 2033 3034; textphone 029 2033 3036
- ✉ cymru@hearingloss.org.uk
  wales@hearingloss.org.uk
- 🌐 www.actiononhearingloss.org.uk/about-us/wales.aspx

**British Deaf Association – Sign Community**

18 Leather Lane, London EC1N 7SU

- 📞 020 7405 0090
- ✉ bda@bda.org.uk
- 🌐 www.bda.org.uk

Campaigns for the rights and opportunities of those who use sign language; provides information and advice services; employs youth workers; and can offer counselling in British Sign Language.

Around the UK:

**BDA Northern Ireland**

Unit 5c, Weavers Court, Linfield Road, Belfast BT12 5GH

- 📞 028 9043 7480; textphone 028 9043 7486

**BDA Scotland**

Suite 58, Central Chambers, 93 Hope Street, Glasgow G2 6LD

- 📞 0141 248 5554

**Deafblind UK**

National Centre for Deafblindness, John and Lucille van Geest Place, Cygnet Road, Hampton, Peterborough PE7 8FD

- 📞 01733 35 8100 (also textphone)
  Advice line 0800 132 320
- ✉ info@deafblind.org.uk
- 🌐 www.deafblind.org.uk

Offers a range of services to deafblind people and provides expertise, professional advice and training. Publications are available in large print, Braille, Moon and on audio-tape. Deafblind UK has regional staff, membership support workers and volunteers around the UK, who help to identify deafblind people in the community, and help ensure their needs are addressed.

Around the UK:

**Deafblind Cymru**

Trident Court, Eastmoors Road, Cardiff CF24 5TD

- 📞 029 2060 1471
- ✉ deafblindcymru@deafblind.org.uk

**Deafblind Scotland**

21 Alexandra Avenue, Lenzie, Glasgow East Dunbartonshire G66 5BG

- 📞 0141 777 6111; textphone 0141 775 3311
- ✉ info@deafblindscotland.org.uk
- 🌐 www.deafblindscotland.org.uk

**DeafPLUS**

1st foor, Trinity Centre, Key Close, London E1 4HG

- 📞 020 7790 6147
- ✉ info@deafplus.org
- 🌐 www.deafplus.org

A charity dedicated to enabling deaf and hearing impaired people to get the most out of life. Working one-to-one, they provide practical advice, support and guidance. They have offices in London, Somerset, Birmingham, Bath, Farnborough and Aldershot.

# DISABILITY-SPECIFIC ORGANISATIONS

**The Ear Foundation**
Marjorie Sherman House, 83 Sherwin Road,
Lenton, Nottingham NG7 2FB
T 0115 942 1985
E info@earfoundation.org.uk
W www.earfoundation.org.uk
Supports and provides activities, courses and resources for children, young people and adults with cochlear implants, their families and supporting professionals.

**Hearing Link Concern**
27-28 The Waterfront, Eastbourne, East Sussex BN23 5UZ
T 030 0111 1113
E enquiries@hearinglink.org
W www.hearinglink.org
Provides advice, information and support to people with hearing loss; promotes communication access; and raises awareness of the issues associated with hearing loss.

Around the UK:
**Hearing Link Scotland**
The Eric Liddell Centre, 15 Morningside Road,
Edinburgh EH10 4DP
T 0131 447 9420
E scotland@hearinglink.org

**National Blind Children's Society**
Bradbury House, Market Street, Highbridge,
Somerset TA9 3BW
T 01278 76 4764
E enquiries@nbcs.org.uk
W www.nbcs.org.uk
Provides information and services for children with a visual impairment from birth to the end of formal education and their families including family support, educational advocacy, CustomEyes large print books, recreational activities and grants for home computers and specialist equipment. For Family Support Information call 0800 781 1444 or email familysupport@nbcs.org.uk.

**National Deaf Children's Society (NDCS)**
15 Dufferin Street, London EC1Y 8UR
T 020 7490 8656
Helpline 0808 800 8880 (also textphone)
E ndcs@ndcs.org.uk
W www.ndcs.org.uk
Provides information and support for deaf children and youths and their families through family officers and appeal advisors, grants, social activities, local groups and their website.

Around the UK:
**NDCS Northern Ireland**
38-42 Hill Street Belfast BT1 2LB
T 028 9031 3170; textphone 028 9027 8177
E nioffice@ndcsni.co.uk

**NDCS Scotland**
2nd Floor, Empire House, 131 West Nile Street,
Glasgow G1 2RX
T 0141 354 7850
E ndcs.scotland@ndcs.org.uk

**NDCS Wales/Cymru**
4 Cathedral Road, Cardiff CF11 9LJ
T 029 2037 3474; textphone 029 2023 2739
E ndcswales@ndcs.org.uk

**The Partially Sighted Society**
7/9 Bennetthorpe, Doncaster DN2 6AA
T 0844 477 4966
E info@partsight.org.uk
W www.partsight.org.uk
Provides information, advice, equipment and clear print material for people with a visual impairment to help them to make the best use of their remaining sight.

**Royal National Institute of the Blind (RNIB)**
105 Judd Street, London WC1H 9NE
T 0303 123 9999
E helpline@rnib.org.uk
W www.rnib.org.uk
The country's largest charity promoting the rights and interests of, and providing services for anyone with a sight problem. Services offered include information, equipment provision, advice on education, employment and leisure, talking books and advocacy.

Around the UK:

**RNIB Cymru**

Trident Court, East Moors Road, Cardiff CF24 5TD

T 029 2045 0440

E cymruevents@rnib.org.uk

**RNIB Northern Ireland and Isle of Man**

40 Linenhall Street, Belfast BT2 8BA

T 028 9032 9373

E rnibni@rnib.org.uk

**RNIB Scotland**

12-14 Hillside Crescent, Edinburgh EH7 5EA

T 0131 652 3140

E rnibscotland@rnib.org.uk

**Sense**

101 Pentonville Road, London N1 9LG

T 0845 127 0060

020 7520 0972 (also textphone)

E info@sense.org.uk

W www.sense.org.uk

A national charity that works with and campaigns for the needs of people who are deafblind. Services include individual assessments, family support, a range of living options, day services and a holiday programme.

Around the UK:

**Sense Northern Ireland**

Sense Family Centre, The Manor House, 51 Mallusk Road, Mallusk, County Antrim BT36 4RU

T 028 9083 3430 (also textphone)

E nienquiries@sense.org.uk

**Sense Scotland**

43 Middlesex Street,

Kinning Park, Glasgow G41 1EE

T 0141 429 0294; textphone 0141 418 7170

E info@sensescotland.org.uk

**Sense Cymru**

Ty Penderyn, 26 High Street, Merthyr Tydfil CF47 8DP

T 0845 127 0090; textphone 0845 127 0092

E cymruenquiries@sense.org.uk

**Signature – Excellence in Communication with Deaf People**

Mersey House, Mandale Business Park, Belmont, Durham DH1 1TH

T 0191 383 1155; textphone 0191 383 7915

E durham@signature.org.uk

W www.signature.org.uk

Undertakes the training, assessment and accreditation of interpreters using British Sign Language and other forms of communication used by deaf people. It publishes an online directory of accredited communication professionals.

Around the UK:

**Signature Northern Ireland**

Harvester House, 4-8 Adelaide Street, Belfast BT2 8GA

T 028 90 438161

E pam.tilson@signature.org.uk

**Signature Scotland**

TouchBase Community Suite, 43 Middlesex Street, Glasgow G41 1EE

T 0141 418 7191; textphone 0141 418 7193

E glasgow@signature.org.uk

SPEECH, LANGUAGE & LEARNING DIFFICULTIES

**Afasic**

1st Floor, 20 Bowling Green Lane, London EC1R 0BD

T 020 7490 9410; helpline 0845 355 5577

W www.afasic.org.uk

Supports children and young people with speech, language and communication impairments and their families and care professionals in England through youth activities, parents' helpline and online forum, workshops and conferences, local groups and training materials for professionals.

Around the UK:

**Afasic Northern Ireland**

Cranogue House, 19 Derrycourtney Road, Caledon, County Tyrone, Belfast BT68 4UF

T 028 3756 9611; helpline 0845 355 5577

W www.afasicnorthernireland.org.uk

**Afasic Scotland**

The Vine, 43 Magdalen Yard Road, Dundee DD1 4NE

T 01382 25 0060; helpline 0845 355 5577

W www.afasicscotland.org.uk

## DISABILITY-SPECIFIC ORGANISATIONS

### Afasic Cymru

Titan House, Cardiff Bay Business Centre, Lewis Road, Ocean Park, Cardiff CF24 5BS

T 029 2046 5854; helpline 0845 355 5577

W www.afasiccymru.org.uk

### The British Stammering Association

15 Old Ford Road, London E2 9PJ

T 020 8983 1003
   Helpline 0845 603 2001 or 020 8880 6590

E mail@stammering.org

W www.stammering.org

Provides information and support to people of all ages concerned about stammering through its library, network of self-help groups and activities. It also has a shop selling specialist items.

### British Dyslexia Association

Unit 8, Bracknell Beeches, Old Bracknell Lane, Bracknell RG12 7BW

T 0845 251 9002

E helpline@bdadyslexia.org.uk

W www.bdadyslexia.org.uk

Campaigns to raise awareness and understanding of dyslexia and the needs of dyslexic people and those with whom they have contact.

### Dyspraxia Foundation

8 West Alley, Hitchin, Hertfordshire SG5 1EG

T 01462 45 5016; helpline 01462 45 4 986

E dyspraxia@dyspraxiafoundation.org.uk

W www.dyspraxiafoundation.org.uk

Provides information and support for children, teenagers and adults who have dyspraxia, their parents and families and for teachers and other professionals working with them. It has a number of local support groups.

### Speakability

1 Royal Street, London SE1 7LL

T 020 7261 9572; helpline 080 8808 9572

E speakability@speakability.org.uk

W www.speakability.org.uk

Supports and empowers people with aphasia, a communication disability caused by damage to language centres of the brain, through self-help groups, online forum, publications and training resources for care professionals.

## OTHER SPECIFIC CONDITIONS

### Attention Deficit Disorder Information & Support Service (ADDISS)

Premier House, 112 Station Road, Edgware, Middlesex HA8 7BJ

T 020 8952 2800

E info@addiss.co.uk

W www.addiss.co.uk

Provides information and resources about attention deficit hyperactivity disorder to anyone who needs assistance, through publications, a website and by telephone.

### Allergy UK

Planwell House, LEFA Business Park, Edgington Way, Sidcup, Kent DA14 5BH

T 01322 61 9898

E info@allergyuk.org

W www.allergyuk.org

Aims to increase understanding of allergy, food intolerance and chemical sensitivity, and help people manage their allergies. They also provide training for healthcare professionals and fund research.

### Ataxia UK

Lincoln House, Kennington Park, 1-3 Brixton Road, London SW9 6DE

T 020 7582 1444; helpline 0845 644 0606

E helpline@ataxia.org.uk

W www.ataxia.org.uk

Supports people throughout the UK who live with the effects of ataxia through information leaflets, events, local support groups and financial support.

### BackCare – National Back Pain Association

16 Elmtree Road, Teddington, Middlesex TW11 8ST

T 020 8977 5474; helpline 0845 130 2704

W www.backcare.org.uk

Provides independent information on the causes, treatments and management of back pain through its helpline, publications and local groups.

### Beat – Beating Eating Disorders

Wensum Housel, 103 Prince of Wales Road, Norwich NR1 1DW

📞 0300 123 3355; helpline 0845 634 1414
Youthline 0845 634 7650

📧 help@b-eat.co.uk

🌐 www.b-eat.co.uk

Provides information and support to people affected by eating disorders, as well as their families and care professionals through self-help groups, online forums and message boards, publications and training courses. Youthline is for people aged 25 or under.

### British Heart Foundation

Greater London House, 180 Hampstead Road, London NW1 7AW

📞 020 7554 0000
Textphone 18001 020 7554 0000
Helpline 030 0330 3311

📧 supporterservices@bhf.org.uk

🌐 www.bhf.org.uk

Provides information and support to people with heart disease and their families through a helpline, online community and network of heart support groups around the country.

### British Kidney Patient Association

3 The Windmills, St Mary's Close, Turk Street, Alton GU34 1EF

📞 01420 54 1424

📧 info@britishkidney-pa.co.uk

🌐 www.britishkidney-pa.co.uk

Provides information and financial support to kidney patients and their families including help with getting a holiday. Applications for grants should be made through a renal social worker.

### British Lung Foundation

73-75 Goswell Road, London EC1V 7ER

📞 020 7688 5555; helpline 030 0003 0555

🌐 www.lunguk.org

Provides information and support to people of all ages affected by lung disease through publications, an online community, pen pals, specialist nurses, and a nationwide network of Breathe Easy support groups.

Around the UK:

### BLF Scotland and Northern Ireland

Suite 104 Baltic Chambers, 50 Wellington Street, Glasgow G2 6HJ

📞 0141 248 0050 or 079 0204 4363

📧 scotland@blf.org.uk

📧 northernireland@blf.org.uk

### BLF Wales

6a Prospect Place, Swansea SA1 1QP

📞 01792 45 5764

📧 wales@blf.org.uk

### British Polio Fellowship

Eagle Office Centre, The Runway, South Ruislip, Middlesex HA4 6SE

📞 0800 018 0586

📧 info@britishpolio.org.uk

🌐 www.britishpolio.org.uk

Provides support and information to people who have had polio, their families and anyone living in the UK wanting information about polio or Post Polio Syndrome. It has a network of local groups and offers grants, welfare services and a holiday programme.

### Brittle Bone Society

Grant-Paterson House, 30 Guthrie Street, Dundee DD1 5BS

📞 01382 20 4446

📧 contact@brittlebone.org

🌐 www.brittlebone.org

A national support group for people with 'brittle bone disease' or Osteogenesis Imperfecta who can provide advice to parents and some specialist equipment on loan.

### Changing Faces

The Squire Centre, 33-37 University Street, London WC1E 6JN

📞 0845 450 0275 or 020 7391 9270

📧 info@changingfaces.org.uk

🌐 www.changingfaces.org.uk

Offers confidential support and advice to people with a visible difference or disfigurement to their face as well as training for care professionals.

## DISABILITY-SPECIFIC ORGANISATIONS

**Coeliac UK**
3rd Floor, The Apollo Centre, Desborough Road,
High Wycombe, Buckinghamshire HP11 2QW
📞 01494 43 7278; helpline 0845 305 2060
🌐 www.coeliac.org.uk
Provides information and support through local
groups, publications, and their website for people
affected by coeliac disease and related conditions.

**Cystic Fibrosis Trust**
11 London Road, Bromley, Kent BR1 1BY
📞 030 0373 1000
📧 enquiries@cftrust.org.uk
    asktheexpert@cftrust.org.uk (medical
enquiries)
🌐 www.cftrust.org.uk
Funds research to treat and cure Cystic Fibrosis
and aims to ensure appropriate care and support
for people with the disease. They produce a range
of publications and provide a helpline service for
advice.

**DEBRA**
DEBRA House, 13 Wellington Business Park,
Dukes Ride, Crowthorne, Berkshire RG45 6LS
📞 01344 77 1961
📧 debra@debra.org.uk
🌐 www.debra.org.uk
Provides support to people with the skin
blistering condition, epidermolysis bullosa
through specialist nurses and social workers and a
range of literature.

Around the UK:
**DEBRA Scotland**
Rex House, 103 Bothwell Road, Hamilton,
Scotland ML3 ODW
📞 01698 42 4210
📧 debra.scotland@debra.org.uk

**Different Strokes**
9 Canon Harnett Court, Wolverton Mill, Milton
Keynes MK12 5NF
📞 0845 130 7172
🌐 www.differentstrokes.co.uk
Established by and for younger stroke survivors of
working age, to provide support and information.
Its website includes a message board where
members exchange information and share their
own experiences of stroke.

**Duchenne Family Support Group (DFSG)**
78 York Street, London W1H 1DP
📞 0870 241 1857; helpline 0800 121 4518
📧 info@dfsg.org.uk
🌐 www.dfsg.org.uk
Brings families affected by Duchenne muscular
dystrophy together for mutual support, sharing
of information and social activities. It organises
holidays, workshops and an annual conference.

**Epilepsy Action**
New Anstey House, Gate Way Drive, Yeadon,
Leeds LS19 7XY
📞 0113 210 8800; helpline 0808 800 5050
📧 epilepsy@epilepsy.org.uk
🌐 www.epilepsy.org.uk
Supports people with epilepsy and provides
information for anyone with an interest in
epilepsy.

In Scotland similar services are provided by:
**Epilepsy Scotland**
48 Govan Road, Glasgow G51 1JL
📞 0141 427 4911; helpline 0808 800 2200
    Helpline text: 077 8620 9501
📧 helpline@epilepsyscotland.org.uk  enquiries@
epilepsyscotland.org.uk
🌐 www.epilepsyscotland.org.uk
Involves people affected by epilepsy in raising
awareness of epilepsy issues and works to ensure
that services are developed to meet their varied
needs.

**Epilepsy Society**
Chesham Lane, Chalfont St Peter, Bucks
SL9 0RJ
📞 01494 60 1300; helpline 01494 60 1400
🌐 www.epilepssociety.org.uk
A national epilepsy medical charity working for
everyone affected by epilepsy, through cutting-
edge research, awareness campaigns and expert
care. It provides residential and nursing care,
respite care, day-care, home services, specialist
training and seminars, and an online forum.

## The Haemophilia Society

1st floor Petersham House, 57a Hatton Garden, London EC1N 8JG

☎ 020 7831 1020; helpline 0800 018 6068
Benefits information 020 7269 0686
✉ info@haemophilia.org.uk
🌐 www.haemophilia.org.uk

Aims to ensure all people with haemophilia and related bleeding disorders receive the best possible care, treatment and support. Particular attention is given to the needs of children, young people, their families and women with bleeding disorders.

Around the UK:
### Haemophilia Scotland

4b Gayfield Place, Gayfield Place Lane, Edinburgh EH7 4AB

☎ 0131 557 5953
✉ dan@haemophilia.org. uk
🌐 www.haemophilia.org.uk/get_involved/
Haemophilia+Scotland

### Headway – The Brain Injury Association

Bradbury House, 190 Bagnall Road, Old Basford, Nottingham, Nottinghamshire NG6 8SF

☎ 0115 924 0800; helpline 0808 800 2244
✉ helpline@headway.org.uk
🌐 www.headway.org.uk

Supports the interests of people living with a brain injury, their families and carers with over 110 local groups and branches.

### Hemihelp

6 Market Road, London N7 9PW

☎ 0845 120 3713; helpline 0845 123 2372
✉ helpline@hemihelp.org.uk
🌐 www.hemihelp.org.uk

A membership organisation offering advice and support to people with hemiplegia and their families through an online message board, home visiting services, workshops, events and activities.

### Huntington's Disease Association

Suite 24, Liverpool Science Park IC1, 131 Mount Pleasant, Liverpool L3 5TF

☎ 0151 331 5444
✉ info@hda.org.uk
🌐 www.hda.org.uk

As well as supporting research into treatment for Huntington's Disease, the Association provides a central information and advice service and a network of Regional Care Advisers. There are local groups throughout the country.

In Scotland similar services are provided by:
### Scottish Huntington's Association

Suite 31 St James Business Centre, Linwood Road, Paisley PA3 3AT

☎ 0141 848 0308
✉ sha-admin@hdscotland.org
🌐 www.hdscotland.org

### Jennifer Trust for Spinal Muscular Atrophy

40 Cygnet Court, Timothy's Bridge Road, Stratford upon Avon, Warwickshire CV37 9NW

☎ 01789 26 7520
✉ jennifer@jtsma.org.uk
🌐 www.jtsma.org.uk

Supports and provides information for children and adults with spinal muscular atrophy and their families as well as funding research.

### Limbless Association

Unit 16, Waterhouse Business Centre, 2 Cromar Way, Chelmsford, Essex CM1 2QE

☎ 01245 21 6670; helpline 0800 644 0185
✉ enquiries@limbless-association.org
🌐 www.limbless-association.org

Provides information and support to amputees, through a volunteer visitor service linking experienced amputees with newly disabled people. They also run a sports development service for disabled children and young people, a panel of specialist legal firms, and local support groups.

**Lupus UK**
St James House, Eastern Road, Romford, Essex
RM1 3NH
T 01708 73 1251
E headoffice@lupusuk.org.uk
W www.lupusuk.org.uk
Provides information and support for people with lupus, or SLE, and their families both directly and through their network of self-help groups around the country. Produces an information pack, a magazine and a range of other publications for individuals and professionals.

**The ME Association**
7 Apollo Office Court, Radclive Road, Gawcott, Buckinghamshire MK18 4DF
T 01280 818 964; helpline 0844 576 5326
E meconnect@meassociation.org.uk
W www.meassociation.org.uk
Represents the interests of, and provides support and services to, people with myalgic encephalopathy, chronic fatigue syndrome and post viral fatigue syndrome.

**Migraine Action**
4th Floor, 27 East Street, Leicester LE1 6NB
T 0116 275 8317
W www.migraine.org.uk
Provides information and support through a helpline, booklets and local support groups.

**Motor Neurone Disease Association**
PO Box 246, Northampton NN1 2PR
T 01604 25 0505; helpline 0845 762 6262
E mndconnect@mndassociation.org
W www.mndassociation.org
Provides information, day-to-day support and services for people with motor neurone disease and their families in England, Wales and Northern Ireland. These include association visitors and befrienders, support groups, equipment loans, financial support, care development advisers who work to improve healthcare professionals' knowledge, and 19 Care and Research Centres.

In Scotland similar services are provided by:
**MND Scotland**
76 Firhill Road, Glasgow G20 7BA
T 0141 945 1077
E info@mndscotland.org.uk
W www.mndscotland.org.uk

**Multiple Sclerosis Society**
MS National Centre (MSNC), 372 Edgware Road, London NW2 6ND
T Helpline 0808 800 8000
E helpline@mssociety.org.uk
W www.mssociety.org.uk
Provides information and support for people with MS and their families through a network of over 300 branches and support groups.

Around the UK:
**Multiple Sclerosis Society Northern Ireland**
The Resource Centre, 34 Annadale Avenue, Belfast BT7 3JJ
T 028 9080 2802

**Multiple Sclerosis Society Scotland**
Ratho Park, 88 Glasgow Road, Ratho Station, Newbridge EH28 8PP
T 0131 335 4050

**Multiple Sclerosis Society Wales/Cymru**
Temple Court, Cathedral Road, Cardiff CF11 9HA
T 029 2078 6676

**Muscular Dystrophy Campaign**
61 Southwark Street, London SE1 0HL
T 020 7803 4800
   Information line 0800 652 6352
E info@muscular-dystrophy.org
W www.muscular-dystrophy.org
Provides information and support on all aspects of life for children, adults and families living with muscle disease through regional advisors, peer support, financial grants, and events.

### Myasthenia Gravis Association

College Business Centre, Uttoxeter New Road, Derby DE22 3WZ

T 01332 29 0219
Helpline 0800 91 9922 (freephone)
E mg@mga-charity.org
W www.mga-charity.org

The Association has a network of local branches and Regional Organisers offering support to people with myasthenia gravis and information to those involved with them.

### National Eczema Society

Hill House, Highgate Hill, London N19 5NA

T 020 7281 3553; helpline 0800 089 1122
E helpline@eczema.org
W www.eczema.org

Provides an information and advice service, an expanding network of local support groups, funds for research and campaigns on behalf of people with eczema.

### National Kidney Federation

The Point, Coach Road, Shireoaks, Worksop, Nottinghamshire S81 8BW

T 01909 54 4999; helpline 0845 601 0209
E nkf@kidney.org.uk
W www.kidney.org.uk

An organisation run by and for kidney patients, it works with associations of patients at individual renal units; campaigns for improved treatment and support services; and provides a wide range of information in print, through its website and by phone.

### Parkinson's Disease Society

215 Vauxhall Bridge Road, London SW1V 1EJ

T 0808 800 0303
Textphone 18001 0808 800 0303
E hello@parkinsons.org.uk
W www.parkinsons.org.uk

Provides support and information to people with Parkinson's, their relatives and carers through a team of information and support workers, local groups, publications and education and training.

### PINNT – Patients on Intravenous and Nasogastric Nutrition Therapy

PO Box 3126, Christchurch, Dorset BH23 2XS

W www.pinnt.com

Provides advice on issues such as treatment, equipment, holidays and benefits; and mutual support through local groups. Half PINNT has been established for younger members and their parents.

### Pulmonary Hypertension Association UK

Unit 2, Concept Court, Manvers, Rotherham S63 5DB

T 01709 76 1450
E office@phassociation.uk.com
W www.phassociation.uk.com

Aims to raise awareness of pulmonary hypertension and support those affected through regional support groups, family weekends, and online community.

### REACH – Association for Children with Upper Limb Deficiency

PO Box 54, Helston, Cornwall TR13 8WD

T 0845 1306 225; 07879 678 909
E reach@reach.org.uk
W www.reach.org.uk

Aims to bring parents into contact with each other, giving them the opportunity to compare experiences and a way to understand how others have coped or overcome problems through local support groups, activities, and outings.

### Restricted Growth Association

PO Box 15755, Solihull B93 3FY

T 0300 111 1970
E office@restrictedgrowth.co.uk
W www.restrictedgrowth.co.uk

A self-help organisation concerned with all aspects of the wellbeing of people of restricted growth. They represent their interests nationally and provide information and support. They also welcome parents and professionals, produce a quarterly magazine, hold a convention and regular social events.

## DISABILITY-SPECIFIC ORGANISATIONS

**Scoliosis Association (UK)**
4 Ivebury Court, 325 Latimer Road,
London W10 6RA
📞 020 8964 1166
✉ info@sauk.org.uk
🌐 www.sauk.org.uk
A national self-help support organisation for people of all ages with scoliosis, it campaigns to raise awareness of scoliosis, provides information and support through publications, an online shop, scoliosis meetings where specialist speak about the condition, and local support groups.

**SHINE (formerly Association for Spina Bifida & Hydrocephalus)**
42 Park Road, Peterborough PE1 2UQ
📞 01733 55 5988
✉ info@shinecharity.org.uk
🌐 www.shinecharity.org.uk
Provides information and advice to individuals, families and carers through advisers in England, Northern Ireland and Wales with specialist advisers in the fields of education, medical matters and continence management. There are local support groups in many areas.

In Scotland similar services are provided by:
**Scottish Spina Bifida Association**
The Dan Young Building, 6 Craighalbert Way, Cumbernauld G68 0LS
📞 01236 79 4500; helpline 0845 911 1112
🌐 www.ssba.org.uk
An organisation created by parents for parents, it employs specialist staff in their Family Support Centre, and offers a multi-faceted service to people affected by spina bifida, hydrocephalus and allied conditions, across Scotland.

**SIA Spinal Injuries Association**
SIA House, 2 Trueman Place, Oldbrook, Milton Keynes MK6 2HH
📞 0845 678 6633; helpline 0800 980 0501
✉ sia@spinal.co.uk
🌐 www.spinal.co.uk
Supports spinal cord injured people and their families through a variety of services including peer support teams, counselling, career advice, online community and publications.

In Scotland similar services are provided by:
**Spinal Injuries Scotland**
Festival Business Centre, 150 Brand Street, Govan, Glasgow G51 1DH
📞 0141 427 7686 or 0800 013 2305
✉ info@sisonline.org
🌐 www.sisonline.org

**Sickle Cell Society**
54 Station Road, London NW10 4UA
📞 020 8961 7795
✉ info@sicklecellsociety.org
🌐 www.sicklecellsociety.org
Works to improve services for people with sickle cell disorders and to create wider understanding of the conditions. Directly or through local support groups, they provide a range of services including information, advice, counselling, financial help, and an annual children's holiday.

**Steps Charity Worldwide**
Wright House, Crouchley Lane, Lymm, Cheshire WA13 0AS
📞 01925 75 0271
✉ info@steps-charity.org.uk
🌐 www.steps-charity.org.uk
Supports people with a lower limb condition such as clubfoot or hip conditions through a contacts directory, database of specialist doctors, online forum, grants and publications.

**Stroke Association**
Stroke House, 240 City Road, London EC1V 2PR
📞 020 7566 0300; textphone 020 7251 9096
Helpline 0303 3033 100
✉ info@stroke.org.uk
🌐 www.stroke.org.uk
Provides UK-wide support for people who have had strokes, their families and carers; promotes research; and campaigns to increase knowledge of stroke and improve services. Community services are available in many parts of the country including communications support, family and carer support, and local stroke clubs.

Regional offices :
**Stroke Association Northern Ireland**
Rushmere House, 46 Cadogan Park, Malone Road, Belfast BT9 6HH
📞 028 9050 8020
✉ northernireland@stroke.org.uk

**Stroke Association Scotland**
Links House, 15 Links Place, Edinburgh EH6 7EZ
T 0131 555 7240
E scotland@stroke.org.uk

**Stroke Association Wales**
Unit 8, Cae Gwyrdd, Greenmeadow Springs
Business Park, Tongwynlais, Cardiff CF15 7AB
T 029 2052 4400
E info.cymru@stroke.org.uk

**Terrence Higgins Trust**
314-320 Gray's Inn Road, London WC1X 8DP
T 020 7812 1600; helpline 0808 802 1221
E info@tht.org.uk
W www.tht.org.uk
Campaigns to raise awareness of HIV. Provides information and support to people affected by HIV through counselling and group support, testing and treatment advice, information on community services, housing, benefits and employment and an interactive website (www.myHIV.org.uk)

# Ombudsmen

Ombudsmen deal with complaints where maladministration has caused injustice. There are a considerable number of different types of Ombudsmen, the ones detailed here refer to the areas we have covered in the various sections of this guide.

**Parliamentary and Health Service Ombudsman**
Millbank Tower, Millbank, London SW1P 4QP
T 0345 015 4033
W www.ombudsman.org.uk
Deals with complaints about central government in the UK, including government departments, agencies and other public bodies. Only an MP can refer a complaint about a government department or agency. Also deals with complaints about services provided through the NHS in England.

**Local Government Ombudsman**
PO Box 4771, Coventry CV4 0EH
T 0300 061 0614
W www.lgo.org.uk
Deals with complaints about local authorities and certain other bodies in England. Ring the advice team to make a complaint by telephone, get a complaint form or get advice on making a complaint.

Around the UK
**Northern Ireland Ombudsman**
Progressive House, 33 Wellington Place, Belfast BT1 6HN
T 028 9023 3821; Freephone 0800 343424
W www.ni-ombudsman.org.uk
Deals with complaints about Northern Ireland government departments and their agencies and public bodies including health and personal social services.

**Scottish Public Services Ombudsman**
4 Melville Street, Edinburgh EH3 7NS
T 0800 377 7330
W www.spso.org.uk
Deals with final stage complaints about the Scottish Government and its agencies and other public bodies including local authorities, NHS, housing associations, and colleges and universities.

**Wales Public Services Ombudsman**
Peter Tyndall, Public Services Ombudsman for Wales, 1 Ffordd yr Hen Gae, Pencoed CF35 5LJ
T 01656 641150
Deals with final stage complaints about the Welsh Assembly Government and its agencies.

# Index of advertisers and supporters

**Disability Rights UK thanks all its advertisers for supporting the publication of its books for disabled people.**